P9-AZW-696

THE EDUCATION OF A COACH

OTHER BOOKS BY DAVID HALBERSTAM

The Noblest Roman

The Making of a Quagmire

One Very Hot Day

The Unfinished Odyssey of Robert Kennedy

Ho

The Best and the Brightest

The Powers That Be

The Reckoning

The Breaks of the Game

The Amateurs

Summer of '49

The Next Century

The Fifties

October 1964

The Children

Playing for Keeps

War in a Time of Peace

Firehouse

The Teammates

THE EDUCATION OF A COACH

DAVID HALBERSTAM

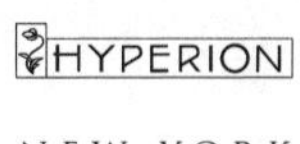

NEW YORK

 Printed in the United States of America. For information address Hyperion, 77 West 66th Street, New York, New York 10023-6298.

ISBN: 1-4013-0154-1

Hyperion books are available for special promotions and premiums. For details contact Michael Rentas, Assistant Director, Inventory Operations, Hyperion, 77 West 66th Street, 11th floor, New York, New York 10023, or call 212-456-0133.

FIRST EDITION

10 9 8 7 6 5 4 3 2

For Gay and Nan Talese

THE EDUCATION OF A COACH

PROLOGUE

That year, in the fall of 1957, when the boy was only five years old, the father had scouted Army at least four times. The father was considered by many colleagues to be the preeminent football scout in the country, and he was gone almost every fall weekend, analyzing Navy's upcoming opponent; he liked to joke after he retired that the only game he had ever watched Navy play in all his years at the Academy was the one with Army, because it was the last game of the year, and there was no other team to scout that week. This was Steve Belichick's second year as an assistant coach at the Naval Academy. In those days, when professional football had not yet become the dominant part of the football universe, the Army-Navy game was still a considerable sporting event, and that year both Army and Navy had formidable teams. Each had lost only one game, Army to Notre

Dame by two points, Navy to North Carolina by a touchdown (it had also tied Duke). That was a magnificent Army team, physical if not versatile, and it featured two formidable running backs: Pete Dawkins, a scholar-athlete and already something of a national hero, and Bob Anderson, who was, if anything, a heavier, more punishing runner. Both were All-Americans. Army was leading the nation at the time in rushing and was ranked second in total offense and scoring. But Steve Belichick did not think it took the most brilliant of scouts to figure out the Army game plan, and he was not particularly impressed with his own pregame analysis and predictions, though they later seemed quite accurate. He thought he had done a good job of detailing the obvious, but there were many other games when his role as a scout had been more important.

For if Army had great strength in its running game, it was not matched by a comparable passing game. The Cadets averaged 323 yards on the ground and only 81 passing. It was therefore an imbalanced offense, one, Belichick suspected, that would be comparatively easy to defend against. The Army coach, Red Blaik, was conservative. He did not like to throw the ball, and in particular he did not like to throw when he got near the goal line. The Cadets preferred a power game to a speed game, off-tackle runs rather than sweeps, and they had been rewarded all season long for the strategy. All you had to do at critical moments, Belichick thought, was pack the defenders in tight and keep the Army runners from getting outside. If you deployed your defenders in the right way, and cut off certain angles and slants, the Army runners could not cut back. An Army quarterback who could throw even a simple pass down on the goal line might exploit so imbalanced a defense, Belichick knew, but he did not think Army had either that passer or the inclination to throw the ball. Belichick's general defensive philosophy was simple: Find out what the other guys do best—which is what they always want to do, especially under pressure in a big game—take it away from them, and make them do things that they are uncomfortable with.

Belichick was watching from the press box that day. Eddie Erdelatz, the Navy head coach, liked to call him "my upstairs coach," because Belichick preferred watching the game from up there, in no small part because he got nervous when he worked the sidelines. Bill, his son, was at home. He was judged to be too young to go to Philadelphia for the game, and so one of his uncles had come down from Ohio to babysit, with the game on the television set, of course. (Bill would see his first Army-Navy game live two years later when Joe Bellino, his first football hero, scored three touchdowns in the first game Bill ever remembered seeing, a 43–12 Navy victory.) Aged five, Bill was still a few years away from helping his father go over film, and still so new to the game that when he was told he was being taken to see William and Mary play, he wondered if William would beat Mary.

On that day in December 1957, Navy stopped a great Army team cold, shutting it out, 14–0. True, it was a muddy field, but that did not seem to matter very much and perhaps should have helped Army. The Cadets gained a total of only eighty-eight yards on the ground, and forty-eight yards in the air. They threw fourteen passes and completed six. The next year, in order to keep the Navy defense from packing in against the run, Blaik came up with his idea of the lonely end—a receiver stationed some twenty yards from everyone else, receiving the signals from the quarterback by, it seemed to opposing teams, mental telepathy. That formation put a great deal more pressure on the defenses, loosened them up significantly, and brought Army a greater measure of success and Dawkins the Heisman Trophy. But the 1957 game was a stunning victory for Navy, and after the game Shirley Povich, the famed *Washington Post* columnist, sought out

Erdelatz to congratulate him on a superlative victory. Erdelatz pointed to Steve Belichick and said, "He won the game for us two weeks ago." Belichick did not think he had done anything exceptional, just done his job, and what he had seen was what any good football man would have seen.

CHAPTER ONE

When the clock was finally winding down, the seconds ticking off, with the Philadelphia team unconscionably slow in getting its plays off, Steve Belichick, always in the background whenever there were television cameras around, left his place behind some of the New England players, back around the 50-yard line. Moving quickly, he headed toward the 35, wanting to share this final glorious moment with his son, Bill, the coach of New England, about to win his third Super Bowl victory in four years. Bill Belichick himself was puzzled at that moment by the slow, almost languid way the Eagles were running their plays, as if they were the ones with the lead, not the Patriots, and they wanted to burn the clock. He kept checking the scoreboard, which said 24–14, as if perhaps he was the one who had the score wrong. He called his assistants, Romeo Crennel and Eric Mangini, on the headphones to make sure the Patriots did indeed enjoy a ten-point lead. "Have I got the score right?" he asked, and they assured him he did. "Then what the hell are they trying to do?" he asked. His assistants did not know, either. The long, slow drive had finally culminated in a Philadelphia score, because of a blown defensive coverage on the part of the Patriots; the correct defense, designed to give up a limited number of yards in exchange for more time off the clock, had not been sent in or used, and Philadelphia scored on a 30-yard pass play. Seeing that his players were in the wrong coverage, Belichick had tried desperately to call time-out, but he had been too late, and the Eagles had scored. Belichick had been momentarily furious, mostly at himself, because he demanded perfection first and foremost of himself. But the score had served only to make the game closer; it had not affected the final outcome.

Steve Belichick got to his son's side just in time to be soaked by Gatorade in the ritual shower of the victorious. That gave him his first great moment of celebrity, coming at the end of a six-decade career of playing and coaching football, and that moment was witnessed by much of the entire nation, live and in color, on national television. One could imagine one of those Disneyland commercials, generally accorded the young and instantly famous at moments like these, when a voice would ask, "Steve Belichick, you've been coaching and playing for sixty years, where are you going now that your son has won his third Super Bowl in four years?"

It was one of the best moments of the entire Super Bowl extravaganza, filled as it is so often with moments of artificial emotion, because this moment was absolutely genuine, father and son drenched together, emotion finally showing on the face of the son, usually so reticent about showing emotion, as if to do so was to give away some precious bit of control, to fall victim at least momentarily to the whims of the modern media trap. Father and son were bonded in this instant by the joy of victory and by the shared experience of a lifetime of coaching, with all its bitter as well as celebratory moments.

Steve Belichick was a lifer, viewed by his peers as a coach's coach. He had never made much money and never enjoyed much fame outside the small hermetically sealed world of coaching. For much of his adulthood he had lived with the special uncertainty of a coach—a world without guarantees, except for the one that no matter how well things were going at the moment, they would surely turn around soon. There would be a bad recruiting year, a prize recruit who said he would come to your school and then decided at the last moment to attend an archrival, too many good players would be injured in the preseason (but only after the national magazines had looked at your roster and predicted a conference championship), or there would be a change in athletic directors and the new one had a favorite all his own whom he hoped to install in what was now his program. In the end, the head coach would be fired and the assistant coaches would have to leave with him.

Bill Belichick had been born in 1952 in Nashville, when Steve, already considered an exceptional coach—tough and smart, original and demanding, way ahead of the curve in the drills he demanded, and, in addition to everything else, an absolutely brilliant scout—was in the process of being fired as an assistant coach at Vanderbilt, even though the team he was part of had done reasonably well. He had been fired, all of the members of the Belichick family later believed, because they and the coaching team they were part of had been not quite social enough for the genteel world of Vanderbilt football, and there had been a deftly organized campaign against them by one of Nashville's more influential (and social) sportswriters.

Thus Bill Belichick had entered the world rather typically as the son of a lifer. When he was a toddler, his family had already given up the lease on their house and put their furniture in storage, and his father was waiting for word on his next job. The head coach they had followed to Vanderbilt, an immensely popular man named Bill Edwards (William Steven Belichick was named both for Bill Edwards and for his father), was well connected in the world of coaching and liked by almost everyone, save apparently one or two Nashville sportswriters, but it was late in the year, and there were not a lot of openings.

It was a difficult moment. On Steve's tiny salary they had not been able to save any money, and they were hunkered down in a house they would soon have to vacate. They had no furniture—moving boxes filled with their possessions served as their tables and chairs. The phone, which was supposed to be ringing with job offers, did not ring. There was talk that Bill Edwards might be offered a job at North Carolina as an assistant to a man named George Barclay, and that if he were, Steve Belichick might become a part of his team, but it was still just talk. Time was running out. Finally a game plan was decided on, one that Jeannette Belichick helped formulate. They would pile everything they had into the car and drive east. Somewhere along the way, they would stop and call the Carolina people. If the job was there, they would continue on to Chapel Hill; if there was no word, they would leave the uncertain world of college coaching, head south, and Steve would try to find a job in Florida, coaching high school football.

In Knoxville, not quite halfway to Chapel Hill, the Belichick family pulled up alongside a restaurant, and Steve got out and called from a pay phone. The Carolina job was his. So they had continued to Chapel Hill, and the idea of coaching high school football was put aside, at least for the moment. The Belichick family loved Chapel Hill, and Steve always regretted that Carolina was not a perennial football power, but to his mind George Barclay was not that good a coach—it would have been better had Edwards been the coach, he thought. Chapel Hill lasted three years, 1953–55, before they were all once again fired.

From there Steve Belichick managed to get the job as an assistant coach at Navy. Bill was three years old when they went to Annapolis.

Steve Belichick loved coaching there, loved coaching the midshipmen, and decided he would stay there permanently if he could. He did not long to be a head coach—he had seen how quickly they came and went, even when they were talented, like his friend Bill Edwards. He did not need the title or the power. He decided everything he needed was right there: a solid program (Navy still had nationally ranked teams in those days), great young men, an attractive community, wonderful colleagues. He was by all accounts a brilliant coach, an exceptional teacher, and arguably the best and most professional scout of his era. No one, it was said, could scout another team and break down their film quite like Steve Belichick; no one could pick up on a giveaway mistake of another team—say, a runner who involuntarily gave a small tip-off before the snap when he was going to get the ball—like Belichick.

He was one of those rare Americans who, though ambitious and exceptionally hardworking, knew when he had a deal that suited him, and had no urge for greener pastures, which in his shrewd estimate might in fact not be greener. Over the years he turned down countless other job offers, from other colleges and from the pros. When Bill Edwards, his great mentor and by then coach at Wittenberg College in Ohio, asked him to come there, he regretfully turned it down because it would be a step backward in terms of the strength of the program. When there was a chance to become the head coach of Navy, he told the committee that he liked the job he already had, thereby taking himself out of the running for head coach. He did another shrewd thing. At Chapel Hill he had become close to the Carolina basketball coach, the legendary Frank McGuire, who had taken a special liking to the Belichick family and especially to its three-year-old son. Basketball practice always stopped when Steve and Bill showed up, and someone was ordered to find a basketball, always brand-new, to roll out to Bill. When McGuire heard that the

Belichicks were going to Navy, he told Steve to do what his friend Ben Carnevale, the basketball coach there, had done, which was to try and move up on a tenure track as a physical education instructor in addition to coaching. This would protect him from the volatility and uncertainty of the coach's life. Steve took the advice, and became an assistant professor first and then a tenured associate professor. That gave him something rare in the world of coaching, job security, and he ended up staying at Navy for thirty-three years under eight head coaches.

He taught thousands of players and younger coaches, many of whom went on to more prominent jobs, but in the end his greatest pupil was his son. He taught him many things, including what position to play—center, because the boy was smart and strong for his size, but he was not going to be very big, not on a football-player scale, and because, even more important, he was not going to be particularly fast. Steve knew that early on because Bill had heavy ankles—that was the first thing he looked for when he was recruiting, the ankles, because it was a tip-off on speed. Center was the right position for Bill because he was smart and would know the game, and a smart center who knew how to read a defense was always valuable. So, as a result, a particular repetitive sound, a kind of thudding, filled the Belichick house in Bill's teenage years: the sound of him centering the ball against a mat hanging from a wall in the basement. Another important thing Steve taught his son was how to scout and how to study film, which Bill Belichick started doing when he was about nine years old.

For if anyone had helped create the extraordinary coach who stood there, soaked in Gatorade, that evening of his third Super Bowl win (both Belichicks subsequently caught bad colds and suspected it was because of the shower), it was Steve Belichick. At that moment his son (still known as Billy to some of the players and coaches Steve had worked with during the Navy years) stood at the pinnacle of his profession. Others in the football world placed him in the pantheon of the NFL's greatest coaches. Maxie Baughan, one of the first men he worked under when he joined the league in 1975, a nine-time Pro Bowl player himself, and a longtime George Allen favorite, was one of the first players to pick up on Bill Belichick's brilliance when he was still a child-coach with the Colts back in 1975. After the third Super Bowl he placed Belichick among the elite three, a new trinity: Lombardi, Landry, and now Belichick. Others were more cautious and added the names of Paul Brown, George Allen, Chuck Noll, Don Shula, and Bill Walsh, among other immensely talented coaches, but of Belichick's excellence and originality and his place among the elite, there was no doubt. Ron Jaworski, who quarterbacked an earlier Eagle team to the Super Bowl in 1981 and eventually became ESPN's most knowledgeable football commentator, thought it was quite possible that Belichick was the best ever, because he had won three times in an era dramatically less congenial to creating a dynasty than before. In the past, there were two principal obstacles faced by a team once it became a champion. The first was the instinct to relax and not work as hard once you had won it all, to think that because you had just been the best, you were entitled to be the best again. The other was the League's draft, the fact that each year the weakest teams had the best shot at the very best players. In the modern era, when there were probably too many teams, the League had decided, consciously or unconsciously, on policies to keep the better teams and better organizations from dominating, and instead to make weaker organizations look better—in effect, to reward the weak and punish the strong. Now the schedule was rigged—the better you were, the tougher the schedule you faced.

The League, it was believed, wanted every team to come in as close to .500 with its record as possible. That was a dramatic change from the past. In addition, free agency and the salary cap worked against dynastic ambitions. Teams that did their scouting better than their competitors could not stockpile players as in the past, and it was harder than ever to keep a good bench, because if you won, other teams stole your starters and your backup people—those you were grooming, but who were probably a bit dissatisfied because they were not starting. The salary cap put a certain pressure on you as well, because as you won, your players felt, not without some justification, that they deserved more money, and it was hard to keep them all satisfied, so some of your role-playing athletes were snatched away at star-player salaries by your rivals. What Dallas, Green Bay, Pittsburgh, and San Francisco did in another era—create a powerful team and add to it systematically—was harder to do now. "There's a volatility to line-ups now that wasn't there before, before free agency and the cap, and no matter how good your organization is these days you're going to lose a number of your best players each year," Jaworski said. "That makes his accomplishments even more remarkable." Or as Bill Walsh, the celebrated architect and coach of the San Francisco 49ers in their glory years, and sometimes called The Genius, said admiringly of Belichick: "He's done it in an age when the dynasties are gone, unless you count the Patriots as a dynasty, which I think they are."

What football men, coaches and players alike, admired about him more than anything else was his ability to create a *team* in an age when the outside forces working against it seemed more powerful every year and where often the more talented a player was, the more he needed to display his ego, to celebrate his own deeds rather than team deeds. A fan could now watch truly bizarre scenes on Sunday—a player, his team down by four touchdowns, making a good catch and dancing around as if his team had just won the championship. Belichick, as much as anyone in football, tried to limit that, and to make New England win and behave at all times like a team. The most obvious example of that old-fashioned emphasis on team came in the first of New England's three Super Bowl victories. The League had asked him, according to tradition, whether he wanted to introduce his offensive or defensive team to both the crowd and the nation at the start of the game, and he had said, neither—he wanted to introduce the entire team. The League officials argued against it, because that was not the way it was done, and told him he had to choose. Belichick was nothing if not stubborn—stubborn when he was right and sometimes just as stubborn when he was wrong—and he refused to budge, so, finally, the League caved.

Out they had come, all the Patriots, joyously and confidently, and it was not just other players and coaches who got it immediately, that this introduction was something different, designed to show this was a team and everyone was a part of it. It was also understood by much of the vast television audience, exhausted not merely by players' excessive egos, but also by broadcasters who failed to blow the whistle on them. A great many people decided then and there that they would root for New England as kind of an homage to the game itself.

As they watched the game, these fans came to admire not merely Belichick, but also the players: These were football players as they were supposed to be. They cared about playing together, they were a team. The fans did not necessarily know the Patriots players at first—McGinest, Bruschi, Seymour, Vrabel, and Brown—because they were not the kind of players whose contract negotiations made the national press; nor did they have signature war dances. But they played with intelligence and grittiness, and they refused to give in to the superior press clippings of the Rams. The Patriots were not necessarily America's Team, as Dallas had so optimistically nicknamed itself in an earlier era, but they were an easy team for ordinary football fans to like in the new era of football.

CHAPTER TWO

The Belichicks are from the coal mining and steel making part of the country, from a culture and a time when nothing was to be wasted, and when everyone, or almost everyone, was poor. Both of Steve Belichick's parents were Croatian; Steve was Stephen Nickolas Belichick. The name was originally Bilicic, and it was phoneticized or Americanized, not, as happened with so many immigrant families, at Ellis Island, by immigration officials reluctant to master the names from the old world, with their weird mixtures of vowels and consonants, but rather by a first-grade teacher in Monessen, Pennsylvania. That teacher, told by Anna Bilicic, Steve's oldest sister and the first family member born in the United States, that her name was Bell-uh-chik, wrote it down as Belichick, thereby earning the undying hatred of Mary Barkovic Bilicic for corrupting the family name.

Ivan (John) and Mary Barkovic Bilicic were both born in Croatia, in the Karlovac region, and John came to this country around 1897, Mary, a bit later. They were already married, and the original idea was that he would come for a time, make some money, and then return to Croatia. "How did he do it?" Steve Belichick asked years later. "How did he come here, not knowing the language, not knowing how to read or write, and somehow manage to make it here, and find work? And how did she find the courage to come here and find him? It's always baffled me. I can't imagine myself being able to do it." John and Mary were supposed to stay in touch, but because he had never been to school (the nearest school had been some eight miles away), he could neither read nor write, and so he could not contact her. In time, she set out for America with her brother, Nick Barkovic, to find him. Not speaking a word of English, the two arrived here and started searching the Croatian enclaves of western Pennsylvania, the coal mining and steel manufacturing part of the country. They went town by town, looking for Ivan, going to one after another of those small ethnic islands in America, places where the culture of the old world was being blended into the very different culture of the new world.

They found him by luck and hard work in Monessen, a tough steel town just south of Pittsburgh, where he worked for Pittsburgh Steel. All five of the Bilicic children, soon to be Belichick, were born there: Anna, the oldest, in 1908, Frank in 1910, Joe in 1913, John in 1916, and Steve in 1919. In time, Anna married a man from Youngstown, Ohio, just west of the state line, when Youngstown (today one of the poorest and most neglected cities in the country) had seemed infinitely more prosperous. In Monessen, the particular combination of weather and smog from the plant seemed to kill all vegetation in the area, and the family was anxious to get away. "The air was so terrible that if we hadn't moved I don't think my father would have made it to forty," Steve Belichick said years later. So, in 1924, drawn to where Anna now lived, and driven out in part by the Monessen air, the family moved to Ohio, eventually settling in Struthers, an extended industrial suburb of Youngstown. Like so many others who came here from that part of Europe, they knew they would have to begin their American journey by doing the requisite heavy lifting, aware that the rewards for their hard work might be minimal; if the fruits of their coming to America were to be enjoyed, the better life they had hoped for, they would most likely have to be enjoyed by their children, and perhaps more accurately their grandchildren.

With a loan from a neighborhood grocer, they bought a small, extremely simple house. There was a garden, but not for flowers—they grew all the vegetables they could, and John, who was good at all handiwork, built an area in the basement to put the jars of canned vegetables. When it was time to preserve the vegetables in glass jars, the entire family helped out. It was a primitive, rather brutal economy—no minimum wage, no social security, no pensions, almost no labor unions. Everyone in the family had to contribute. The family code was a simple one: When things were working out, and John Bilicic had work, it was important to save money for the moment when things would go bad. John walked five and a half miles a day from Struthers to Youngstown and five and a half miles back each day to and from his job with the Youngstown Sheet & Tube factory. There his job was making wire; he was what was called a wire drawer, pulling huge rolls of wire out of a giant oven by pulleys, and then cooling them by pouring water on them. "They poured the cooling water into the Mahoning River," Steve Belichick remembered. "I think there were thirty-eight factories in the immediate area, and all thirty-eight poured all their dirty water into the Mahoning, making it probably the brownest river in America. Nothing could live there."

It was an unbearably hard job, but it was worse when there was no work. The Depression was brutal—it was as if work stopped throughout the entire region, and thousands and thousands of men were laid off without any protections. There were three years, just as Steve Belichick was in junior high, 1932–34, when John was laid off. But the family endured. Everyone played his or her part. They took in boarders—two Croatian men, of course, to live in an upstairs bedroom. The boarders worked different shifts so that one could sleep while the other was at the mill, one working 7 A.M. to 7 P.M., the other 7 P.M. to 7 A.M. Mary was always washing and ironing and cleaning and cooking and canning. John was, in addition to other talents, a self-taught butcher, and the word got around to some local farmers, so the farmers brought him their animals, which he would clean and butcher, doing it for no fee, but getting in return some part of the meat. All of the children had jobs, and if Steve and his next older brother caddied at the golf course—55 cents for nine holes, 90 cents for eighteen holes—they were allowed to keep 10 cents, with the rest of the money going into the family kitty. What probably saved them in those years, Steve remembered, was the fact that his older brother Frank quit school and took a job with the gas company digging ditches—the work was steady, so there was a small base income.

The process of Americanization was led, as it was in so many immigrant homes, by the children, while the parents struggled both to survive and to understand so different and complex a society, one so hard and yet so much freer than that of the old country. At first the only language spoken in the house was Croatian, but then as Frank, the second child and oldest son, began to grow up, the language started to change to English—the parents, by now becoming Belichicks instead of Bilicics, would still speak Croatian, but Frank, and soon the others, spoke English back. In time even the parents tried to speak English at home, though they often lapsed into Croatian. The older children, unlike their parents, understood not only English, but also the American ways and that doing American things did not necessarily mean that the younger kids were spoiled. If the parents had been harder on the older children, they were looser with the younger ones; the older children marveled that when the family went for walks, if Steve, still very young, got tired, he would ask his father to carry him, and John Bilicic would in fact pick him up and carry him. The older three children would not be able to go to college, but the younger two, largely because of their athletic abilities—most certainly not because of any family affluence—would.

The values of that era and of that particular ethnic culture were basic. You worked hard. You saved. You did not waste anything. If possible, you grew your own food. You did not complain. You did not expect anyone to do anything for you. Discipline was not so much taught as it was lived, as an essential part of life for which there was no alternative. It was, says Bill Belichick, "a Draconian unsparing world." In those years, when Steve Belichick was going to high school, the union was trying to organize, and the Belichicks were all pro-union. It was done secretly at first; no one was to know whose side you were on until the right moment. Union organizers would come to the homes to spread the gospel, and then finally the men would show up at work sporting a big pro-union button.

The entire region of western Pennsylvania and eastern and central Ohio was great football country, both high school and college football. Everyone seemed to care passionately about the game. This was, after all, a part of the country where tough men endured great physical hardship to earn a living—only the strong succeeded, and not surprisingly, they produced big, strong, athletically gifted children, who had no fear of ferocious physical contact—indeed, they seemed to relish it. In the era before the coming of the great black athletes, when power was blended with speed and the game stayed just as physical but got a lot faster, no area produced as many great football players or as many distinguished coaches as this region. For the children of the steel mills, whose parents barely spoke English, it was often the first step in the Americanization process, the first recognition as successes they or their families would get, and in some cases the first ticket out of the steel mills and coal mines, a chance for a college education.

So it was with the Belichicks. Steve Belichick loved football from an early age. He played every day after school in the Struthers sandlots, and when he was on his way home from those games he was still practicing, putting moves on trees along the streets, juking them, faking left, and cutting right—no one could put a better move on a tree than Steve did, hearing as he did the imagined roar of the crowd. He started playing in junior high school, and continued in high school. He was not that big, perhaps 165 pounds when he reached college, but he was tough, and he was very fast. Coaches noticed, and he became a very good high school player at Struthers High.

CHAPTER THREE

Bill Belichick was a star who did not want to be a star, a celebrity in search of privacy and the right to do his job without any public interference. Unfortunately for him, on a playoff weekend, upward of 40 million Americans cared about him and what he and his players did. The camera had long since let the entire nation into his world, and it had created an appetite, healthy or unhealthy (he thought it was unhealthy), to know more about him as a celebrity, something he most demonstrably did not want to be. That on an ordinary Sunday some 15 or 16 million people wanted to watch him at work—and that the figure swelled to 90 million for a Conference championship and to around 135 million for a Super Bowl—moved him not at all. He was a man for better or for worse, remarkably without artifice. He had little gift or interest in modern public relations—if anything, he seemed almost uniquely resistant to it for someone so much, however involuntarily, in the public eye. He was about one thing only—coaching—and wary of anything that detracted from it, and in his mind, much of the modern media, especially television, did precisely that—not just because it took up time that could be better spent doing other things, like watching a bit of film for the tenth or eleventh time and working with assistant coaches, but because it was singularly dangerous, it fed egos, and swollen egos detracted from the essence of football, which was the idea of team. Modern media created a Me-Me-Me world, whereas he insisted on a We world.

He feared the celebrity culture's addictive force, which was particularly dangerous to athletic endeavors, though much less of a problem in baseball, rooted as it was in individual accomplishments, and a little less of a problem in basketball, where (as in the case of Michael Jordan) an individual accomplishment and team accomplishment could often be merged, and where there were so few players on a team. But football was a sport based entirely on the concept of team, where as many as forty players might play important roles in any given victory—yet the television camera might celebrate the deeds of only one or two. Thus, a great deal of time and energy in the world of the New England Patriots went into selecting players who were at least partially immune to displays of ego and self. This did not mean Bill Belichick was without ego—far from it. His ego was exceptional, and it was reflected by his almost unique determination. He liked being the best and wanted credit for being the best, a quiet kind of credit. But his ego was about the doing; it was fused into a larger purpose, that of his team winning. It was never about the narcissistic celebration of self that television loved to amplify.

He was about coaching; he did not exist in a world of one hundred new friendships, created instantly by his success, or friendships with other celebrities. His friends were people he had known at Annapolis, Andover, Wesleyan, and his early coaching days. His friendships were based on trust, and they were to be kept private, if at all possible. He shielded family and friends alike from public scrutiny. He did not do particularly well with the media, lacking the desire and the skill to create the artificial intimacy that worked so well for many others. Some very good, hardworking reporters thought he was unacceptably rude to them; as much as he wanted respect, he did not, in their view, treat them or what they did with proper respect. He was not good at challenging reporters and keeping them on the defensive as one of his mentors, Bill Parcells, had been, and he did poorly in dealing with the media in his first head coaching job, in Cleveland, in part because he tried to be like Parcells. This was a significant mistake, because he was not Parcells, did not have Parcells's sharp, acid tongue, and most important, he had not yet won as a head coach—for much of Parcells's style with the media, challenging them and on occasion bullying them with singular skill and getting away with it, was successful because he did it *only* after he had started winning.

Bill Belichick did not do small talk well. He did substance much better. To those reporters genuinely interested in football, he could be exceedingly helpful, giving an immense amount of his time, drawing up the plays his teams had run. At such times he was the coach doing what he did best, teaching (both his mother and father, after all, had been teachers), pouring as much energy into a chalk talk as if the reporter were a rookie linebacker from a small school, where they had not had quite enough in the way of linebacker coaches. He was not a man of charisma, as one expected of coaches, but rather a quiet man of chalk.

Bill Belichick was the most stubborn of men. He did the things he wanted to do the way he wanted to do them, because in any given instance it was something he had thought about for a long time, and he had decided his way was right for him. Almost nothing could change him and make him act differently, and he did not easily forgive those who offended him. A commentator on ESPN named Tom Jackson had once said of him after a Patriots defeat that his players hated him. Belichick neither forgave nor forgot, and he could be very hard on other ESPN reporters, some of whom were equally appalled by Jackson's carelessness. He was uneasy about and distrustful of the world of modern media and public relations precisely because he saw it as a world of people wanting to know the wrong things about him and his players. It wanted him to be more charismatic. There was a great contradiction here: He was ferociously driven, and his drive had made him a singular success, and his success had made him a celebrity, but he had little interest in the excessive rewards of fame. The more successful he was, the more those rewards poured in. Then the more distrustful he became of those rewards. Most comparable figures enjoyed being celebrities, and understood the uses of fame, that it could make things easier. Some were completely seduced by it, a sure sign that they would begin to slip in their chosen professions, and the rewards would quickly be pulled away. You could fall from celebrity in contemporary America almost as quickly as you had achieved it.

He wanted no part of that. Ever wary of distractions, with the exception of an unusual friendship with the musician Jon Bon Jovi, a certifiable football nut and owner of a team in the Arena League, he avoided celebrities. He wanted to be with the people who had always been his friends. He wanted to avoid the trappings of a celebrity life. He dressed as simply as he could—his attire was as gray as he could make it, with the grayest of sweatshirts, and, as the television host David Letterman once said, he looked like a sherpa guide on the sidelines; his lack of sartorial elegance was a favorite subject with journalists. There was no stylist to the Boston elite eager to take credit for his haircuts. Though all kinds of auto dealers in the New England area competed to have him drive the fanciest and most elegant of cars, he drove a Volvo station wagon, which seemed appropriate, parked as it often was in the open fields alongside his children's schools; it looked very much like the cars belonging to the other parents of teenaged soccer and lacrosse players. The voice on his phone message—"Sorry to have missed your call"—was singularly flat, as if he might be apprenticing to be an undertaker, and it seemed not at all sorry to have missed your call, and might in fact be delighted to miss it once again.

He was, all in all, an unadorned man. He wanted that to be not just his hallmark, or lack thereof, but the hallmark of his team. They were not to excel at media sound bites, which often came at the expense of team, or were at the very least fodder for opposing teams eager to be fired up by the slightest sign of disrespect. Their mission was as unadorned as possible. It was about football and nothing else. Belichick coached because he loved coaching, and for him it was virtually an end in itself. He wanted to bring his players to the highest level of preparedness, hand them an edge in a world where everyone was so evenly matched that any edge might determine the outcome.

He would have been just as happy coaching in high school or at some small college, his close friends thought; he would have worked just as maniacally if there were no giant stadium filled with fifty or sixty thousand people, not to mention dozens of television cameras broadcasting the games to an audience of millions more. The great reward of winning the Super Bowl was neither the money nor the fame that followed, but the fact that his team had beaten the best; it was not that the rewards were greater, but that the challenge was greater. His personal challenge, each week, was to see if he could do it all one more time: study the opposition like a pathologist using a powerful microscope and pick up on the one or two little telltale signs that would give his team the one or two extra bits of information that represented the fateful edge.

In a world where attention to detail was probably as important as sheer brilliance, where the people who took care of the tiniest details tended to be rewarded for it, the little details added up until they represented significant differences. He was the king of Post-it notes. Nothing slipped through the cracks with him. In attention to detail he was a lineal descendant of some of the most obsessed men in America, those great NFL coaches—most notably George Allen, who coached successfully in both Los Angeles and Washington, and among whose other peculiarities was the fact that he seemed to eat nothing but ice cream. "I think he likes it because he doesn't have to chew it, and it doesn't take any time," his wife, Etty, once said. "Chewing it would take his mind away from football."

Of Allen's Ten Commandments for a coach, number one was "Football comes first," and number five was "Leisure time is that five or six hours when you sleep at night." (There were, of course, those who thought that Allen was less the workaholic than the image he presented, but that he wanted the people around him, especially his players, to believe that he had no other life, as if to shame them into not having other lives, either. It was said by these skeptics that he would sneak off on occasion and have dinner with his family, and when the office phone would ring, he would turn on the projector so the sound would be in the background when he answered and he could tell the caller, "Wait just a minute while I turn the projector off," to make it seem he had been viewing film.)

"You can understand Bill Belichick's value system the moment that you walk in the door here," said Dean Pees, one of his assistant coaches, describing the offices of the Patriots. Pees was a longtime coach who, like Belichick, came out of the great tradition of Ohio football coaches; he joined the Patriots this past year as a linebacker coach, after coaching at Kent State: "It's as if it's an anonymous office. You'd never know our offices were here. It doesn't say anything on the door about being the offices of the Patriots' coaches. And in the outer room there are no trophies—you'd think there would be all kinds of trophies or other symbols of our success. But there's nothing there. And more important, you'd never know we were at a pinnacle of the profession. If you didn't know before you got here how low-key it was, I think you'd expect something like a Donald Trump office, with all kinds of things advertising and promoting the ego of the institution, the ego of the team, and the ego of the coach. There would be all kinds of signs of our success, all kinds of trophies displayed in a case. But not here. There are no symbols of what the Patriots have done in the past, no celebrations of the past championships. That's all done with, that's the given. Everyone here is working in T-shirts and shorts. There is no celebration of any victory in the past—we're all working for the next victory, the one yet to come. That's all Bill—he doesn't want the trappings of the past, doesn't need them. He knows they lead to complacency. He does not allow complacency."

The person who has to lead the fight against complacency, Belichick had learned, was the man at the top. Some three years into his career, after he had finished working at more or less entry-level positions in Baltimore and Detroit, he was at something of loose ends. The group he had been a part of in Detroit had all been fired. His colleagues at both places had understood how talented he was, that he was a young coach with the rare ability to take film and turn it into a living profile of an opposing team, that he produced scouting reports of exceptional value. Because of his Ohio connections, Don Shula, then one of the two or three ranking coaches in the game, was a possibility. Shula, too, had come out of the Paul Brown alumni association, and Steve Belichick, if he had not actually played for Brown, was connected to him because Bill Edwards had once roomed with Brown and had been an assistant coach under him. The name Belichick would be known to Don Shula in Miami. So Bill Belichick had contacted Shula, explained what he thought he could bring to the job, and given his references, which were already glowing, especially for someone in his mid-twenties. Shula was gracious and listened carefully. Then he said, "I'm afraid you're exactly what I don't want. I don't want someone like you doing film. I want my coaches to do it themselves. I don't want them delegating responsibility to their assistants and distancing themselves from what is happening. I want them right on top of it." With that Shula apologized, and there was no job offer—it was an interesting lesson; Belichick had been rejected for being able to do something important too well.

By the time he took the job as head coach of the Patriots, he had finally learned how to delegate a good deal of the work, but he held on to the most elemental job of all: looking at film. It was as if a journalist managed to become CEO of a great newspaper and then announced that in addition to running the paper, he would continue to function as the paper's police reporter; or a great general, having become chief of staff of the Army, announcing he wanted to serve as the point man for a rifle platoon as well.

CHAPTER FOUR

He was at once both optimist and pessimist, optimistic that if you got the right players and did the right things, you could win it all; pessimistic because he felt that any overt public optimism might endanger his chances of success. "Gloom," his colleague Bill Parcells, so good with nicknames and with whom Belichick had a complicated, almost tortured relationship, called him. As in the phrase "Where's Gloom?" which Parcells said upon arriving at the offices of the Cleveland Browns when Belichick was coaching there. Smile too much and people got the wrong idea, that you were not taking it seriously enough; laugh too much and your players might think you were an easy mark.

His determination to reach the pinnacle was nothing less than a lifelong pursuit. When the first Super Bowl victory (over the St. Louis Rams) took place on February 3, 2002, it had been going on for twenty-seven years, which was the length of time that Bill Belichick had been coaching in the NFL (though arguably it was more like forty-one or forty-two years, which went back to the time when Bill was about nine years old and working with his father, breaking down game film at Annapolis).

In that journey, the victory against the St. Louis Rams was something of a landmark, the high-water mark of his career, the best job of coaching in a single game he had ever done, Belichick would later say. It is important to remember the context of that victory: The Rams were already the *Rams,* one of the NFL's true golden teams; they had already won the 1999 Super Bowl, scored 526 points; they missed the Super Bowl in 2000 because their defense was not nearly as good as their offense, but in 2001 they had once again dominated almost everyone. The Patriots were, by contrast, an unlikely Super Bowl visitor. They had started slowly, and had changed quarterbacks early in the season when their star quarterback was seriously injured, forcing them to go with a virtual rookie for the rest of the season. That season their opponents had cumulatively made more first downs, rushed for more yards, and passed for more yards than the Patriots, and looking at their statistics they seemed more like an 8–8 or perhaps even a 7–9 team. Belichick had been to the Super Bowl three times before, twice as a defensive coordinator of some powerful New York Giants teams, and once as an assistant head coach—but not defensive coordinator—for a different Patriot team, one coached by Bill Parcells. In the second of the two Super Bowls with the Giants, he had estimated that the opposition Buffalo Bills, with an exceptionally versatile and explosive offense, probably enjoyed a slight edge in pure talent. But now, as he surveyed the Rams and the Patriots, he thought the Rams were a better, more explosive team than the Bills had been, and his Patriots not as talented as those Giants. The gap between the Rams and the Patriots seemed vast.

The Rams had a brilliant quarterback, Kurt Warner, a great passer whose personal narrative at that moment was the foremost Horatio Alger story of college and professional football. He had been a very good high school quarterback in Iowa and had hoped to go to the University of Iowa. But on a recruiting trip there he had been completely ignored by the all-powerful Hawkeye coach, Hayden Fry, who did not even deign to shake his hand. (In his autobiography, *All Things Possible,* Warner referred to Fry as the King of Iowa, or simply the King.) His hopes dampened, Warner went to Northern Iowa, where he sat on the bench too long and played for serious amounts of time only in his senior year. He was not drafted by the pros, but showed enough ability for scouts working the bottom of the talent chain to recommend him to the Green Bay Packers, who paid him $5000 to show up at their training camp as a free agent. That was not a lot of money to invest, especially for a team looking at a number of other young quarterbacks, and that year he got only fourteen snaps in five weeks of seven-on-seven football. Then the Packers cut him loose. He stayed on the periphery of football for a few years, playing (and starring) in the Arena League for the Iowa Barnstormers, and then he moved on to the European League, while continuing to make some money on the side back in Iowa in the off-season by packing groceries at Hy-Vee, a regional food chain.

But he always had faith in himself; he had a good arm, and he always managed to impress a few coaches. The time spent in the Arena League, where he played faster-than-a-speeding-bullet football on small fields against defenses that closed ever so quickly, sharpened his reactions and prepared him well for a shot at the big time. He made it back to the NFL in 1998, and the next year he was listed by the Rams as a backup, and then got his chance when the starting quarterback, Trent Green, went down in the preseason. By then he had a formidable arm, a great touch, and he made very quick reads. He starred immediately and took the Rams to the Super Bowl. His regular season numbers seemed to mock every player personnel man and coach in the NFL. In sixteen games he completed 65 percent of his passes, for 4353 yards, and 41 touchdowns, and only 13 interceptions. His touch seemed almost magical: The ball always seemed to arrive just where it was supposed to be just when it was supposed to get there, and he had wonderful receivers—Isaac Bruce, Torry Holt, Az-Zahir Hakim, and Ricky Proehl—some of them shockingly fast, men who could run brilliant routes and seemed wired to Warner by some kind of extrasensory perception, so that he could throw to spots where they would miraculously arrive at just the right instant. The Rams had, in addition, a great running back, Marshall Faulk, always dangerous, a player with speed and balance and power, who posed an extra threat because he was such a marvelous receiver, able to take a short pass of six or seven yards and turn it into a 20-yard gain.

On the eve of the Super Bowl game in early 2002 Marshall Faulk was twenty-eight, at the very peak of his abilities, playing in an offense perfectly suited for his multiple talents. He made the rest of the offense—those exceptional wide receivers, all of them it seemed unusually fast—more dangerous, and they in turn, with the defense's need to concentrate on them, made him even more dangerous. It was not his pure power that made him so dangerous—there were other more powerful, more muscular running backs in the game—nor was it his speed. "What sets him apart from everybody else is that he can go from a standing start to full speed faster than anybody I've ever seen," said Ted Marchibroda, who coached Faulk when he had first come into the League with the Indianapolis Colts. "When he runs the ball and is forced to hesitate, his next step is full speed." The other thing that made him special was his unusual vision and the way he used it as an extension of his running ability. "He runs with his eyes probably as well as any back in pro football, probably in the history of pro football," said Charley Armey, the player personnel man of the

Rams. "His legs allow him to do what his instincts and eyes tell him to do." Warner himself was dazzled by Faulk's versatility and his ability to see the entire field. "He thinks like a quarterback," he once said. "You put him in any situation and he sees the whole field, knows whom he has to pick up, and how he can help out, because he's aware of everyone's assignments." He was quite possibly, Warner thought, the best multipurpose back in the history of the game. Entering the Super Bowl, Faulk had just become the first player in NFL history to average over two thousand yards in plays from scrimmage, both running and receiving, for four straight years. He simply killed defenses.

The St. Louis offense labored behind a very good offensive line. It was bad enough to play them on any given field, but they would play on artificial turf that Sunday of the Super Bowl, and on the turf the fast became even faster. The Greatest Show on Turf, the Rams were called, and regrettably for the Patriots, cows could not eat the field in New Orleans. Nor were the Rams vulnerable on defense. They were not carried by their defense, but it was good and it did not pose any essential weaknesses for them. "They were very explosive—that's the right word for them—as explosive a team as the NFL probably has ever had," Belichick said later, "certainly one of the great NFL teams of all time."

By contrast the Patriots were not yet the *Patriots,* the dynastic team, and Belichick was not yet *Belichick,* the genius, which he was later often accused of being, a tricky charge against which there was no real defense, a charge as much burden as praise. (The genius talk made everyone in the Belichick family a little nervous. When writers began to suggest in print that Bill, like his lineal predecessor Bill Walsh, might be a genius, Steve Belichick wisely demurred. "You are," he said, "talking about someone who walks up and down a football field.") He had been a brilliant defensive coach in his years on the Giants, always under the considerable shadow of Bill Parcells, who was like a giant tree under which no other smaller trees ever got much sunshine. Yet the Giants fans and other football aficionados knew that Belichick was something special, a man not to be underestimated, that there was a signature to a Belichick team: Whatever the opposition did in the first half, his team tended to take away in the second half. But then in 1991 he got a chance to become the head coach at Cleveland, and there he was judged to have fallen on his face, although under closer inspection he had done a good deal better under rather difficult circumstances than he got credit for. The Cleveland tour had created a view that he might be the perfect defensive coordinator, but somehow lacked the requisite charisma—a vital word in those days—to be an NFL head coach, that he was something of a genius-nerd, someone who was doomed to make a more charismatic coach (Parcells) look better; he had found his level in the NFL constellation and it was not as a head coach.

Besides, the Patriots themselves were not taken that seriously. They had gotten to the Super Bowl, it was believed, by a fluke, a very bad call in a playoff game with the Raiders. They had a de facto rookie quarterback, Tom Brady, who did not seem to match up well with Warner. Still, the Patriots had been improving week by week, they had beaten some very good teams on their way to New Orleans, and they had a very good defense, very physical and yet quite nuanced in its sense of the game. Their coach was brilliant at situational football—more than any other team in football, they made adjustments week by week according to the strengths of the teams they were playing, meaning they were not as predictable as most teams. But none of that seemed to enter the calculations. Serious football fans simply did not think they belonged in the Super Bowl, that most sacrosanct of games—it was almost as if they were seen as intruders. For those betting on the game, the spread was two touchdowns, and any serious fan, one suspects, probably thought St. Louis would win 28–14 or 35–14.

The Rams had played the Patriots earlier in the season and had handled them easily. The score was relatively close, 24–17, but the game was not. The Rams had been completely in charge of the tempo of the game, had gained 482 yards from scrimmage, 401 of them from Warner's passes—he was a cool 30 of 42 that day. At the end of the game, with 7:46 left on the clock, the Rams had controlled the ball almost leisurely as if they were toying with the Patriots, who were never able to get their hands on the ball to try and tie—not that, given the way the game was going, it would have made much difference. The game had ended when, with the Rams on the Patriot 12, and with the Patriots out of time-outs, Warner had burned the last two minutes of the clock by kneeling down three times in a row.

Afterward, Belichick believed that he had coached badly. He had been preoccupied with other issues that week—his quarterback coach Dick Rehbein had died suddenly in the preseason and that had thrown the coaching staff a little out of order and out of their normal sequence of responsibilities. In addition, they were still in the process of breaking in Brady after a serious, midseason injury to Drew Bledsoe, the team's signature player, a quarterback blessed not with great mobility, but with a powerful arm, the kind most coaches salivated over. Bledsoe could deliver a brilliant strike down the field at just the right moment, and the fans loved him. In the week before the Rams game, Bledsoe had finally returned from his injury, the two quarterbacks had shared the snaps in practice, and Belichick later regarded that as an added distraction.

Looking back on the regular season, Belichick decided that he had been preoccupied with too many other things, that his game plan had been flawed, and that the Rams had handled it all too easily. The Patriots had blitzed—that is, systematically sent in linebackers and defensive backs as if they were pass rushers—but because the Ram offensive lineman had picked up the blitzes, nothing had broken Warner's rhythm, and he had enjoyed something of a free-fire zone, throwing into the Patriot secondary. Belichick had gone back and looked endlessly at the film of that game and of all the other Ram games, looking for a way to throw the Ram offense off-stride, to break their timing, to take away their comfort zone. Forty-two Patriot blitzes, he saw, and they had handled them all.

For the Super Bowl, the NFL demanded that the head coaches and the players be there by Monday, and Belichick had flown down to Louisiana along with the team, with the rest of the coaches coming a day later. He was accompanied by his assistant, Ernie Adams, an enigmatic, almost mysterious figure in football circles. He had been a close friend and adviser of Belichick's since 1970, when they were both seniors at Andover, not exactly a football powerhouse—rather, it was a boarding school more likely to produce senators, governors, and writers than professional football coaches. Not even all the people who understood the Belichick operation understood exactly what Adams did, and that included some of the Patriot players. Once during a team meeting, a giant photo of Adams had been punched up on the immense screen, instead of a play, and under it was written "What does this man do?" That was the same question that Art Modell, the owner in Cleveland, had often pondered, once saying to his staff, "I'll pay anyone here $10,000 if they can tell me what Ernie Adams does. I know he does something, and I know he works for me, and I know I pay him, but I'd love to know what it is."

The answer, of course, was that Ernie Adams was Belichick's Belichick, the film master's master of film. He was supremely knowledgeable about the history of the game—no play was ever forgotten, and his brain was like a little football computer, always clicking away, remembering which defense had stopped which offense, and who the coaches and the players had been. He was in a class with his boss in breaking down film and finding little things that no one else saw, and just as good at understanding the conceptual process that drove another team. He was, for a coach with so cerebral an approach to the game, a comforting figure, since he shared Belichick's views and his passion.

He was one of the very few men that Bill Belichick liked to test his own view of a game against, trusting completely Adams's truly original mind and his encyclopedic knowledge of the game; if they differed in a strategy, if they came out on different sides—which happened rarely—then Belichick took Adams's dissent seriously. He might not ultimately adapt to Adams's view, but he would always weigh it carefully. They had been through a great deal together, playing next to each other on an unbeaten Andover team (about which, as his senior project, Adams, who already had his own rather considerable collection of football films, did a study breaking down Andover's tendencies on offense) and then coaching together in New York, Cleveland, and New England.

As the friendship went way back, so did the trust, and so did the tendency to see the game in much the same way. Adams, the son of a career naval officer, was already in his fourth year at Andover, one of the truly great preparatory schools in the country, when Bill Belichick arrived there to do a fifth year of high school—it was called a PG or postgraduate year. Adams was already as advanced a football junkie as Belichick; he had an exceptional collection of books on coaching, including *Football Scouting Methods* ($5.00 a copy, published by the Ronald Press of New York City, and featuring jacket quotes from, among others, the legendary Paul Brown: "Scouting is essential to successful football coaching."), the only book written by one Steve Belichick, assistant coach of the Naval Academy. The book was not exactly a best seller—the author himself estimated that it sold at most four hundred copies—nor was it filled with juicy, inside tidbits about the private lives of football players. Instead it was a very serious, very dry description of how to scout an opponent, and, being chock full of diagrams of very complicated plays, it was probably bought only by other scouts and the fourteen-year-old Ernie Adams.

That year, just as the first football practice was about to start at Andover, Coach Steve Sorota posted the list of the new players trying out for the varsity, including the usual number of PGs—the list included the name Bill Belichick, and Ernie Adams was thrilled. That first day Adams looked at the young man with a strip of tape that said Belichick on his helmet, and asked if he was from Annapolis, Maryland, and if he was related to the famed writer-coach-scout Steve Belichick, and Bill said yes, he was his son. Thus were the beginnings of a lifetime friendship and association sown that day on the playing fields of Andover.

Ernie Adams, it should be noted, was a coach even before entering Andover. He had gone to elementary and junior high at the Dexter School, a private school in the Boston area (where John F. Kennedy had gone), and being more passionate about football than the teacher who had been drafted to coach the intramural team there, he had ended up giving that teacher more suggestions than the teacher wanted to hear. Finally the teacher, in desperation, had turned to Ernie and said, "Well, if you know so much, why don't you coach?" That was an offer Ernie Adams could not turn down, and he ended up coaching the Dexter team quite successfully.

At Andover he had already befriended another football-crazed classmate, Evan Bonds, with whom he talked football constantly and with whom he diagrammed endless football plays and with whom he jointly did the senior project breaking down and analyzing all of Andover's plays from their senior season. Bonds had also read Steve Belichick's book and was equally thrilled that the scion of such a distinguished football family was about to become a teammate. "Because we were such football nerds, it was absolutely amazing that Bill had come to play at Andover, because we were probably the only two people in the entire state of Massachusetts who had read his father's book," Bonds said years later. Bonds felt that although his own life revolved completely around football, Adams was already a good deal more advanced in his football obsessions, going off on his own to coaching clinics where everyone else was at least ten years older, collecting every book written by every coach on the game, the more technical the better, and collecting films of important games: "Ernie already had an exceptional football film collection, sixteen-millimeter stuff, the great Packer-Cowboy games, Raiders-Jets, films like that, which he somehow found out about through sports magazines, and had sent away for, and for which he had enough primitive equipment so that he could show the films," Bonds said. "It's hard to explain just how football crazed we were, but the year before Bill arrived, when we were in the eleventh grade, and it was spring, the two of us went down to Nickerson Field, the old Boston University field, because BU was having an intra-squad spring game. We were up there in the stands taking notes, these two seventeen-year-olds—can you believe it?—scouting an intra-squad game at BU on our own, and I still have no earthly idea what we would have done with the notes. Anyway, pretty soon a BU assistant coach came up looking for us, to find out what we were doing, and why we were doing it. So we said we were from Northeastern, as if that would give us extra legitimacy, and the coach said what we were doing was illegal, and we had to get out then and there."

Ernie Adams was even then a truly remarkable young man, a brilliant student, a true eccentric. After all, who else could be so passionate about football and also the school's best Latin scholar? He was almost alone in the school in taking fifth-year Latin, which on occasion interfered with football practice, but Latin came first. He would always remember what Dr. Allen Gillingham, the Latin teacher, said about learning the language: "If you have to write it down, you don't know it well enough," a phrase Adams would later use about the team playbook before various professional quarterbacks and offensive linemen, though he would never reveal the source of the quote. He was a scholarship student with very little money at a school where a lot of young men were, in fact, very rich. But he was also self-assured—lack of money notwithstanding, he was an Adams, and somewhere back there, generations earlier, there had been some Adamses who had more or less founded this country. He was so generous and sweet, so interested in other people and what they were doing, and his interests were so wide-ranging, that he got along with almost everyone there. In the fierce political divide of that era (1967–71), when the differences over the Vietnam war were at their height (and when the school was closed down briefly because of protests over the invasion of Cambodia), there were on one side, according to Michael Carlisle, a student there and later an important literary agent, the freaks and on the other, many of the jocks. Still, Adams, whose own politics were quite liberal, managed to get along with everyone. "The key to Ernie was his incredible personal integrity, the fact that he was always true to himself," said Carlisle, who was Adams's roommate. "You knew where you stood with him. He was incredibly honest and open and in no way manipulative, very confident of who he was, and nice to everyone. There are not that many people who are that interesting and that nice when they are young."

That Adams was football obsessed had been obvious from the time he had arrived at Andover and had sat in the back of some of his classes—more often than not science classes—and had pleased the teacher by seeming to be the most diligent and enthusiastic note taker in the class. Sadly, it would turn out, and much to the irritation of the teacher, these were not science notes but turned out to be sketches where eleven Xs took on eleven Os. In time the teacher notified Helen Adams, Ernie's mother. She was not surprised, because Ernie's housemaster, Hale Sturges, had already written her of his own concerns about the narrowness of her son's interests: "I wish he would expand his horizons. His interest in football has assumed such proportions that it seems to be closing doors on other areas of endeavor." (At virtually the same time, an eerily similar scene was taking place at Annapolis High, where Bill Belichick was taking French; some thirty-five years later Jeannette Belichick happened to stumble over some of her son's old notebooks, including one from French class, and eager to see what he had been doing in a subject that she had once taught, she opened it, finding inside not very much in the way of French verbs but a lot of football plays that had been diagrammed, part of his secret world of Xs and Os.)

At Andover the connection among the three of them—Belichick, Adams, and Bonds—was immediate and lasting; they were a club of three, although it became increasingly clear that Belichick and Adams were more committed to the idea of being football coaches and that Bonds, by their standards, was a bit soft and given over perhaps to interests in other things. They were inseparable that last year. "Others would be at the library doing trig or history, and the two or the three of them would be off to the side in a corner, and you'd look and they'd be X-ing and O-ing, always doing their football plays," said Bruce Bruckmann, the halfback on that Andover team. For a time Evan Bonds thought about trying some coaching. When he graduated, he went off to Duke, but he was disappointed with the football program there, and he discovered he was just as passionate about music as he was about football. Eventually he became a music professor at nearby Chapel Hill.

For Adams, there were two high points of that year. After helping beat vaunted Lawrenceville to maintain an unbeaten record, he rushed into the Lawrenceville locker room, still in his uniform, and bearing a pen, he had asked the Lawrenceville coach, Ken Keuffel, a great authority on the single wing (and an Andover graduate himself) to sign his book, *Simplified Single-Wing Football.* The other great day was when Steve Belichick showed up to scout Boston College and took the boys out to dinner. He was duly impressed by the passion and commitment of young Adams. "What do you want to do for a career?" Steve asked, and Adams answered that he wanted to be a football coach. "Where do you want to go to college?" Steve then asked. "Northwestern," Adams answered. "Why?" Steve asked. "Because they have the best Latin department in the country," Adams answered. The last answer quite surprised the elder Belichick, and he looked at Ernie Adams, surely a new breed of football coach, and said, "Well, if you go there and study Latin, you'll be the only coach in the country who can speak Latin."

Adams did go to Northwestern, a major Big Ten program then enjoying some of its glory years under a famed coach named Alex Agase. Agase was a great Chicago area favorite, having played college ball at Illinois; a very rugged physical player, he was a kind of Dick Butkus before Butkus arrived. He had been a very tough football player, fought as a Marine on Okinawa, and emerged as a complicated, rough-hewn, and yet surprisingly tender man. When Jay Robertson, one of his favorite assistants, prepared to go off to fight with the Marines in Vietnam in the mid-sixties, Agase gave him a brief but valuable warning, one earned the hard way from a previous war: "Look, I know that kind of war. You're never going to see the bastards who are shooting at you. So keep your head down." That, translated from Marine-talk to English, meant, don't try and be too big a hero, don't learn from the John Wayne movies, just go out and do your job and don't underestimate the enemy.

That year Agase was a little surprised when he received in the mail, unsolicited, an unusual document, beautifully bound as if it were a college senior thesis. It turned out to be a treatise on the importance of the drop-back quarterback in T-formation football.

(Drop-back quarterbacks, classic quarterbacks who dropped back to throw in systems that were built around passing, were then more in vogue in the pro game than in the college game.) It was written by a young man then eighteen years old named Ernest Adams, who had been a manager earlier that fall (his chance to become a manager eased because even before he arrived there had been a letter to George McKinnon, the Northwestern baseball coach who had been an assistant football coach in the past, from an old pal of his at Annapolis named Steve Belichick saying that Adams was very, very smart—a letter like that never hurt). Adams mentioned in the letter that he would like to help coach at Northwestern in some form or other. Most coaches would have thrown it away, but Agase gave the thesis a glance and then handed it to Robertson, a young assistant on his staff, who read it and was impressed by it. Robertson, in fact, thought it could have been written by any number of rather distinguished college or professional coaches. When Agase told Robertson that it had been written by one of the managers, Robertson remembered a very young-looking freshman with curly hair, who always seemed to edge his way unusually close to the huddles so he could hear everything that Robertson said (and apparently, Robertson learned later, that night would call his two friends, Bill Belichick at Wesleyan and Evan Bonds at Duke, both coaching hopefuls themselves, to tell them what he had learned that day).

If you like the thesis, Agase told Robertson, follow up and see if we can use him. Robertson did and was immediately impressed by Adams as a person and as a football mind. In those days most of the scouting was live, and colleges were allowed two scouting trips a year, one two weeks before a game and one the week before the game. As such, you needed two scouts, and Robertson and a man named Bill Dudley were doing the scouting at the time. If Adams was as good as they hoped, Agase suggested, he could become one of the scouts, and it would free another coach up to be with the team on game day. Agase told Robertson to go out and talk to the kid and find out the depth of his knowledge. "That was thirty-three years ago, and he was eighteen, I think, and I still don't know what the bottom of his knowledge is, what it is that he doesn't know, because he knows so much," Robertson said recently. "I was impressed by everything about him—his intelligence in all areas, his almost unique knowledge of football, his discipline, his work ethic, and his innate decency."

They decided to let him break down film, which he did with great skill in the catacombs of the football offices in a dark, grim little converted ticket room they called the Dungeon. Carrying his little briefcase (the other coaches checked it out, and it always contained three things: a small folded-up umbrella, a sandwich, and a copy of the *New York Times,* but never, as far as they could tell, a single textbook), he would arrive every day around noon, after his last class was over, and leave four or five hours later. He proved to be immensely talented at analyzing the film, and it appeared he might be a wonderful scout, but there was still one question: Could he do it live? It was after all one thing to sit next to a projector, running film over and over, and quite another thing to do it in a stadium, when there was no chance for replays. So Robertson and Dudley decided to let him scout the Notre Dame spring game. Ara Parseghian was the Fighting Irish coach back then, and it was an interesting challenge because he might show you nothing or he might show you everything and try to overwhelm you with too much.

They went to South Bend, and Robertson and Dudley gave Adams a bunch of cards on which to mark the plays, and they put him in a separate booth, so he could scout by himself. At halftime, they would compare cards to see if he had missed anything. Just to see if they could throw him off, they had put in some cards describing plays that never happened. But he got everything right and caught the imaginary plays as well. They were greatly impressed. The only problem was that to scout you had to drive, and he did not have a driver's license yet. So he went back to Massachusetts to get his license, and then for his first road game, which was in California, Robertson had to go with him to teach him how to handle airports, rental cars, hotels, and sports information officials. Though only eighteen, Adams was a full-fledged scout for a big-time team. For the Andover group, it was a marvelous moment: The first one of them had gotten his foot in the door in coaching. He was a very successful scout, and was soon a de facto coach as well, coaching the scout team as it ran opponents' plays in practice, in effect coaching his classmates. He was so successful that when Agase left to go to Purdue, after Adams's sophomore year, he asked his young assistant to come along with him. But Adams chose to stay at Northwestern, with the new group of coaches headed by John Pont.

Sometimes in those days Robertson would invite select Illinois high school coaches to the games as his guests, to help strengthen regional ties for recruiting trips, and then at the last minute he would be called to another assignment. So he would turn the coaches over to Adams, and he could see the disappointment on their faces: They were not going to be taken around by a bona fide college assistant, but by some kid. Twenty minutes later, Robertson would look over to see this small, intense group gathered around Ernie, the chalk would be flying on the blackboard, and sometimes when those coaches came back, they would go directly to Adams, not to Robertson.

By his senior year it was clear that all Adams wanted to do was be a football coach, that nothing else interested him. In those days it was part of the Northwestern assistants' responsibility to do some recruiting in the Chicago region, something very important in the college game, and something that Robertson sensed the shy Adams was extremely uncomfortable with. He was not a person who liked to go around selling anything, particularly himself or his school. Football to him was a great chess match. One Friday they had visited a local high school, and driving back to Evanston, Robertson looked over and saw that Adams, normally quite ebullient, seemed rather depressed. Robertson finally said, "It's the pro game or nothing, isn't it, Ernie?" "Yes," Adams had answered.

The pro game it had to be. But though some of the other coaches in the Northwestern group tried to help him, what they were suggesting—a professional job for a kid who had not played a single down—seemed a bit of a reach, and there were no quick offers. Adams tried getting a job with Cincinnati, which was where he wanted to be more than anyplace because not only was the great Paul Brown still coaching there, but even more important, the newest wizard of professional football, a rising young offensive coach named Bill Walsh, was there, too. But, the answer came back, as he later said, "No, we don't do that, not now, not ever, please don't call us again. Period."

Through Robertson, his closest friend among the Northwestern assistants, Adams finally landed a job in New England, even though it was without pay. Robertson had called a friend of his, Hank Bullough, who had coached at Michigan State, a Big Ten guy, and told him how valuable, indeed how invaluable, Adams was. Some of the pro teams were just beginning to hire young assistants to do what was called quality control, which was breaking down film. "My guy is perfect for that. You'll be impressed," Robertson told Bullough.

The Patriots' head coach at the time was Chuck Fairbanks, who had come from Oklahoma and the college game, which meant, Adams thought, he might be more amenable to graduate assistants. The way Steve Belichick, with his ear to the ground in the coaching world, understood it, was that someone had told Fairbanks that Adams was really smart, and he would work for free, and Fairbanks had replied that he had coached for some thirty years and that anyone who would do anything for no pay was not worth a goddamn. But what Fairbanks told

Adams was that they were glad to have him, and while they were not going to pay him, they were not going to carry him either. If he could do the work, he could stay; if not, he was going to be out of there very quickly because no one had the time to teach him.

By chance it was mid-June, the one time in pro football when almost everyone takes a vacation. Everyone in Boston did that year, save Ernie Adams, who had the facilities all to himself and who spent the next two weeks studying their playbook and their films, so that by the time they all returned, he knew it all, it was as if he had photographed it and then computerized it. Soon after, Fairbanks called Adams to the blackboard and asked him to draw up one of their more arcane coverages. He did it flawlessly, of course. It was a piece of cake. If there was any young would-be coach who could break film down even better, he had not yet been hired, and he was temporarily living at home with his parents back in Annapolis, waiting for the phone to ring.

When Ernie Adams was hired by the Patriots, he immediately called his pal Bill Belichick. At that moment Belichick, newly graduated from Wesleyan and hoping to get a job as a graduate assistant in the college ranks, thought he had a job lined up at North Carolina State under Lou Holtz, but Holtz was forced to pull it at the last minute because of competing demands from Title IX. When Adams called to celebrate his own success, he suggested that Belichick try for a professional job, which he did, ending up as a virtually unpaid assistant with the Baltimore Colts.

◆ ◆ ◆

Now, thirty years later, Adams and Belichick were flying to New Orleans to play the Rams in the biggest game of the year. The blitzing had not worked in the regular season. Forty-two times they had blitzed, and nothing had come of it. Belichick faulted himself for his coaching in the first game with the Rams that season. The only thing that was close was the score. The Rams had been successful 57 percent of the time on third down, a hard statistic for Belichick to swallow about one of his teams. They had averaged—he did not need to look at the stats to check—9.2 yards per pass, "almost as if they didn't need a second down," he said. "The score could as easily have been 50–14," he believed.

This time Belichick intended that it would be different. He was all too aware of the vast imbalance in terms of sheer talent between the two teams, that the matchups were not that good. The key, both he and Adams decided independently of each other, was in trying to stop Faulk, the great running back–receiver of the Rams. That Ernie Adams agreed with him was comforting to Belichick. The Rams offense might look like it was flawless and unstoppable, but all offenses have weaknesses. The job is to find them. In addition, the Rams were so accustomed to being successful, to having things their way, that if someone could make a partial stop on them, they might not react well and might become flustered.

But stopping them would be extremely hard. Their offense was different from most offenses, in that they did not have a set playbook based on certain tendencies—they were as likely to call a certain play at first and ten as they were on third and two. But all offenses had their needs, and at the core of the Ram offense was Marshall Faulk, so great a football player that he could control a game if you did not control him. The Rams might be a team without a predictable set of tendencies, but there were going to be times when they went to Faulk, and these were going to be the critical moments of the game; if the Patriots could stop him on these critical plays, they could probably stop a Ram drive. But that was much easier said than done. He was unusually dangerous. Five-yard dump-off passes became long gains with him. The game plan was to key on him and wear him down on every play. They were going to hit him every time he had the ball and hit him every time he didn't have the ball. The phrase they used was "butch the back," which meant hit him every time, or, as Belichick later said, "knock the shit out of him." In addition, they planned for the pass rushers "to set the edge," which meant don't let Faulk get to the outside, where he could do so many different things and cause so much havoc. Make him stay inside.

And so that week—a short one-week preparation because of the September 11 terrorist attacks, instead of the traditionally exhausting two-week extravaganza of relentlessly boring promotion—was given over to practicing how to stop Faulk. It began with Belichick telling his players that he had screwed up and done a poor job of coaching the last time. "I'm not going to screw up again," he promised them. The first and most important thing they were going to do, he said, was know where Marshall Faulk was at all times. Was he at home? That is, was he right behind the quarterback? That meant it would be a run or a play action pass, in which the quarterback faked the handoff and threw to a receiver. Or was he off to the side, which meant that he was likely to be a receiver. And so all week the scout team lined up and ran Rams plays, and a player would imitate Faulk, and there would be Belichick standing behind his defense and yelling out, "Where is he? Where is he?" It was that way all week long, with that constant yell before every practice play: "Where is he?" Finally one of the defensive players turned around and yelled, "Shut the fuck up," which even Belichick appreciated, because it meant that they had it down. Later that day they were all filing into a team meeting, and some of the players were walking just behind the head coach, and he heard one of his players yelling, "Where is he? Where is he?" That reassured him: Whatever else happened, Marshall Faulk would be a marked man on Sunday.

There were other things they had worked on. The first was to slow the game down. Encourage the Rams to run. Hit their receivers hard at the line of scrimmage and hammer them when they caught the ball. Run the ball themselves, as successfully as they could, and thereby shorten the game. Each run took roughly forty seconds off the clock, and that was time taken away from the Ram passing game, and time, therefore, when the Patriot defense did not have to be on the field. The other thing was to deal with the Rams' speed. If the Patriots got in a track meet with them, they would flat-out lose, Belichick thought. But the Patriot secondary had to be prepared for that speed, for the fact that it all happened a lot more quickly than it did in most games, and so Belichick lined the scout-team receivers about three yards ahead of the normal line of scrimmage, effectively in Patriot territory, just to give his defensive backs a sense of how quickly it all happened. And, just to make sure his offensive line also understood the speed of the Rams, even when they were on defense, he had the scout team defensive players line up offside, on the Patriot side of the ball.

The Xs and Os are fine, but the Xs and Os don't always work like they do on a chess board. The Xs don't get to where they're supposed to get to, and the Os turn out to be smarter than you thought. But on game day it all worked. Marshall Faulk gained only seventy-six yards. It was a great victory for the Patriots—the game plan was not just brilliant, but they had managed to pull it off. "We hit Faulk hard every time he had the ball," Patriot linebacker Tedy Bruschi said afterward, "and we hit him hard when he didn't have the ball." The Patriots Xs had stopped the Rams Os when they were supposed to. New England had led for almost the entire game, then held off a late St. Louis charge at the end just enough for Adam Vinatieri to kick a field goal in the final seconds for a 20–17 win.

Watching that day was Stan White, a talented linebacker who had been just three years into the pro game in 1975, when he worked with

Belichick, newly arrived at his first job with the Baltimore Colts. "I was sure he was going to try and take Marshall Faulk out of the game," White said. "He would want to stop Faulk and throw the timing of those great receivers off just a bit. Make Warner throw to places where the receivers had not yet arrived. Even back in Baltimore, when he was a kid, he was thinking of what the offensive teams were going to do and how to stop them. They say these days that if you give him too much time to coach before a game, he'll kill you. If he has a full week before a game, your chances are slim, and if he has two weeks, like they usually do in the Super Bowl, he'll kill you—there's no chance against him then."

Of the media people covering the Super Bowl that day, the person who understood most clearly what Belichick and his staff had done was ESPN's Ron Jaworski, who was a kind of Belichick of the media, taking the tape of a game afterward and running it relentlessly to study what had happened and, perhaps more importantly, why it had happened. You had to do that, he told colleagues, because otherwise there was so much small stuff you might miss, especially on a Belichick-coached team, and those little things would show you how he had thrown another team's timing off. After eight hours of screening the Patriots-Rams film, he pronounced it "the best coaching job I've ever seen." Not just that season, not in a Super Bowl, he said, but in twenty-nine years of playing and watching football.

He also broke down the Rams-Patriots game of the regular season and was fascinated by the difference between it and the championship game. By his count, which was slightly different from Belichick's, in the first game the Patriots had sent five or more players after Warner thirty-eight times, or 56 percent of the time. In the Super Bowl they had done it only four times. Instead of going after Warner, they had gone after Faulk. "I've never seen anything like it," said Jaworski. "One of their defensive ends or linebackers, usually [Willie] McGinest or [Mike] Vrabel, wouldn't care about Warner. He would go after Faulk and drill him. No matter where he was! It was brilliant. Here's the key: The Rams rely on timing and rhythm, but everyone thinks that rhythm runs through Warner. Belichick and [offensive coordinator] Romeo Crennel decided that the Rams rhythm depended on Faulk. So they hit him and kept hitting him. There was even one time when Faulk tried to leak through the middle of the line—and bang!—there's Richard Seymour and he nails him."

The Patriots, Jaworski noted, had used five or more defensive backs 74 percent of the time. Sometimes they used seven defensive backs. "Think about that—there are teams that don't carry seven defensive backs," he said. With all those defensive backs out there, Jaworski pointed out, the Rams would have had better success running the ball more at the smaller backs (he referred to them as "pissant secondary guys"), but they failed to do that. "They [the Rams] should have tried to overpower them." In that sense, Jaworski believed, Belichick had outsmarted the very bright Rams coach Mike Martz, forcing Martz to stay with an offense that was not going to work that day, but that he was more comfortable with. "I talked with Ricky Proehl [one of the great Rams receivers] after the game," Jaworski said, "and he told me that the Rams players were all on the sidelines during the second half, screaming at the coaches that the Patriots were playing five and six defensive backs, that they had to run the ball, that the run was there every time. But Martz was telling them, 'Fuck it, I'm going to win it my way.'" Chalk one up for Belichick.

What had happened, Jaworski added, was not a fluke. "Belichick is the best in the game today, maybe the best ever."

CHAPTER FIVE

Steve Belichick had been a very good high school football player, fast and tough. He ran the forty-yard sprint, the measure of speed in football, in about 4.6 seconds, which was fast for that era. Years later he was voted into the Struthers High School Hall of Fame. He played fullback, and the school paper was immensely admiring of his exploits for the Big Red, if not absolutely sure of how to spell his name, for sometimes it was Belitchich, other times it was Belichik, sometimes it was Belechich, and once in the same article in the school paper it came out Belitchich, Belchich, and Belechich. He had always loved football, and if Struthers was not exactly a powerhouse, it generally held its own with the surrounding high schools. The coach, Mike Koma, whose roots were Slovakian, was a man the young Belichick greatly admired. A good athlete himself, he gained the respect of all the boys and always treated them well.

Of Steve's brothers, Frank Belichick, the oldest boy, was a fine boxer with fast hands and quick reflexes, but from the start, he was overwhelmed with family responsibilities; Joe, the next oldest brother, had to deal all his life with a rheumatic heart; so John, who preceded Steve at Struthers High, became the first Belichick to do well in athletics. As a 185-pound tackle, he was good enough to win a tryout with Duquesne, then a football power. In those days, the major colleges would hold tryouts for prospective players, with perhaps ten young men showing up and only three being given scholarships. But the names of the others would make the *Pittsburgh Post Gazette* as having shown up, and thus other, smaller schools in the region would then contact the players. In the case of John Belichick, it was Geneva College of Beaver Falls, Pennsylvania, that called and offered him a scholarship.

Soon, Steve started to gain some local fame as a high school football player. His parents did not try to stop him from playing—John had made the breakthrough—but neither did they applaud him by coming to his games. Sports, especially an American game such as football, were an alien thing to John Belichick Sr. His life was exhausting enough—twelve-hour shifts when he got work, the long walks home. His relaxation came with the chance to stop and have a beer with pals or to work in his garden.

But Frank and other members of the family came to the games, and they were impressed with Steve; there was so much pride in hearing a large crowd cheering for your brother. Steve was aware of how hard times were, how little money they had, and he did not think college was in the cards for him. That was too bad, he thought, because in his heart of hearts from the moment he met Mike Koma he had wanted to be a football coach. He had always gotten good grades—none of the Belichick children was careless at schoolwork, because they knew their father had never even had the chance to go to school.

But he did not try for the college-preparatory route, and in his junior year the principal and the superintendent of schools called him in. "You haven't taken physics or chemistry," the principal noted. Belichick said that was right. "Why not?" the principal asked. "Why should I take them?" Belichick answered. "I'm only going to work in the steel mills anyway." "Well," said the principal, "you never know—maybe there'll be something else out there for you." He did not take physics or chemistry, but there was, as the principal suggested, something else out there for him.

By chance, the basketball coach at Struthers, Barney Francis, was getting his master's degree at Columbia University in New York, when he ran into Bill Edwards, the coach at Western Reserve in Cleveland. Edwards was a man already somewhat famous because he was a pal and a former roommate of Paul Brown, the great high school coach at Massillon, Ohio, perhaps the most famous high school coach in the country at that time. Brown almost always won in that football-crazed part of the country, his final record there being 80–8–2. Western Reserve was not yet a powerhouse, and Edwards could not compete with the surrounding Big Ten schools, like Ohio State, or the great independents, like Notre Dame, in recruiting. But he was shrewd about getting good kids not quite big enough for the major colleges, and he was in the process of producing some good teams that played at a surprisingly high level. So when Barney Francis told him about this high school running back—very tough, with good hands, and fast, very dangerous in the open field—Edwards trusted Francis, and when he got back to Ohio, he made an appointment to visit the Belichick family. Accompanied by his wife, Dorothy, and very properly dressed (this showed he was a serious family man), he turned up at the Belichick house, with a football scholarship to offer Steve, plus a job—working outdoors, digging ditches and cutting foliage, whatever it took—to pay whatever other costs there were. It was a hard time in that house. In 1937 the Depression was at its peak, and John Belichick had spent much of the last four years out of work. So this was a glorious moment, and Edwards seemed like nothing less than a god that day.

If there had been any need for a reminder of Steve's good fortune, it came from the job he took in the months right after he graduated from Struthers High and before he entered college. In January 1937, he went to work in the mills. He was paid 49½ cents an hour, turning coal into coke, which became a fuel that could cook at a temperature much hotter than the impure coal. It was, Steve believed, the dirtiest, hardest job in that area, filled, as it was, with so many other exhausting, brutal tasks. Almost all of his coworkers were black, which meant that it was a job that whites, even down-and-out whites, did not want. Some of the men fed the coal into giant ovens, and then the newly created coke was dumped into a hopper; it was Steve's job to dump water on the coke in order to cool it. The heat in the place was so bad that there was a constant danger of passing out, and all the men wore wooden clogs about an inch and a half thick under their shoes, lest they get burned through their shoes. The air was filled with an odious black dust created by the collision of the water and the red-hot coal. Steve left there after about five months, exhausted and grateful for any opportunity that could get him out of the mills. To this day he has a serious cough, which he believes was produced by those months cooling the coke.

Western Reserve, later Case Western Reserve, was an oasis for Steve, a very good college that opened the door to a very different America for him. The football program there did very well under Bill Edwards, going 49–5–2 in his six years there, and he was soon seen as one more of those talented coaches from America's football epicenter whom other, larger colleges competed for. For Steve Belichick, going to college was a life-changing experience. He had grown up among men and women who had no choices in their lives, who worked in the hardest, most physically demanding jobs that the society had to offer. They worked until their good luck ran out and they were either laid off or they could no longer physically do the work. At Western Reserve many of the students were the sons and daughters of successful people, for whom it had always been a given that they would go to college and then choose the careers they wanted. Belichick repaid the coach who had rescued him from the mills and brought him into this new world by excelling in every way—listening more carefully, working harder, knowing more about what was going on than anyone else. In effect, he became almost like an assistant coach.

Edwards ran the single wing, and in his particular version he ran most of the plays through the fullback, who handled the ball. It was a system that suited Steve's talent because he had very good feet and hands. "The best fullback I ever coached," Edwards once told Gordon Cobbledick of the *Cleveland Plain Dealer,* words that Steve Belichick could remember more than sixty years after they had been uttered. It was high praise, indeed, because Edwards had also coached Ray Mack, a superlative athlete, who later played second base for the Cleveland Indians. The friendship between Edwards and Belichick was to be one that lasted a lifetime, and they would be together at three colleges.

Edwards was always keeping an eye out for his young protégé and opening doors for him. The first time came in the fall of 1941, right after Belichick had graduated from college. War was imminent, and the draft had been instituted. Steve, who wanted to be a teacher and coach, had a low draft number, and because of that, he could not in good conscience get a job as a teacher or coach. In the fall of 1941 Edwards left Western Reserve to take a job as head coach of a professional football team called the Detroit Lions, which was part of the then-fledgling National Football League. Aware that Belichick was marking time before being drafted, Edwards called him up and asked him to come up and be his equipment manager. It was all very primitive: They practiced on the field at an abandoned grade school, and the lockers were for little kids. The equipment manager did not have a lot to do, except collect the towels, the socks, and the jocks for the laundry. Because Edwards had little in the way of assistant coaches, Belichick, who knew the system well, almost as well as the coach, was soon helping to coach. Milt Piepul, the team's starting fullback, had been a star at Notre Dame, a two-time All-American, but he did not handle the ball particularly well, largely, it turned out, because he was the first player among them who wore contact lenses, primitive ones in those days, and it soon became clear that Belichick handled the ball better, so he was soon playing fullback as well. Some of the players were very good, Steve remembered, especially Byron (Whizzer) White, a Rhodes scholar just back from Oxford who had been an All-American at Colorado. Each of the players was paid about $115 a week, "but remember you could buy a car for $600 back then, though most of us did not have cars," Steve remembered. Most of them stayed in a hotel, which cost $7 a week, and they went out for meals costing 50 or 60 cents, and they could buy beer for 10 or 15 cents.

Steve Belichick loved the life, even though he did not get a full season at it. Though he did not play every game, he ended up with the team's best running average, 4.2 yards a carry, better even than the immensely talented Whizzer White. There were many days full of satisfaction and rewards, but also days bitter and full of pain. There had been a day when they played the Chicago Bears, who were always tough, and there was a Chicago player named Dick Plasman, who was big, strong, and viewed by opponents, if not by himself, as mean as hell. "He was the last guy to play in the NFL without a helmet, if that places him for you," Steve Belichick said years later. Plasman had taken his giant forearm, which seemed to be made of oak and was the size of most players' legs, and whacked Belichick in the nose, becoming either the sixth or seventh opponent to break it. But he did it with such singular violence that Belichick bled, in his own words, like a stuck pig, and they had to cram tissues up his nose to stop the bleeding. But he kept on playing. The next week he scored two touchdowns in New York against the Giants, and then the week after was the greatest day of all, because they played Green Bay, with the great Don Hutson at end. At one point Green Bay punted to the Lions, and in those days they did not use a single safety but kept three men back. They had tried to kick to the return man in the center, but it went wide toward Belichick, and he was already moving when he got the ball, and it came to him on a wonderful bounce, one you dreamed about. Everyone else was over in the center, and he never broke stride, going down the sidelines some seventy-seven yards for a touchdown. It was his third touchdown of the season, but soon the season was over, and he went into the Navy.

He played a lot of football for a year in the Navy, on a spectacular team that had been gathered at the Great Lakes Naval Station. All kinds of superior college athletes were being funneled through Great Lakes on their way to other duties, so they had a kind of all-star team that did very well playing against some of the best college teams in the country. Then he was on his way to the war, on merchant ships making the Atlantic crossing and the crossing between England and France after D-Day. When he came back after the war, he was more sure than ever that he wanted to coach. Bill Edwards told him about a job at Hiram College, a small liberal arts college about forty miles from Youngstown, and he ended up taking it. He did not know at the time that the brand-new professional football league, the All-America Football Conference, had just held a secret draft, and he had been drafted by the football New York Yankees to play fullback, although apparently they were more interested in some of their other players and never notified him. He learned about it only later when Paul Brown, then the coach of the eponymous Cleveland Browns, a great team in the new upstart league, called him in and told him how much he would love to have him, but that the Yankees had his draft rights. Well, what Paul Brown said was both true and not true: His rights did belong to New York, but what Brown wanted, he tended to get, and he was speaking with a bit of a forked tongue, because he could easily have traded for Belichick's draft rights. The truth was that he did not need a fullback, for he already had a formidable one, Marion Motley, the first of the great black running backs in the modern era. A man who had played at Great Lakes, he was one of the first blacks to play in the new postwar incarnation of what would become the NFL. Motley was so impressive a physical specimen that when the Browns assembled at a player tryout for positions, a young man named Bud Grant, who up to then had thought of himself as a fullback, spotted Motley and decided to try out for whatever position Motley did *not* try out for. So when they called for the fullbacks to step forward, and Motley stepped forward, Bud Grant instantly decided to become an end.

That he was not playing professional football did not weigh too heavily on Steve Belichick, because he liked being at Hiram, where he coached, in addition to football, four other sports. One of the things he liked most about Hiram was the fact that it was so small, you knew all the other faculty members, and he was soon much taken with an exceptionally vivacious young woman who taught French and Spanish there, Jeannette Munn. In time, he asked her out, and, playing to his strength and what he knew best, he took her to Cleveland to watch a Western Reserve game. She was always eager to learn and thought this would be a wonderful way to learn about football, which everyone else in Ohio seemed to take so seriously, except that Steve Belichick did not talk very much during the game. He just sat there, and smoked a cigar, and did not speak. Afterward, they went out for a sandwich at a local college hangout, and she became irritated, because all sorts of people kept coming up to their table to talk to him, but he never introduced her to them. She thought it poor manners. But later, he apologized and said he had not introduced her because they were absolute strangers, and he did not know their names. He was, she realized, something of a celebrity in the area.

She had grown up about eight miles away, in Chagrin Falls, a suburb of Cleveland. Her people, unlike his, had been in this country for many generations, and some in her family had done very well in the land, lumber, and gravel business. She was middle-class, as he was not. She was gifted at languages and had gone to Middlebury College in Vermont for graduate work in them. During the war, she worked in Washington, using her language skills to translate military maps. After they were married, she decided that it would strengthen their family if she could speak to her in-laws with ease, and so as a kind of gift to her husband, for it was the sort of instinctive natural kindness that seemed to define her life, she learned Croatian. She and Steve were an unlikely couple. She was small and delicate, immensely vivacious and quite sophisticated, and he was rough-edged, though aware of what he did not know in the world beyond football. She did not think him particularly good-looking, but she sensed there were other things to admire about him: a drive that was unusual and a special kind of honor that she considered more important than looks. There was, over the more than fifty years of their marriage, an ongoing low burner debate between them over the question of whether he had ever pushed her to give his football players a break on their grades when they were back at Hiram. "I never asked for anything for them," he would say. "Yes, you did," she would answer, "but you did it subtly—you would ask how the player was doing, but I knew what you wanted, you didn't fool me a bit." "Okay, maybe I did, but you never helped any of them," he would answer. Eventually she quietly mastered football and became extremely knowledgeable about it; that allowed her to mix easily in a world where all the men were coaches who spoke of little else but their work. Late in life she even helped her husband scout. In years to come, as their son became a celebrated coach, there were many people who saw Bill as his father's son, but others, who knew both parents well, thought he was every bit as much her son. She had been an exceptional teacher, and their son, above all, loved to teach, seemed to be born to do it. Moreover, his attention to detail reflected her own—no one, for instance, was allowed to help take care of her home; she did all the cleaning herself.

No outsider was ever more important in the Belichick family than Bill Edwards. Even when Steve was still dating Jeannette, she was introduced to Bill and Dorothy Edwards. In 1947 Edwards had gone to the Cleveland Browns as an assistant coach. There he coached the tackles for Paul Brown, the first coach, it seemed, to have an assistant coach for every position. That was obviously a great stepping-stone, to be at the right hand of the very best that there was. Then, in 1949, Edwards was offered a job coaching at Vanderbilt, an elite private college playing in the Southeastern Conference (SEC). One of his first acts there was to ask Steve Belichick to come to Nashville as his defensive coach. Belichick accepted readily, and in August 1950, he married Jeannette. "All her friends were shocked—she loved classical music and foreign languages, and she was marrying a football coach?" Belichick remembered. Taking the job in Nashville was a big step up on the football ladder, and a significant financial boost as well—his salary went from $3100 a year to $4900, enough for a man to get married and start a family back then.

Edwards, like his mentor Paul Brown, was in the process of abandoning the traditional formation of that era—the single wing. Though it was still evolving and new variations continued to be worked on it—innovations that emphasized greater speed and more deception—the single wing was, at its heart, a power football formation. By contrast, in the forties, the T-formation was gaining ever greater acceptance, especially with younger coaches, and it was Paul Brown, using a variety of innovations, flankers and split ends, who brought speed, deception, and explosiveness to the T-formation. Brown, as much as anyone, was the father of modern (post–World War II) football. He was innovative in countless ways, such as integrating his teams racially, using players as messengers to bring plays to the huddle from the coach, and testing his players on their playbooks. He was ahead of the curve in almost everything, including his fears that their relatively small salaries would prove corrupting and pull the players away from the true spirit of the game. He had told the assembled players at the first Browns' camp, "We will be the most amateur team in professional sports. I don't want you to think of the money you'll be making; rather I want you to think of the game first and the money second."

Many of his disciples became legends, too, and one of the last ones was Bill Walsh, who had coached under him in Cincinnati, and who was called the Genius. At San Francisco Walsh eventually created what became known as the West Coast offense, an offensive alignment done without a tight end, which emphasized an ever quicker, more open passing game. Walsh himself hated the name West Coast offense, because as he said, it made it sound like everyone was going down to the beach to play touch football. But there were many coaches, including Ernie Adams, who looked at the West Coast offense and saw its origins in the handiwork of Paul Brown in Cleveland. In fact, Adams believed it should be called the Lake Erie offense, in honor of Brown.

Edwards and Belichick did well at Vanderbilt, but it was never easy. The SEC, in the era before it started playing the region's exceptional black athletes, was a good if not great conference—not, as it is today, arguably the best football conference in the country. Vanderbilt had to play against some very good football schools: Georgia, Georgia Tech, Alabama, LSU, Auburn, Ole Miss, and, above all else, Tennessee, its traditional rival. The school's biggest problem, back then as today, was that it had significantly tougher academic entrance requirements than many of its rivals, and thus could never compete in recruiting the requisite raw talent. Essentially Vanderbilt should get out of the SEC, because it will never be able to compete in football; it ought to play at another level, against a group of comparable private schools. But the financial rewards of playing in the SEC are so compelling that it has never been able to make the move.

Bill Edwards had followed a very talented and very popular coach named Red Sanders, a Vanderbilt graduate, who had coached the single wing, and who had gone 8–2–1 before leaving for UCLA. That was a tough act to follow, and Edwards was considered very much an outsider, a man with no Southern roots in a place and time when that really mattered. He quickly replaced the single wing with an offense modeled on Paul Brown's, and he did very well with it, given the considerable odds against him there. His teams beat Alabama three times, and Ole Miss three times, but they never beat Tennessee. ("Well, Red Sanders only beat Tennessee once in six years," Steve Belichick noted years later.) His teams were exciting and original, flankers right, flankers left, flankers in motion, creating great pressure on the defenses of teams nominally much stronger. "The offense that Edwards and Belichick brought in was so modern that they were probably two or three years ahead of their time, and, in some ways, it worked against them—a lot of the players already there did not readily fit into so different a system, and the fans weren't really ready for it," said Mac Robinson, who had played halfback under both Red Sanders and Edwards. "To them it was about flash rather than deception, and they were uncomfortable with it; they wanted a more traditional, more conventional single wing offense, a kind of football they had grown up with and had always seen in the past. If Edwards and Belichick had arrived a couple of years later, and they had not had to make that major switch from the single wing to the Paul Brown T at the very beginning, it might all have gone better."

No one doubted they were good, but Edwards had none of the smooth manner expected of a Southern coach. He was likeable, gregarious, optimistic, and often even joyous, surprisingly open with his players, but he was not a good ole boy; he was more like a Northern politician about to run for mayor or congress. He intended to have some fun for himself, and, despite all the pressure, he would on occasion play jokes on his colleagues, as he had at North Carolina when he was working with an assistant named Marvin Bass. One day Bass got an angry phone call from a Carolina alumnus who criticized him for his behavior on the sidelines, which the alumnus said was unbecoming and unruly. Why couldn't he be like Bill Murray, the head coach of Duke? Now there was a gentleman. A great school like Carolina deserved a gentleman like Murray, not some redneck like Bass. Soon Bass began to lose his temper, and the alumnus became more insulting, and before long they were cursing each other. Finally, Bass challenged the fan to meet him in a fistfight outside the practice field. Steaming mad, he had barely put down the phone when Edwards and Belichick showed up with a bottle of wine. It was Edwards, egged on by Belichick, who had played the part of the irate alumnus over the phone.

Unlike Red Sanders, Mac Robinson pointed out, Edwards did not coach through fear and intimidation, but through a certain optimism. He would tell his players what they needed to do and add that they could do it, that all they had to do was remember what they had been taught. He was not an emotional coach, and his pregame speeches did not seem to vary much: Oh, he would say, to be as young as they were on that day. Oh, to have their opportunity to go out there and play college football before all those fans. Oh, to be able to have the pleasure of knocking down an Alabama or a Tennessee lineman. . . .

He was good at making fun of himself. If during practice they were about to separate and break down into smaller groups, he would deliberately use certain malapropisms he had stolen from Ernie Godfrey, a colleague on the Browns: He would tell them to scatter out in bunches, or pair off in threes. When they were tense before a game, he would mangle their names just a little bit when he gave them the starting lineup. Mac Robinson, for example, became one word, Macrobinson. "It's two words, Coach," Robinson would say. "Mac. Robinson." "Okay, Macrobinson, got you," he would answer. Carl Copp, the team captain, became George Gopp. When Marshall College, hardly a football power, came in, and Vandy was heavily favored, Marshall ran none of the plays that they had previously shown on film and took an early lead. Edwards, making sure every player on his bench heard what he was saying, spoke as loudly as he could through his phone to his assistants up in the press box: "Come on down, boys. The game's already over—they're going to whip us," a zinger that worked, and Vanderbilt soon asserted itself.

Steve Belichick was, some of the players thought, perhaps an even better coach, a man of exceptional intelligence, commitment, and knowledge, a man whose true potential had not yet been realized. He was an original teacher, and he had a rare skill in preparing them for a game, because he was unmatched as a scout. "The best scout I've ever seen—the amount of detail and knowledge was unmatched. What he had was like nothing we had ever seen before," Robinson said. "If Steve said something was going to happen in a game, then it was going to happen in a game." Other players agreed. "Best scout in the pre-computer age that football ever had," said Don Gleisner, who played defensive back at Vanderbilt and then played in the NFL. "Nothing was left to chance." Steve did not prepare with broad generalities, but with minutiae, detail after detail. Each player, he felt, should go into a game feeling he had a distinct advantage over the player he was matched up against. For Robinson there had been one memorable game, against Alabama, in which he had played fifty-nine minutes and could barely walk off the field at the end. Alabama had an end named Al Lary, a kind of stealth player. He would get off the line of scrimmage somewhat slowly and come at the defensive back as if he were no threat; then he would explode, and in that millisecond, he would be gone. The previous week against Tulane, as Robinson recalled, Lary had caught three touchdown passes. So Belichick and Robinson worked on it and worked on it, and Robinson dropped off the line a few extra yards and was ready when Lary turned it on. He caught no touchdown passes that day as Vanderbilt beat Alabama.

In contrast with Edwards, always affable and accessible, Belichick seemed tougher on the surface, capable of giving a player a scorching look—a glance no one wanted to receive. But, in the end, the players decided his gruff exterior masked genuine warmth, which was apparent once a player showed any kind of real commitment. Like Edwards, he was original and inventive. When Don Gleisner, who had been a quarterback in high school but eventually became a defensive back, was trying out for the quarterback job at Vanderbilt, he had a tendency to throw sidearm. So Belichick had some sawhorses made, except that they were much higher than the normal sawhorse, and he placed them right where Gleisner's hand would finish up in its follow-through. If Gleisner didn't keep his arm up and at the right angle, his hand would hit the wooden bar of the horse. That quickly cured his sidearming. Another drill was to make Gleisner walk down the sidelines, while Belichick walked parallel, constantly holding up different numbers of fingers. The player was expected to tell the coach how many fingers were up—a lesson in how to expand and exploit your peripheral vision. The drill was done first at a walk, then at a jog, and then at full speed. There were other lessons for defensive backs, how to go up for a contested pass, and how to bump the receiver with your body, but not your hands, which the refs were more likely to see.

But Edwards and his group were never really accepted, Steve Belichick believed. That they were very good coaches, and that their teams did well, did not matter. Bill was born there in April 1952, and his father was fired from his job eleven months later, in early March. Within the world of coaching, the timing was considered unfair and discourteous because it gave the released coach almost no chance to find another job; the positions had all been filled earlier. The story of how Vanderbilt treated the Edwards group was to become an important part of the Belichick family lore, an example of the dangers of coaching. It suggested that being good was not necessarily enough, and that college athletics was rife with politics and favoritism.

The politics were partly the result of the complicated relationship between Vanderbilt University and the two formidable, bitterly feuding newspapers in Nashville. The *Banner* was conservative and tied closely to Vanderbilt, with its equally conservative board of trustees, and also to the wealthy Belle Meade community, which was disproportionately important at Vanderbilt. The *Tennessean,* the more liberal paper, was already a dominating player in statewide politics, but much too liberal to be influential in Vanderbilt's internal politics. The columnists from the two papers' sports pages could not have been more different. Freddy Russell, the *Banner*'s extremely gifted columnist, was a protégé of the famed Grantland Rice and for a time thought to be his heir; he was well connected in Belle Meade. By contrast, Raymond Johnson, the sports editor of the *Tennessean,* was in no way gifted, a man whose cigar, rarely lit, seemed always to precede him into a room, likeable to a great many ordinary people, a very decent man who was an unusually poor writer.

Of the vast gap in their talents there was no doubt. More important, Russell had been a close friend of Red Sanders because they had gone to Vanderbilt together. When Sanders was coaching, all the important football stories had been channeled directly to the *Banner*. Bill Edwards had put a stop to that. When he first arrived, he called both journalists in and said he was going to divvy up the news as best he could. With that, he made a powerful enemy out of Russell. "We never really had a chance," Steve Belichick said years later. "There was always a part of that community which did not accept us and fought us, and when it came to fighting us, Freddy Russell led the charge—he always wanted us gone." Russell's official line was that Edwards never beat Tennessee, Belichick said, but it was always "about who we were, where we were from, and how Bill Edwards had tried to even the playing field between Freddy and Raymond."

They lasted there four years, and their record was 21-19-2, which, given Vanderbilt's stricter academic admissions policies, was remarkable. Vanderbilt in the ensuing half century would have a parade of talented young coaches who struggled with the same problem; they would arrive in Nashville and hold press conferences in which they spoke optimistically about their plans to change the program. But they soon ran into the same concrete wall and quickly left town, some of them of their own volition, others fired. As a result there were a total of eleven head coaches in the last fifty years at Vanderbilt and only Steve Sloan has a winning record. Nor did Bill Edwards's successors do much better against Tennessee; in the last fifty-three years, Vandy has beaten the Vols six times.

It was a hard lesson in the Belichick family and eventually a very important one for young Bill Belichick, then not even a year old, that the world of football was one of great insecurity. In addition to the usual pitfalls—the injuries sustained by key players, the coveted recruits who went elsewhere, and the bad calls by referees (there had been a lot of them in a game with Tennessee in 1949, a game they all felt they should have won), there were other forces, like politics. Men like Freddy Russell, who had not necessarily ever played a down of ball in his entire life, could help lose you your job. The Belichick family took the firing hard, and years later Steve Belichick was still irritated with the people, the head of the school and the board of trustees, who ran Vanderbilt's athletic program, who put the entire burden of the discrepancy between an optimistic hope for a winning record and the reality of the admission policies on the coaches. To him it had a bitter ending; Bill Edwards, not as hard-edged, was a little more forgiving, and about a decade later at a convention of football coaches, Don Gleisner spotted Edwards, by then the coach of Wittenberg, having dinner with, of all people, Freddy Russell. Afterward Gleisner went up to Edwards and asked how he could dine with someone who had practically run him out of town. "Always kill them with kindness, Don," Edwards answered. "Always kill them with kindness."

For a brief time after Vanderbilt it appeared that Belichick would become the head coach at the University of Toledo; there had been some phone calls, and his old friend Barney Francis, the man who had originally connected him to Bill Edwards, was coaching basketball there. Belichick even spoke to Gleisner, one of his favorite players, about coming on as an assistant. But then he was never even interviewed for the job. What he felt, though he would not say publicly at the time and could never prove, was that in that era there was a certain prejudice against someone who was Croatian, that other people, sometimes of lesser talent, with names easier to pronounce might have had an advantage in getting a job.

The job at North Carolina came just in time, but there was a problem there from the start, because George Barclay, the head coach, had neither the talent nor the passion of his two new assistants, and because the Carolina alumni clearly wanted Jim Tatum, a Carolina alumnus, to come back to his old school. "We were always under a shadow," said Marvin Bass, who was there when Edwards and Belichick arrived, "and the shadow was that of Jim Tatum." When, after three years, it was over again, Edwards eventually headed back to Wittenberg, and he asked Belichick to come with him. But Belichick was reluctant to go; he had sampled the aura of a big-time football operation, and he had liked it. What some people at both Vanderbilt and Carolina began to figure out after the Edwards team left was that they had been very good under difficult circumstances, and that Bill was an exceptional coach. But, if you paid attention and didn't think in terms of hierarchy, then Steve Belichick might even be the more talented of the two—certainly, he was more driven and passionate about it.

Belichick had met Eddie Erdelatz at a college all-star game, where he had been in the company of Bill Wade, who had played quarterback at Vanderbilt. Belichick and Erdelatz instantly liked each other, there being an extra bond because Erdelatz, wonder of wonders, was also Croatian. They had stayed in touch, and in 1955, after the North Carolina job ended, Belichick heard that Ben Martin from Erdelatz's staff was going to Virginia, so he called to see if Erdelatz would put in a word for him with Martin. Erdelatz said he was glad to, indeed; in fact, he would do better. "I've got a slot open here," Erdelatz said. "Do you want it?" "Damn sure I do," Belichick answered. So in 1956, when Bill was four years old, the family moved to Annapolis. Steve and Jeannette Belichick loved it from the start: the community, which was both a city and a small town, so near to both Washington and Baltimore; the beauty of the harbor; the feel of the community, so nicely entwined with a great institution like the Naval Academy; and the Academy itself, with those exceptional young men who were on their way to the service and who were totally committed in all that they did.

It was the perfect place to raise a family, and it was a perfect place for someone like Belichick to coach because there was such a rare intersection of values between those the Academy demanded of its young men, and those any football coach demanded of his players. Coaching there, he said, "was like dying and going to heaven."

After Vanderbilt and North Carolina, he had become shrewder about it all, figuring out how to take care of himself and protect himself, aware that what might seem like the best job was not necessarily the best job, at least for him. He was always careful about raising his own expectations too high. One of the things he had told Don Gleisner in those days reflected his own tempered view of life: "Don, one of the greatest things you can learn about yourself is your own limitations—how much you can eat at any given meal, how much you can drink, and how much you can get out of life. It's very important to know them and not go beyond them."

He understood both the plus and the minus sides of staying at Annapolis—that Navy was not necessarily going to get as many great athletes as other schools but that the young men who came there were wonderfully motivated, and that made up for the lack of pure talent, in his view. He became an expert at explaining to younger coaches how the Academy worked, telling them not to expect the players to drop by a coach's office as often happened at other schools, because they had no time to do that. But watch them during practice, he would say, always running from one drill to another, never wasting any time. And understand that you cannot here, as at other places, leverage them by threatening to take away their scholarships, because that could not be done—every student in the place was on scholarship. The most important thing any young coach could learn, he said, was how much football meant to them. It was the one break in the day when they could have fun, and let loose from so pressurized an existence. Motivation here, he said, was not a problem.

Years later Bill Belichick would understand what made his father so good a scout: the absolute dedication to his craft, the belief that it was important, and the fact that so many people—the people who paid his salary, his colleagues, and the young men who played for him—were depending on him. But it was not just about the superior work ethic; it was about natural abilities. Steve Belichick had been blessed with great eyesight, 20/15, he was told. He had come to believe, though no one had ever measured him on this, that he had great peripheral vision, as well, because when he played he had been able to see the play as it opened up, and the dangers that existed for him on the periphery. He could see clearly where other people had black areas. But it was more than just a gift of exceptional vision; it was the ability to use that vision, to be able, as a scout, to anticipate the play and read it. No one did that better than Steve Belichick. The key, he decided early on, was to watch the center, for the center almost always told you so much: whether it was a pass or run, and which way the play was going. Then your eye flashed accordingly to the flow of the play, out to the end and the linemen on the side to which the center had tipped you, and you had to do all this quickly, almost before the play developed, because otherwise you would be too late, and then your eye would not see the entire play unfolding.

Steve Belichick was also incredibly smart. "It was the superior intelligence, too," said Bill Walsh. "Steve has superior intelligence and intellect, and he not only saw the game as very few scouts did, but as he was seeing it, he *understood* it as very few scouts do." Scouting seemed to come so naturally to him, not so much an end in itself, as some of his colleagues who watched him thought, but more accurately as a game within a game, one which he was always determined to win. Most of the other scouts were assistant coaches who did not really want to be scouting. They wanted to be back with their teams on Saturday, watching their handiwork in action, and their work habits showed it. They were, Bill Belichick remembered from watching them when he was a boy, "all so casual about it, talking to each other, paying attention but not really paying attention, doing a lot of coaching small talk, gossiping really. Not really paying attention to the game, but thinking that they were. Instead they were halfway interested. There were a lot of questions they would be asking each other, like 'Hey, did the guard pull on that play?' It was like a social occasion for them, and they would be ordering hot dogs and coffee. And, by contrast, he was always working. Every minute. He was like a hawk up there. And by watching him, I learned to see the game, how well prepared you have to be and how quickly your eyes have to shift. He had his own sheets which he had created himself to make it easier to get the information down, and he could get the basics down, the rest to be filled in later. The other guys were barely operating off the programs. He had it all laid out—the plays, the downs, the tendencies, the different yardage needs on different downs, the different formations, all of it. He had such quick eyes, a great field of vision, and such great anticipation, play after play. If he could not get everything noted in time before the next play was run, he could make some little note to himself that probably only he could understand, and then he would fill it in at halftime or after the game. The others might have one or two pencils and one lawyer's pad, but there he would be with thirty pencils, all of them sharpened." He was, his son said, "the first great scout." "What I learned, going with him," Bill Belichick added, "was that it was not just a game, it was a job."

He was always working. Bill remembered one year when he had been allowed to make the trip to Philadelphia with his father to scout Penn. They were the first to arrive and Steve did not waste a minute, immediately checking out the players in the pregame drills, the punters, how long they held the ball, how they dealt with the wind, and finally what kind of returns they were setting up on punt returns. There was, Steve Belichick taught his son, always something to learn.

His name was never known to those in the larger society, even to those who thought of themselves as football junkies. What he did was rarely written about, and few journalists or broadcasters sought him out for halftime interviews. He greatly preferred it that way, since probably not very much good would come of it—fame for an assistant coach was not usually regarded by the head coach as a good thing, and it could easily be viewed as the beginning of a move on a head coach's job. Belichick's feeling was that all the people who needed to know about his talent already knew, and those people were other coaches. There were other offers, often for much more money. Earl Blaik wanted him to come to West Point. Hank Stram wanted him to come out to Kansas City and work for the Chiefs. When Eddie Erdelatz was fired at Navy and went to Oakland as an assistant with the Raiders, he pushed hard for Steve to join him. But Belichick was reluctant to leave.

He was all too aware of the politics at the Academy, which had made him wary of ever wanting to be a head coach. Eddie Erdelatz had done very well there, had put together great teams and had beaten Army four times, but he got in a power struggle with the athletic director at one point because he was perceived as getting too much credit; that went against the culture of the place, where credit was to go to the institution, not the coach. There had been one terrible moment when some of the coaches were gathered in the head coach's office and Erdelatz took a phone call and got in a very heated conversation with someone on the other end. He finally shouted, "Well, fuck you too," and slammed down the phone. "Who was that?" one of the assistant coaches asked. "The Athletic Director," Erdelatz answered. Then, after a loss to Army—only his third in nine seasons—the authorities finally had an excuse to squeeze him out. Wayne Hardin, one of his assistants, replaced him, and he beat Army four out of five times and then lost and was fired. All of that taught Steve Belichick the uses of caution.

That he was always an assistant coach did not mean he was always a compliant one or that he felt he should not have strong opinions. He was intense, stubborn, opinionated, absolutely sure of when he was right. He was capable of towering arguments with Erdelatz over strategy, and he won most of them on defensive strategy—over, for example, rotating the defensive secondary toward the strong side. Particularly memorable was the fight the two men had at the Cotton Bowl on New Year's Day 1958, following Navy's 14–0 defeat of Army. In the Cotton Bowl, Navy had taken a 20–0 lead over Rice, a team that had two very good quarterbacks, King Hill and Frank Ryan, the latter eventually a star with the Cleveland Browns. Because Navy had such a big lead, Erdelatz had started substituting much sooner than Belichick thought safe. Those two quarterbacks, he thought, made Rice an unusually explosive team, one capable of scoring quickly and often, and Navy could all too easily lose its momentum. He argued with Erdelatz from the press box when the substitutions began, telling the coach he was being precipitous; he watched Rice score once, argued with the coach again, and then saw Rice go on a long drive that ended on the Navy 2-yard line when the clock ran out. He was so angry with Erdelatz that day that he refused to ride on the team bus back to the hotel; he decided to walk back, the better to burn off his anger.

Even after he retired he went back and coached. No one coached punters better than he did, and long after he retired, other coaches would call him for tips on how to handle their punters, who were somehow believed to be different from all other football players. Dean Pees, then coaching at Kent State, once asked Steve Belichick about a punter who kicked brilliantly in practice and poorly in games. How does he prepare in practice? Belichick asked. "Well, he punts and punts and punts, one after another," said Pees. "Have him practice the way he kicks in a game," Belichick suggested. "Have him punt, and then take a fifteen-minute break, and then punt, and then take another break." Pees did, and the problem was solved. On other occasions Pees called because he was having trouble with another punter. This punter was not able to do the two-step, which was the generally approved approach; he needed a three-step. Whenever he did the two-step, his punting suffered. "Have you timed him on the two-step?" Belichick asked. Yes, Pees had, and he came in at 2.3 seconds, a little above the ideal, which was 2 seconds. "And what about the three-step?" Belichick asked. "He does it in two seconds," Pees said. "Well, there's your answer, just let him be," Belichick said, and Pees thought, of course, how simple, and then he thought, no wonder the son is so smart and wastes so little of everyone's time.

◆ ◆ ◆

Both Steve and Jeannette Belichick thought that Annapolis was a good place to raise a son, and from an early age Bill liked to hang out with his father at practice. Steve enjoyed that, too—some coaches, he knew, did not like having their sons at practice, but he was more than comfortable with it. He was gone so much of the time scouting that he liked being around his boy when he could. Bill liked practice, and he would, in the years when Roger Staubach was there—and was always the first to arrive at practice and the last to leave—catch passes that Staubach threw, or take snaps from the great center Tom Lynch, who eventually went on to become the superintendent of the Academy.

The Belichicks were careful in the way they lived, because the salaries were never that big, even if his pay had been gradually going up. At North Carolina he had been paid $6000 a year, and at Navy he started at $7000. The Navy paid for their move from Chapel Hill, which was the first time anyone had done that. But the shadow of Struthers, the steel mills, and the Depression was always there. In that era, coming out of the Depression, small increments of success were to be valued, for they were not necessarily small. When Steve Belichick, as a young Vanderbilt assistant, had recruited eighteen-year-old Don Gleisner in 1949, visiting him on his farm near Oberlin, Ohio, Gleisner was fascinated by the idea of someone who made a living by coaching. "I think I'd like to do that too," he said. "Any money in it?" Belichick pointed at his new car. "That's a '49 Chevy, son," he answered proudly, "and there's not a penny owed on it." Nothing was ever to be wasted. No food to be left on anyone's plate. There was never any doubt, Bill once said, where that value system came from. He knew all of his father's stories, which had been told again and again: the grandfather who walked back and forth to work every day (the distance seemingly growing longer with each telling), the caddying for the family kitty with only 10 cents to go to the caddy himself, the older brothers who had been forced to leave school and go to work before they graduated, the Sunday chicken as the one meal to look forward to. When Bill Belichick grew up, it was with the most natural conflict imaginable for someone of his generation, who was living in an ever more affluent America, yet was acutely aware of the hardships that had shaped the previous generations, and how those hardships had made them stronger, and how much they had sacrificed to make him successful. Out of that, eventually, an exceptional work ethic was fashioned in a young man whose life was infinitely more privileged than that of his parents and grandparents.

If America was fast becoming a disposable culture, in which broken things—radios, television sets, vacuum cleaners—were thrown away rather than repaired, that was never true in the Belichick home. There was a friend of Steve's living in Annapolis who seemed to be able to fix any kind of electrical device, and he had a regular customer in the Belichick family. Everything was saved, including hundreds of copies of the *New Yorker* magazine, which Jeannette Belichick subscribed to faithfully. Nothing was to be bought on credit—if you could not afford the price, you didn't buy it. The one exception was their house, which with the aid of low-rate loans from the Navy they built themselves. They found the perfect piece of property on the outskirts of town and bought the land for only $5000—the town would eventually grow and come to them.

When Steve Belichick scouted, he almost always drove, unless it was a cross-country trip, and in many of those years the government paid 8 cents a mile. He always deposited the reimbursement check in a separate banking account, which was to be used only to buy the next Belichick family car. The one big expense that lay ahead of them, they were aware, was Bill's college expenses, and so each year, starting relatively early in his career, Steve ran a football camp at a nearby college for a few weeks, with the proceeds, which were hardly huge—perhaps $1000 a year—ticketed specifically for his son's college expenses. (Later when he was a junior at Wesleyan, Bill Belichick decided he wanted to take a break for a year and go to Europe. That was fine with his father—as long as Bill paid for the final year himself. A college education was so important, that he did not want to take any chance of his son not finishing on time or, worse, dropping out.)

Jeannette Belichick enjoyed living in Annapolis, too, and though she did not go back to teaching, she loved taking Bill and the other kids in his class to the Smithsonian in Washington for school trips. The other kids were always comfortable around her; she was a comforting figure, tender and kind, a considerable contrast to her husband, who had a crusty exterior, a booming, gruff voice, and a look he could give that seemed to say "Prove to me that you haven't done anything wrong," as his son interpreted it. If on occasion he could seem like something of a hanging judge, Jeannette was the defense lawyer, who could get everyone off.

Bill Belichick actually had two childhoods: a normal, American childhood and then a football childhood as well. As a boy, he spoke two languages—English and coach-speak, football version. Other kids had their hobbies; some collected postage stamps and others had baseball cards, but Bill studied football film. It seemed natural to him, and he had a great aptitude for it—plus, it allowed him to spend a good deal of time with his father. But he had plenty of friends and he played other sports besides football. He hung out a great deal at the home of his pal Mark Fredland, whose father was a professor of economics at the Academy. There were five Fredland boys, and that made the Fredland house a center of kid activity, a kind of informal boys club. As a boy, Bill played a lot of lacrosse, which was a big sport in suburban Maryland. In some ways it was even more fun than football, since football practices were mostly about repetition and drills, whereas in lacrosse practice you were, more often than not, actually playing the game.

The first Navy game Bill could remember was the Army-Navy game of 1959, when Joe Bellino, his first hero, who would eventually win the Heisman Trophy, ran for three touchdowns in a Navy victory. (Some forty-five years later, as a head coach with the Patriots, Belichick would have Bellino come by every year and talk to his players at the start of camp; Bellino would tell them that what they did in college did not matter, that in the pro game no one cared if they were All-Americans or had even won the Heisman.) Bill started hanging out with his father at Navy practices when he was about six or seven, and by the time he was nine, he would make a scouting trip with him once a year—a reward for the fact that his father was away so much on weekends scouting. He loved making that annual trip; it was a chance to bond with his father, who seemed so important a figure in a world that he admired and was gradually coming to understand. On Monday nights, after his father had scouted an opponent, he was allowed to go with him to the Navy players' meeting (if his homework was finished) to do the breakdown of the upcoming opponent. He would sit there, transfixed by the serious way these wonderful athletes listened to his father and the respect they showed him, as he discussed the strengths and weaknesses of Saturday's opponent.

In a way it was as if he were part of a larger family. When Ernie Jorge, the Navy line coach, did the final game plan on Friday night, he always made an extra copy and put it in an envelope with *Bill* Belichick's name on it. "He'd get the report and go up to his room and study the plays. I think he was nine at the time, but he knew 28 was a sweep, 26 was off tackle. He knew all the pass plays, the banana and the down and out," Steve Belichick said years later. What Bill Belichick remembered about his father in those years, perhaps the most important thing of all, something that lasted with him, was that he seemed to come home from work happy each night, a sign that he loved his work, and always seemed eager to go to work, and that the other men, the men he worked with, obviously respected him greatly. Bill Belichick liked the feeling of camaraderie that they had, of seeing these men working so well together, bonded by a sense of common purpose. There was, he decided, an exceptional richness to his father's life.

◆◆◆

Very early on, Bill Belichick, not surprisingly, started seeing the game through the eyes of a coach. Studying the game and scouting off film is exhausting, repetitive work, which can quickly turn into drudgery, as there is no shortcut: You have to run the film forward, run it back, run it forward again, and run it back again two or three more times. To most people, a quick view of what another team did is enough. But for Steve Belichick and soon enough for his son, that quick view was a ticket into a secret world, in which you could find so much more than what was on the surface: the way different players lined up for different plays, the difference in cadences for running and passing plays—all those things that might give you an edge. Wayne Hardin, the Navy head coach after Erdelatz, could remember father and son coming into the coaches' room to work on film. Steve Belichick would be tracking the quarterback on a given play, and he would say, "Bill, would you check the tight end, and what he runs," and Bill would answer that he had faked a block and then run a square in, and Steve would chart it on the diagram. "My kids would come in and see the same film being shown and look closely at it and say 'Oh, we've already seen this movie,'" recalled Hardin years later, "and go back out and play, but Bill would be absolutely transfixed; he loved helping his father." Hardin was, in fact, very good with him when he was just a boy, asking him from time to time, "How do you think we did today, Bill? Was that a good practice or were they dragging a bit?"

Bill Belichick was never going to be a great football player, they both understood early on. He was never going to be that big, and more important, he lacked the speed which had driven his father's career and gotten the family out of Struthers. But he understood the game from the start and that allowed him to play at a higher level than he might have otherwise. Starting in the sixth grade, he played in the 110-pound league, and then in the eighth grade he played in the 135-pound league. Barry Carter, who was a teacher in the junior high and later an assistant superintendent of schools, and whose son Chris was a running back and a friend and teammate of Bill's, remembered that when Bill was ten he was already an apprentice coach. He already talked exactly like a coach. "He would come by the house and we would be talking about our team, and we would be talking about our next opponent," said Carter. "He would talk about a particular defense we planned to use, a wide tackle six, which was a balanced six-man front, no one over the center, with two linebackers, which he said would be just fine, as long as we were up against a running team; but, if we went against a passing team, if, as he said, they flooded the zone, our linebackers would not be able to deal with it." Perhaps, Bill had added at the time, they ought to go to the Oklahoma, a slightly different defense better suited to a passing team—a five-man front with two linebackers, and the four defensive backs arrayed like an unfolded umbrella. He wasn't being pretentious, Carter thought, it just came naturally. It was simply the way he had been raised. "He was already talking back in those days of trying to stop other teams, and he was saying that most scouts looked at other teams and thought that the most important thing was to find out what their weakness was, but the right way to do it was to search for their strengths and try to take that away from them, and make them do what they don't want to do," recalled Carter. "He was either ten or twelve at the time, and that obviously came directly from Steve. I think back to that all the time now. I remember watching the playoffs this year, when they went against the Indianapolis Colts, the 20–3 game. I was watching what his defenses were doing and thinking he hasn't changed very much."

The first of the coaches other than his father who had a major impact on Bill was Al Laramore, the coach at Annapolis High School. Laramore was a very tough guy, who coached at a very tough school. He was about six feet tall, weighed a little over three hundred pounds, and not all of it, Belichick remembered, was muscle. Annapolis was a large public high school which, when Belichick entered it in 1966, was undergoing its own difficulties because of integration decrees. Bates High School, the black school just two blocks from Annapolis High, had been closed down, and the two schools had been combined. There was a good deal of social tension at the school in those early, difficult days of adjustment, a lot of skirmishing among whites and blacks, but Al Laramore made sure that none of the skirmishing took place in his football program. He was nothing if not intimidating. He had a rough voice and a kind of grumpy look that kept kids at a certain distance. Things were run his way. "My way or the highway," as his wife, Dorothy Laramore Coyle, later noted, "was probably his favorite expression. They either toed the line or they were gone—he wasn't going to debate them about any rules."

The first rule was that all his players had to go to class, or he would cut them from the team; the second was no smoking or drinking—if you did, you would also be dismissed. For a good deal of that time he had no assistant coaches, which was amazing, given the size of the school and the other responsibilities he carried, including being the head basketball coach and on occasion the head lacrosse coach. (He was the only man, Belichick believed, ever to win the state championship in all three sports.)

To the degree that Laramore had a role model, it was Vince Lombardi, who believed in power football executed flawlessly, and whose Green Bay teams were at the height of their success at that time. What Laramore did was not always pretty, and it was rarely deceptive. Instead, it was very basic—four plays really: 22 Power (which could be called either right or left), 24 Quick Trap, 28 Counter, and then Sprint Right, the basic pass play. He did not, as Belichick noted, believe in a lot of razzle-dazzle. Opposing teams tended to know exactly what was coming on each play; the challenge, because his teams were so tough and in such good physical condition, was in stopping them, even when you knew what they were going to do. What Laramore generally aimed at was to wear the other team down, and he often did. He was not into Xs and Os. If he threw the ball five times a game, it was a lot.

"They'd open with the same three plays each time," said Barry Carter, whose son ran some of them. "Twenty-eight Counter, the sweep, the first play; 22 Power, the second; and 24 Quick Trap, the third. One time the coach of the Severna Park High School told a reporter for one of the newspapers that he was going to stop our 22 Power play, the off tackle run, if he had to put the entire band out there on the field in the tackle slot. So, I said to my son Chris, who was the halfback, 'I guess you're not going to run the 22 Power this week,' and he said, 'Oh, we're going to run it—they're the ones who have to try and stop it!' "

Laramore did not believe in the star system. No one, in the time Bill Belichick played there, wore a uniform with his name on the back. Given the talent available—so many kids who wanted so badly to play football for him—the system worked. "In the Laramore system the coach was king," as Belichick noted, "and had been king in the past, and was going to be king in the future." Rarely did players start as sophomores. Occasionally, very occasionally, they started as juniors. Mostly they started as seniors. The good thing about the system was that it was fair. If you worked hard, practiced hard, you tended to get rewarded with playing time; the kids who worked out with weights at the school during the semi-voluntary summer sessions had an advantage in making the team. It was not mandatory, the weight lifting, but Laramore always knew who was playing by his rules, and who was working out.

Practices were tough, deliberately so, as much to scare away players who might lack the requisite character as to toughen those who survived. Those who played for Laramore had to survive the summer sessions, which were brutal. They practiced on a dirt field, devoid, it appeared, of a single blade of grass or for that matter trees on the side, which might cool it ever so slightly; there was just dirt, which was in the process of baking into dust. There were days out there when they all thought they were going to die, days when there were no individual bottles of water and no giant containers of Gatorade, just one large bucket of water, ever so quickly heating up in the sun, and a ladle. If Laramore did not like the way the practice was going, he would shout at them, "You guys stink." And then he would kick over the bucket, and there would be no water that day. That was the way he was, and that was the way he coached, and you either bought into his system, or you did not play football for him. If you screwed up on one of those terribly humid days, then the whole team had to run laps. If he spoke to you, it was rarely in a calm, reassuring voice; rather, it was loud, and his face tended to be about three inches away from yours.

There was a drill that taught the players to keep their bodies low to the ground, which involved a kind of cattle chute with lead pipes just above the chute. You ran the chute with your helmet off, and if you did not stay low enough, you hit your head on the pipes. There was the linebacker/running back drill, where two linebackers waited within a short strip of yardage marked off by orange cones, and went at one running back, whose job it was to negotiate his way down that short, violent passage. And, finally, there was the bullring, in which a group of players circled one player and took turns coming at him from different angles, trying to knock him down, while he fought them off—a drill eventually discarded for being a bit too primitive.

It was a rather crude way of coaching, Bill Belichick thought, but it probably suited Laramore's very difficult situation of dealing with a great many kids who might otherwise have challenged the rules. Any other set of rules, anything more permissive, Belichick thought, might have backfired: "It was, when you thought back about it—given the difficulties under which he worked, how little he had in the way of support, and how tough a situation it could have been—very impressive. It was very fair, very democratic, very much based on hard work, and you only got rewards after you had proved a commitment to the program. No one was going to be bigger than the team or, for that matter, the coach. It was quite well thought out."

Laramore himself would surely have agreed. "What he always sought with them," his widow said, "was what he called a kind of 'distant closeness'—he did not think he could get closer to them without diminishing his authority. He was trying to motivate them, to teach them how to make a commitment to something, without losing his control." He believed, first and foremost, that he needed to establish the totality of his authority, letting the players know that it could not be challenged. If he needed to shout, he would shout. To prove a point, on a couple of occasions, he banged the chalkboard with his hand so hard that he broke the board. His view was that even if he was wrong, he was right. "There was no extra pay at first for coaching, it was called voluntary duty, but he loved it, and he did it because he loved the young kids," Dorothy Laramore Coyle said.

Laramore had been there about four years when Bill Belichick arrived, and his teams were already experiencing considerable success. He had coached kids who were the sons of Academy coaches before, he told his wife, but he had never coached one who had arrived already a coach in the making. "He doesn't even start yet," he told her when Belichick was a junior, "and he already knows so much—he's like a coach. I think he's going to be a coach, but in a way he already is a coach." Bill actually did become something of an assistant coach, although he was always wary of undermining Laramore's authority. But the head coach, located on the sidelines, often has one of the worst views of the game, and on occasion when what Laramore thought was happening on the field was not happening, Belichick would quickly pick up on it. He talked with his father about how to let Laramore know about the needed adjustments, and Steve Belichick suggested that he never do it in front of the other players, lest he embarrass Laramore; instead, figure out the right, private moment when he could sidle over to the coach and make whatever suggestion he had, which is what he did.

CHAPTER SIX

Going to Andover for a postgraduate year allowed Bill Belichick to watch a very different kind of coach, working in a completely different environment. That, he thought, was an invaluable lesson, two very different men coaching in totally different situations, each in a very different way—the style of each was the reverse of the other—but each was maximizing totally different situations. It was a fascinating way of watching two very different coaches in action, seeing how they made their adjustments to their material, to the culture in which they operated, to their own value systems, and that of the schools they operated in, and that of the young men whom they taught.

The decision that Bill should go to Andover had grown out of Steve Belichick's recruiting days. Often he would see a talented young man eager to go the Academy, a young man with some athletic talent and reasonably good grades, but, Steve suspected, he was going to fall just a little short of the entrance requirements. These young men, often accompanied by their parents, would come to Annapolis for a visit, and sometimes drop by the Belichick house. There, in a setting where Steve could be a little more relaxed and personal, he would tell the young man that he didn't think he was quite ready, and he would suggest a postgraduate year. If the young man tried that track, Belichick suggested, he would surely become physically stronger and would have better grades from a better college-preparatory program, and those things might help him get an appointment. Bill heard that speech many times and had not really taken it seriously, except at the end of each school year, when Steve would bring some of the Academy seniors over to the Belichick home for a farewell dinner, and there would always be one of them saying, "You know, Coach, I can remember when I was trying to get in here, and you suggested a year of prep school, and I didn't want to go there at first, but I went there because you suggested it, and it was the best year of my life, because I learned how to study, and I grew up a lot."

◆ ◆ ◆

Bill Belichick had done very well academically at Annapolis High, and had been the starting center on the high school football team. He wanted to play some college ball, but he and his father were well aware of Bill's physical limitations, so they decided that he should, if need be, go to a good, small boarding school for a year if that was what was needed to get into the right college. A lot of hard work and planning had gone into putting aside the money for his college expenses, and the game plan was this: In his senior year at Annapolis he would apply to four schools—Yale, Dartmouth, Amherst, and Williams. If he got into at least one of them, he would go to college immediately. If he didn't, he would PG for a year at either Lawrenceville or

Andover, where the family had connections. It turned out he did not get into any of the four schools—his combined SATs were about 1200—so he set out for Andover, his choice because one of the assistant coaches there, Dick Duden, had been a great player not only at Navy, but for a coach at Andover named Steve Sorota, a man who was himself a quiet kind of legend. Bill did well academically at Andover, and when he retook his SATs a year later, he raised his scores by only about two points, which greatly amused Steve, who thereafter liked to boast that he had paid $2700 for a two-point jump in his son's SAT scores.

◆◆◆

Steve Sorota coached for forty-two years at Andover and was much loved by several generations of men who had competed under him in football and in track. He had been a blue-collar mill kid, growing up in nearby Lowell when that was still a vibrant manufacturing area; his family roots were in Poland, not in Italy, as many who knew him thought. His story—how he had gotten out of that vast pool of turn-of-the-century immigrants and made his way into the luckier, more successful part of America—was eerily similar to Steve Belichick's. Sorota's father had worked in the Gillette factory in Lowell, and the family had been quite poor. But, like Steve Belichick, Sorota was fast and strong, and he was a talented, if not very big, running back at Lowell High. His services had been coveted by several college scouts, including one working for Jim Crowley, the coach at Fordham, then a rising football power. In those days—the early thirties—Crowley had put together several great teams, who played before sellout crowds in the vast Polo Grounds in New York. Sorota entered Fordham two years before Vince Lombardi, who had been a star on teams that featured the famed Seven Blocks of Granite, which meant that Sorota and Lombardi played together for one season. Sorota was very amused by how much excitement Fordham football generated in New York, appealing, as it did, to the vast Catholic population of the city, so many of whom had never been to college themselves. He liked to tell how the Fordham team gathered in the school's locker room up at the Bronx campus, and how Crowley would dole out two subway tokens to each player, one to get from Fordham to the Polo Grounds, the other to get back. He was proud of what he had accomplished on those teams, and though he was not a boastful man, he later told Ernie Adams, when Adams and Bill Belichick were going to work for the New York Giants' new head coach Ray Perkins, a onetime Alabama receiver, "Now, Ernie, be sure and tell Mr. Perkins that you were coached by a man who played for Fordham when it knocked Alabama out of the national championship in 1933."

Sorota graduated from Fordham in 1936, and, in the spring of his senior year, Andover Academy, which was near his hometown, was looking for an assistant football coach. Those were the worst days of the Depression and jobs were hard to come by. He went up to Andover that spring, stayed for a week, and in effect auditioned for the job before they finally gave it to him. The offer of the job was thrilling, because it meant that he and his fiancée, Stephanie, could get married. He started as an assistant at the school in the fall of 1936 at, she remembered, a salary of about $1000 a year, and became head coach three years later. He coached there through three wars—World War II, Korea, and Vietnam. In that time the school changed dramatically, and perhaps more importantly, so did the attitude of the young men toward authority. By the late 1960s, when a dean or a coach made the rules, it was no longer a given that the young men would automatically obey them. In those years Steve Sorota barely changed at all; he had always been a formidable authority figure, but luckily, given the dramatic social changes taking place around him, he wore his authority lightly. His power came from his intelligence, his subtlety, and his kindness, not from his position in the hierarchy. He coached through persuasion, not through orders and yelling. He would always, in a calm, low-key voice, explain to his players what they needed to do in a given game, and which part of their mission he expected them to figure out and execute on their own.

When he had first arrived at Andover in 1936 to coach football, the school's headmaster, Claude Moore Fuess, had given him marching orders very different from those given to most new coaches: "Your job is to *teach,* not to win a lot of football games." That, Sorota would later say, was the perfect message for a young coach, because it meant that his job depended not on his won-and-lost record, which actually turned out to be exceptional, but on his teaching, which he did with great skill, and on his effect on the young men, which was exemplary, for he reached into the deepest part of them, their character, and helped shape it. The headmaster's challenge allowed him to let his young players find their own way. He did not, like so many high school coaches, call the plays for his quarterbacks himself; instead he allowed them to make these decisions on the field. That was something that might have gotten him fired elsewhere. If they called the wrong play and made a mistake, they might in the long run learn more from the mistake than from having their coach call the perfect play. But had he been under pressure to win, he once told a colleague, he might have done the play-calling himself.

He loved coaching at the high school level and thought, if anything, it was more important than coaching at college, because it took place at a more formative time in the boys' lives. You could do more good—or more damage—at that age, he believed. By the time they got to college, their attitudes were already formed in most cases. In the years right after the war, he received a tantalizing offer from one of the area's better colleges to become the head coach. It was a big program, and it would mean a good deal more money, more than twice as much as he was making, and he spoke of it at some length with his wife, but, in the end, he turned the offer down. He already had everything he needed, he told her.

It was never about ego with him. He never seemed to lose his temper with the players. There had been one moment in Bill and Ernie Adams's senior year, when they had gone to play at Lawrenceville. Lawrenceville, because of the considerable skills of its coach, Ken Keuffel, himself an Andover graduate who had been coached by Sorota, was always a tough game. If Andover won, they would have had an unbeaten season. The players were all sleeping on mats in the Lawrenceville gym, and, excited about the freedom they were enjoying on this trip, they got a little noisy—young men on the brink of something big. Sorota came in, clearly irritated, and, without raising his voice, told them to hold it down and get some sleep if they wanted to win the next day.

He was very respectful of his players, and he understood how complicated life could be for a young man struggling through his teenage years, that the fact that a young man looked strong, and had a strong body, did not necessarily mean he was strong, that an adolescent boy was often dealing with all kinds of interior problems and pressures and doubts, almost all of them emotional, none of them readily visible to a coach. These were young men who, despite their noisiness, and on occasion braggadocio, were still unsure of who they were. The job of a good coach was to encourage a boy's better self, to let his confidence grow, but to do it ever so gently. The conventional wisdom, Sorota once pointed out to a younger man named Joe Wennik, who played under him and who eventually became the school's athletic director, was that football demanded the most courage of any sport, because it was so physical a game. But that was not necessarily true, he said. Every sport had its own special demand for courage: the sprinter and the swimmer waiting tensely for the starter's gun, the miler or the rower knowing the pain he would have to face near the end of the race. Wennik took those words to heart; it was a sign, he thought, of how respectful Sorota was of all kids, of how aware he was that all of them deserved admiration for what they were doing, of how important he believed it was not to take any young person for granted.

He was protective of his kids; he did not want college recruiters or scouts or media people around. There was, he suspected, already enough pressure on them. He wanted, thought Wennik, to create an atmosphere in which football was played well, where excellence was valued, but where it was always fun. There was never to be too heavy a price paid if you made a mistake. He knew that though football was important at Andover, it was perhaps not so important in the greater world. He understood that many of these young men were going on to important careers, few of which would be in football. If you missed practices, you missed practices—sometimes the kids had heavy schedules involving other classes that conflicted with football. The school's schedule and player's decision came first.

Sorota's program could not have been more different than the one at Annapolis, Bill Belichick later reflected, and there were serious lessons for a young coach-in-training in all of this. Each method suited the environment, he realized, and neither method would have worked at the other institution—yet, somehow, the right coach had surfaced at each school.

His practices reflected his personality. His players did not do a lot of hitting. His philosophy was that a great deal of the hitting in high school ball was wasted, that you only wore the kids down, and detracted from their ability by having too many scrimmages. Why increase the possibility of injuries? He expected his players to be in good shape and to listen to their coaches—if they did, they would do it right. Monday and Tuesday were devoted to going over what had happened the week before and who they were playing that Saturday. On Wednesday there was usually a scrimmage. Then, on Thursday and Friday, it was generally a light practice, more about the philosophy of the coming game than anything else. Just to make sure that the players had fun, Sorota instituted what he called the sandbox drill, in which he would take the entire team, put them on the field, throw out some footballs, and let them fool around in a totally unstructured practice—defensive tackles throwing passes, linebackers placekicking. This occasionally had the unexpected benefit of discovering a player's hidden talent, but, most of all, as Wennik said, it was about "letting football be fun, letting young men who work so hard at everything most of the time, both sports and schoolwork, enjoy themselves."

Sorota never belittled a player, and never, as far as many of his assistants and former players could remember, needed to discipline one. The rules were set, they were clear, and no one fooled around on Steve Sorota's time. If something went wrong, if they had run the wrong play for the situation, he might suggest that they try another, and he would give them the play—the next time. He once lost his temper with Lou Hoitsma, one of his favorite assistants. It was the week of the Exeter game, and Hoitsma had had the team running sprints. Afterward, he had allowed them to do a little hitting, and a varsity center had hurt his shoulder. Sorota was not pleased. In his mind Hoitsma had violated one of his cardinal rules—he had pushed a kid a little too hard in practice.

Sorota was not very big, about five-eight and 160 pounds, but he had played well in college in what had been a big-time program, and he had done it by using his intelligence as much as his sheer power. He had great footwork and balance, and he knew how to leverage his body; it was, thought Hoitsma, "as if he were as much a professor of physics as a football coach in the way he coached, because leverage mattered so much. Leverage to him was more important than size." He understood how to maximize your power, that the right angle for a block or a tackle might be as important as the pure strength; comparably, in coaching track, which he also loved to do, he could in a few lessons take a strong kid and turn him into a pole vaulter or a discus thrower.

His teams played a surprisingly hard schedule, because in addition to a handful of rival prep schools, Andover often played the Harvard, Yale, and Dartmouth freshmen. Those were tough games—they had players who were, in general, a year older, which was a big edge at that age. One of the things Sorota did with considerable skill was to blend the talented PGs that Andover got each year with his regular students, who had been part of his program for two or three years. That was, as the writer Buzz Bissinger, a classmate of both Belichick and Adams, called it, Andover's dirty little secret. The PGs were, more often than not, very talented athletes. Unlike with Bill Belichick, who had come for an academic boost and was not on an athletic track, they were mostly there to help persuade an Ivy League coach of their value. Feeding ten or twelve players, who expected to be college stars, into an existing program of hard workers who had earned their playing time (and for whom prep school football might be the end of the line), without creating resentment and bitterness, was a difficult assignment. But, somehow, Sorota managed to do it, converting players from one position to another if need be, always finding room for his new talent, while making sure that his older, loyal players were not shortchanged. A player named Bruce Bruckmann had thought he was going to be the team's quarterback in 1970, but then Milt Holt, an immensely talented passer from Hawaii, showed up. He was clearly a vastly superior talent (Holt eventually became a great star at Harvard), and so Bruckmann switched over and became a key running back, and Andover went undefeated. The process of integrating the PGs, thought Bruckmann, "could easily have been toxic, but Sorota made it work and work well for everyone—everyone who deserved a place seemed to find it."

Typically, he did not hype games; nor did he go in for passionate motivational speeches. When a game was unusually important, as with the annual Exeter game, Sorota would take it up just a notch. "This is the week we play for keeps," he would say. One of his favorite stories, one that he particularly liked telling players who had just come out for his teams, was about the time in 1956 when he did not have a good team, and Exeter had run the score up, 45–6. The following year was marked for revenge, he said. Late in the game, with Andover far, far ahead, and time running out, Andover scored. That made it 44–6. Suddenly, without his knowledge, his players called time-out and huddled on the field. Then they lined up and kicked the extra point, making it 45–6. "What was that time-out about?" he had asked his players as they came off the field. "We were deciding whether we wanted to win 46–6 or 45–6, and we were taking a vote," they said. Those in favor of kicking the point won the vote, and there was a lesson in there, Sorota suspected, for everyone, most particularly the Exeter players and coaches.

Bill Belichick enjoyed Andover, though he found the academics hard at first. He had always thought of himself, though not in a boastful way, as one of the smart kids at Annapolis High. What happened to him when he went from an ordinary American public high school to an elite private school was a many-times-told story. At Andover, the students knew how to take notes during class, how to write papers, and how to write essay exams. He, by contrast, was a complete novice, and it was a bit frightening for him to go from being smart and fast to feeling dumb and slow. "When I first got there, I thought it was going to be easy. I looked at the schedule, and there were only three classes a day, and the rest of the day you were free to study," he said. For the first time in his life, he felt intellectually limited. "I thought I had been good at French—I had taken four years of it at Annapolis—so they put me in French three at Andover. We had to translate *Les Misérables,* and we were supposed to do a chapter a night, but I had to look up every word, and it was more like a page a night. I came to hate that guy, Jean Valjean," he said. "I thought I was good at math, at trig and calculus, but I struggled with *everything* at Andover." If it was a hard, new world, it was also a wonderful world, classes with ten or eleven students, all these gifted teachers who had the luxury of time and good students. What they did, Belichick understood much later, was "they challenged you, challenged you to reach for more, to work harder than you thought you could and always to think for yourself." He got a B average there, which he was very proud of. It was, he later said, like jumping from Annapolis into his first year of college, it was so different and demanding. Thankfully, he had few social problems. He got along with everyone, and he had, some of his friends thought, a nicely developed sense of irony and humor.

At Andover, thought Bruckmann, it was interesting how purposeful Belichick already was about coaching. "You could tell from the start that he lived and breathed football, nothing less than twenty-four hours a day seven days a week," he recalled. That was intriguing because until Belichick arrived, everyone had thought that it was Adams who was going to be the coach. "Andover is the kind of place, all those young men with all that talent and ambition, where everyone knows who is going to be who in later life," said Bissinger, who himself became a very successful writer and won a Pulitzer Prize. "We know who is going to be a senator or governor—this was after all, a class which produced Jeb Bush and Lincoln Chafee. We know who is going to be the great lawyer and the star of Wall Street or the CEO or the great doctor and the great biologist. And Ernie was going to be the coach, he loved coaching, he was always doing Xs and Os, and he read every book that came out on football, and he had his own collection of game films that he sent away for. And then Bill showed up and we had two coaches."

If anyone knew Bill Belichick in those years it was Adams, and Adams had no doubts about Belichick's future. "I was absolutely sure of it, because that was what he cared about, and he was always critiquing the games we watched on television, judging the coaches and the players—'Did you see that call, did you ever see a more predictable third and short call?' he would say, or, 'Did you see how poor a route that tight end ran?' When we watched football games he was already coaching." He had the talent for it, Adams thought; he had a great eye for the game, and a great sense of its tempo. But he also, Adams added, was willing to work harder than anyone else. "He had the gift for it," Adams said, "and he had the discipline, and he understood from the beginning the one great truth about film, that the more you ran it, the more you saw."

The experience they had at Andover, Ernie Adams thought, was almost unique: a wonderful coach who knew the game, had great confidence in his players, was immensely sensitive to them, and above all never lost his calm, who always in the midst of the most dramatic and tense moments in a game seemed to be the calmest person there, a calm that reassured his own players and steadied them. Years later, watching Bill Belichick on the sidelines during big games when things were not necessarily breaking well for the Patriots, seeing him so calm and never emotionally out of control, Adams was sure he was watching a partial reincarnation of Steve Sorota.

CHAPTER SEVEN

Wesleyan was exactly the kind of New England college he wanted. This time, a solid B student from a demanding prep school, he got in everywhere he applied: Bates, Duke, Middlebury, Wesleyan, and Wittenberg (where Bill Edwards had finished his career coaching), even Penn, which had a naval ROTC program that interested him, but which, unfortunately, demanded an engineering track when he wanted to major in the humanities. He chose Wesleyan because it fit all his needs and also, in no small part, because his close friend Mark Fredland had just finished his freshman year there and had liked it very much.

Belichick's years there were by and large happy ones. Wesleyan was a small school where the teaching was very good, and where he could continue to study with unusually accomplished people, a privilege he was very much aware of. Football was less pleasant for a time.

He played on the freshman team, and went out for the varsity in his sophomore year, but even in a small and not very distinguished program (traditional rivals Williams and Amherst always seemed to maximize their football programs, as Wesleyan did not), he did not do very well. His size was against him, as was, even more than at Andover, his lack of speed. No one worked harder, but as a sophomore he played relatively little. There were other problems as well. One assistant coach, he believed, had it in for him, seeming to think that because of his Naval Academy connections, Belichick might think he knew more than the coaches. Having a coach who was a bit edgy with you, whose attitude seemed to say, *Prove to me that you don't have an attitude problem,* Belichick thought, was bad enough, but the coach did something even more troubling. He went off to some coaching seminar, where another coach had been teaching a chop block—a block that was, if not actually illegal, certainly ethically dubious—and he tried to install it in, of all places, Wesleyan's program. The chop block took place against a center who was momentarily blindsided. There was one practice when Belichick was a sophomore and playing center, and they had run the chop block play again and again, using it against the center perhaps ten times, Belichick remembered. Finally, someone had gotten him, one player grabbing his leg, another player falling on him, and he had broken his leg. It was, Bill thought, totally unnecessary, "borderline ethically at best, and not something you should do to an opponent and really stupid to use against your own players." That took much of the taste of football away from him, and he did not play his junior year, though in his senior year he came back and played, this time as a tight end. The coaches were the same, but this time there was a certain sweetness to it, because he knew it was the last time he would ever play the game competitively; he was saying good-bye not just to playing the game, but to the special kind of friendships you made playing it, to the camaraderie it generates.

The sport he enjoyed most at Wesleyan was lacrosse, because he admired the coach, Terry Jackson. What made that interesting was that Jackson was not really a lacrosse coach, but rather a soccer coach, who out of last-minute necessity had been drafted into taking the job ("coaching by default," he later said). He had no real knowledge of the game, understood that he had no knowledge of the game, but knew exactly how to handle his players and how to listen to them and use them well. He put them on the field, and let them play, and above all did not get in their way. "You can't teach what you don't know," Jackson noted years later. What intrigued Belichick was that when he first arrived at Wesleyan, the talent was better than it would be under Jackson and they had a coach who was a certified lacrosse man, but they had not done that well. Then, under a coach who did not know the game and with less talent, they had done much better. Belichick flowered in the lacrosse program, as he had not in the football program. "With Bill it was like having a great assistant coach," said Jackson. His knowledge of the game was exceptional, even if his speed, in a game based on running, was marginal. "Have you ever seen him run?" Jackson asked. "When he's running fast, it's like he's jogging to everything." But he was inventive and shrewd about the game, and there were two younger players who were very fast, Mike Celeste and Dave Whiting, and he played well with them. Jackson decided to put one of them on each side of Belichick and let them learn the game while they were playing. They had the speed, and he had the knowledge, and he was like a talented but slow NBA point guard, playing with two very fast forwards. Even opposing teams knew how smart he was. The scouting report on him, a bit primitive because lacrosse scouting reports were not that sophisticated, said Kevin Spencer, who played against him for Springfield College, and later coached football and lacrosse at Wesleyan and then coached for Belichick at Cleveland, was: "Not very fast, and not very good himself. But very smart. Makes everyone around him better. A coach on the field."

In his senior year, with a month to go, Belichick broke his thumb, and the doctors put a cast on it. With the playoffs approaching, he went to the Wesleyan doctors to see if he could get the cast removed so he could play, but they refused. So, on his own, he went down to the Naval Academy, where he saw the Navy team doctor, who looked at it and, knowing Belichick's passion for the game, removed the cast. That, thought Jackson, was about sheer love of the game. They went to the Eastern College finals, but lost to Bowdoin in the final game.

Unlike his close friends at Andover, Belichick's very close friends at Wesleyan had no idea that he was being pulled toward a career in coaching. They knew he loved sports, that it was a passion, but they had no sense of it being a profession. They knew he was ferociously competitive—he hated to lose, and when he lost in racquetball, he would, on occasion, break his racquet in anger, smashing it against the wall. (He got his racquets free at the Naval Academy when he went home, as many as six at a time, until Steve Belichick finally told him that the Academy would not be an endless source of racquets, so he had to set some kind of limit on himself.) To Belichick's college friends, his father seemed a bit tough, short-listed among those parents not to be trifled with. Once Bill sneaked off to Mardi Gras in New Orleans, without bothering to obtain parental permission, it appeared. This involved cutting a good many classes, and the other members of the Chi Psi fraternity house tried to protect him when an increasingly irate Steve Belichick kept checking in, looking for his son. There was also one memorable evening when a bunch of them decided that they wanted to see *Gone With the Wind,* but in order to get through so long a movie they decided they needed a case of beer. Belichick solved the problem of sneaking the beer into the theater by strapping some of it onto himself, and then wearing his down jacket, which even under normal conditions bulged out, and which bulged even more that night.

It was always going to be a coaching life, for the arrow always pointed in only one direction. There were other possibilities, but there was always only one dream. He had considered a business career and there was a good offer from Procter & Gamble, but there was a powerful pull toward coaching, and at the very least he wanted to try it. He had sent out some letters, and he thought there was a job at North Carolina State working as a graduate assistant with Lou Holtz. That meant he could pursue the future on a double track, getting a masters in economics, while getting his start in coaching, but then, at the last minute, Holtz called to tell him the job was off, because he had been limited by Title IX. For a short time, right after graduation, he was a bit adrift, but then Ernie Adams called to tell him about his own job with the New England Patriots and suggested that his old friend try something similar with the pros.

Belichick, after all, had a network, one based on his father's twenty-five years as an assistant and scout. Out of that network would come two important connections to the Colts. Steve Belichick, after all, knew most of the great coaches of the era: Paul Brown, Don Shula, and Weeb Ewbank, among others. If he did not know Ted Marchibroda, just taking over at Baltimore, which was nearby, then he knew one of his assistants, a man named George Boutselis, who was coaching the special teams. So calls were made, and Marchibroda said to have Bill come up there. "I think," Steve Belichick said years later, "that Ted was thinking the kid could come up and break down film for him and maybe get four tickets per game."

Bill Belichick did not know Ted Marchibroda personally; nonetheless, there were some valuable connections with three of Marchibroda's assistants, who had taught at one time or another at Steve Belichick's summer camp. Connections in the world of coaching are incredibly important; they are like the strands in a giant spider's web. At any given moment everyone in the coaching world knew who was up and who was down, which meant that it was important for those who were up to help those who were down, because the order could be so readily reversed, at the whim of an athletic director. Those at the top might soon descend, and vice versa. In a profession where there were very few safety nets, and where one coach's victory was another coach's defeat, collegial courtesy was not just important, it was mandatory. Coaches tended to look out for one another. But there was one additional Belichick family connection to Marchibroda, and it reflected the web at its ultimate. It went through Marchibroda's son, Ted, who had played for a man named Jerry Falls at Jeb Stuart High in Falls Church, Virginia. Falls had played with Steve Belichick back at the start of World War II on some Great Lakes Navy teams. So Bill Belichick had known Jerry Falls all his life, because Falls was always coming by the house to talk ideas with his father. Now Jerry Falls called Marchibroda's son, who in turn called his father, and so it was that Bill Belichick, having just graduated from college in June 1975, landed on the doorstep of the brand-new coach of the Baltimore Colts.

At first, Marchibroda had talked about something very minor, perhaps working just on the weekends, keeping stats, but Belichick said he was looking for a bit more. They went back and forth on what it would be, and finally Belichick said, "Look, you don't have to pay me, but give me something real." Those were magic words at that moment in Colts history, and he was quickly taken on.

The Colts, it should be noted, were at that moment an extremely cheap organization. The glory days of the fifties and sixties when they were one of the elite teams of the NFL, with great defenses, and the legendary Johnny Unitas at quarterback, and a wonderful corps of receivers, were gone. They might be a football power again one day, but at that moment they were just starting to rebuild. Ted

Marchibroda was a George Allen protégé, who had been hired to bring the very successful George Allen system to Baltimore. He had spent nine years under Allen, five years in Los Angeles, and then four years with Allen as he rebuilt the Washington Redskins, getting rid of draft choices and younger players for veteran players whom he knew, and who knew his system—the Over the Hill Gang, as it was known. Marchibroda was a talented, indeed quite daring, offensive coach, but not very much interested in defense, which he handed over to others. The job ahead of him in Baltimore was exceptionally difficult, for George Allen was in some ways, at least, a disciple of Paul Brown; he believed in the virtues of specialization, and that demanded a great many assistant coaches—about eight, in his most recent incarnation in Washington. "I gave George an unlimited budget," Edward Bennett Williams, the principal owner of the Redskins, said a few weeks after hiring Allen, "and he's already exceeded it."

So Marchibroda was charged with putting in a complicated football system that depended on a large number of assistants and doing it on a very tight budget. For, unfortunately, the general manager in Baltimore, Joe Thomas, was exceptionally cheap. "Actually," noted Maxie Baughan, the defensive coordinator on those teams, "fanatically cheap. There was one year in the Joe Thomas years when we won the division championship, and they gave us each a $50 bonus, and we gave it back, because earlier in the year they had criticized us for drinking too much coffee—we were working around the clock there, and we needed the coffee—so we gave the bonus back and told them to keep it and pay for the coffee instead."

That season they badly needed someone to break down film on opponents, which was critical to the Allen system. Earlier on, Thomas had told Marchibroda he had a cousin who would do it. But the cousin found other work, possibly work that actually paid a salary. Whenever the subject of hiring additional coaches came up, Thomas tended to proclaim a bit too loudly and too frequently that he had coached in an era when he had only two assistants. So Marchibroda badly needed to find someone to do the film for no pay—and there was young Bill Belichick, Billy to Marchibroda then and forever, knocking on his door, wanting work, and not interested in being paid for it.

By chance the night he got the job, Bill Edwards, Steve Belichick's great mentor and friend, along with his wife, Dorothy, were visiting the Belichick home, so there was a great celebration, because Bill, without being pushed by his father, was going into coaching. It was, Bill remembered, a great family moment, everyone so proud and happy. Still, Steve Belichick, it should be noted, was more than a little dubious about the professional game; he was a college coach, and he thought the college game was better, and he believed that most of the good professional coaches all came out of the college game.

The job was a perfect fit, Bill Belichick thought later, and it summed up the Colts under Thomas: "All work and no pay was their motto," said Belichick. That was not entirely true. Because he was so good, they soon started paying him $25 a week, and by mid-season when the Colts were doing very well, and on a long winning streak, Joe Thomas came by and told Belichick how well the coaches were speaking of him, and he was therefore going to raise his pay to $50 a week, but not to spend it all in one place at one time.

All Belichick had wanted was a foot in the door. He was absolutely sure he could do the work, especially any work having to do with film. Marchibroda's family was still back in the Washington area, where he had been working for George Allen, and he was living with some of his staff near the Baltimore stadium. There were four of them staying at a new Howard Johnson's: Marchibroda; Whitey Dovell, the offensive line coach; George Boutselis, the special teams coach; and Belichick. Because the manager was a friend of Marchibroda's, they got their rooms for nothing.

Training camp in those days, before players worked out on their own or under team supervision in the summer, was long and hard. It lasted a full two and a half months. There were three scrimmages with the Redskins and, Belichick remembered, six preseason games. It was the way the players got into shape back then. It was hot and muggy in Baltimore, and there was not enough water, and the entire training camp took much too long, but Bill Belichick, all of twenty-three and the newest coach on the staff, loved every minute of it. Marchibroda was a man of rituals: He ate breakfast at the same time every day, and it was almost always the same thing; he went to Memorial Stadium at the same time every day, and one of Belichick's jobs (when he did not spend the night sleeping on a desk in the offices at Memorial Stadium) was to drive him to work, and be with him at all times. Belichick could almost save some money once the $25 a week started coming in, for he ate all his meals with Marchibroda on the head coach's tab. "Ted could probably have declared him as an income tax deduction," Steve Belichick said later. It was for him the beginning of the greatest football seminar imaginable; he was part of the highest level of football coaching all day long, privy to the coaches' talk, seeing how they worked and taught. If they got through work early enough, they went back to the Howard Johnson's, and talked football all through dinner and into the night. No one talked about anything but football. It was the life he had always hoped for. "He was like a sponge, taking it all in, listening to everything," said Maxie Baughan. "He didn't say very much, but he didn't miss very much either."

The year in Baltimore turned out to be one of the most exciting years in Belichick's life. No one worked harder. He kept asking for more, and they kept giving him more. He was doing what he had always wanted to do and discovering that he was good, that his skills were real. Marchibroda was hugely impressed. "You gave him an assignment, and he disappeared into a room and you didn't see him again until it was done, and then he wanted to do more," he said. Soon Belichick's duties expanded and became more interesting. At first they would send him to the airport to pick up film being shipped in, that and other donkey work, but then they decided that he was too valuable, that if he went to the airport they would be wasting two hours of his workday.

That, Belichick decided, was one of his big breakthrough moments, when the coaches knew they needed him. In fact, they needed him badly in Baltimore. There were only three coaches on defense: Maxie Baughan, as well as a defensive line coach and a defensive safety coach. Baughan, the old Los Angeles Ram linebacker, a coach on the field as a player, was a man whose sense of George Allen's complicated defenses was so advanced that he had called defensive signals for Allen, and then had coached under him in Washington after injuries forced the end of his playing career. He then became Marchibroda's defensive expert. Baughan was not just the defensive coordinator, but given the way Marchibroda coached, he was, in effect, the head coach for defense. When Belichick first arrived, no one knew much about him. He had been at a school that did not have a football reputation. "And in pro football in those days not many people came in by the kind of route he did," Baughan remembered, "mostly it was from having played at a high level yourself. But he did have the pedigree because of his father, we all knew that." When Baughan asked him to break down the film, he had done it so well and so quickly that Baughan was so impressed, he asked Belichick if he had ever done it before. "Yes, I helped my dad out once in a while," Belichick answered.

Indeed he had, Baughan thought, indeed he had. "I think he was the forerunner of something new, that professional football was not just a game, but that it was a profession, like the title said, or was going to be a profession," Baughan said years later. The hunger was there from the start. "What was important about him was not just that he saw what we were doing, and bought into what we were doing, but that he bought in *100* percent. That's the important part. A lot of guys come in, players and coaches alike, and they buy in 50 or 75 percent. But you can't do that. You have to buy into the entire thing. A lot of players come in, and they've played at a high level, and so they think they know everything, because they've played at big-time schools. But the truth is they don't know very much at all, because the game is always changing and because the systems are always changing. But Billy knew that already, and that you had to adapt game by game; he knew that everything was always changing. That was one of the things that set him apart. And another thing was the work ethic. It was always a great work ethic. You could always give him more—he always wanted more. He always wanted to get better. A lot of other young wannabe coaches, they always want the stuff that has the glory to it—you can spot guys like that a mile away—but he was different, probably because of the way he had been raised, the way Steve had taught him, and because of the value system of the Naval Academy. He wanted the grunt work. He understood that the key to success, the secret to it, was the mastery of the grunt work, all the little details. There are not a lot of people out there like that. In some ways, he was like us, the men at the top, because he worked around the clock. You did not automatically go home at six or seven o'clock, or nine o'clock, you went home when the work was done, and that meant often we'd work until three in the morning, checking on the film. Some of us would grab mats from the workout room and sleep on them at night in these tiny offices in Memorial Stadium. I think Bill slept on the desk a few times. With him it was not 'It's 2 A.M. and I want to go home,' it was 'It's 2 A.M. and what more can I do?' I can remember him working once; we were all sleeping in the bowels of the stadium on our mats, and it was about 3 A.M., and he woke me up because he had just found something on the film at 3 A.M., something he thought I could use—and he was absolutely right."

What Belichick also had, Baughan believed, in addition to the work ethic and the skill with the film, was what Baughan called "a great cognitive instinct." He could watch all the film and not only get down what each play was, but perhaps more importantly, he understood what it all meant, what the thinking on the other side of the ball was. That is, he could then think like the opposing coach. From the preseason on, the coaches knew they had landed a young coach who was special, someone who had skills that almost no one else had. By the time the preseason was over, he was a real coach with a real job, no longer an intern, but a coach, someone the others depended on. By Thursday of each week he was the best prepared person on the field, and all the players understood that, understood that he knew more about the opposing team than anyone else. "All the things that he does now that have helped him win the Super Bowls," Baughan said, "the core of that was in place even back then."

He was at the right place at the right time, because given their system, there was an unusual dependence on someone who could break down film and chart what the other team was doing, especially the other team's offense. They were running, as best they could, the George Allen defense, and Allen was the leader in that era of figuring out the tendencies of the opposition. In those days they were called breakdowns, and Allen himself had apprenticed in Chicago under George Halas, one of the League's original owners and coaches. Halas had been a pioneer in doing breakdowns and keeping them year by year, when the League was much more primitive and still based on a kind of primal physical power; no one back then did that much in the way of sophisticated scouting. But Halas began, in a fairly elementary way, charting other teams' tendencies over the years and keeping the records. Then Allen, branching out on his own in Los Angeles, took the breakdowns much further, focusing on tendencies in situations, play by play, based as well on different field positions and different amounts of time left on the clock. "In a way," Marchibroda said recently, "Halas began it, and George Allen took what he did even further, and then Billy, when he became a head coach, took what Allen did even further. But there is a major connection from Allen to him; he is George Allen–connected, even if he never worked for Allen. So, back in Baltimore, we had the perfect system to employ his special talents."

The key to the George Allen defense was not to be reactive, not to wait for the offense to make its moves and then react, but to be proactive, for the defense to seize the initiative. That demanded an exceptional knowledge of what the other team was planning to do, its formations, its tendencies, down by down and situation by situation. "If you use the George Allen defense, you cannot be reacting to the other team—you had to be a split second ahead, to know what was coming, to know who they had on the field, what formations they would use, and what they were likely to do in each situation. And Bill was very good at it, the best we had ever seen," said Bruce Laird, one of the Colt defensive backs. "Bill would bring the film to Maxie Baughan, and it would all be there, a reel on what they did on screens, what they did on draws, what they would do when it was third and long, and third and short. And it was funneled into us very quickly, and gradually we mastered it, and that was critical, because the better you came to know it and master it, then the more it all became instinct. That meant we were not back on our heels, letting the offense have the initiative, but we were attacking, and we felt we knew what they were going to do. That's one of the reasons we got better as the season went along; we started 1–4, and then won eight in a row. A lot of it was Bill—he prepared us so well. What he gave us became part of our reflex."

Actually, the offense had been good from the start. It was the defense that got better, week by week, and most of the credit went to

Maxie Baughan. He had understood quite quickly that the Allen defense was too complicated for the players they had, most of whom were young. It had been designed for experienced players, who had been together a long time. So he had simplified it, and Bill Belichick felt very much a part of that success. By spending fifty to eighty hours each week studying the opponent, he knew more about the opposing team than anyone else on the Colts, including the other coaches. And, he had one more advantage: He was always a week ahead of the rest of the coaching crew. If the Colts were going to play the Jets on the coming Sunday and Miami the following Sunday, then he was working on Miami while everyone else was still working on the Jets. So when the Jets game was over, he was the one person who was already an expert on Miami and its tendencies. Thus he was the oracle, or at least the oracle for a week. They were filled with questions on their upcoming opponent, and he had the answers, and as their need for him grew, so his own confidence grew. Suddenly he did not seem so young to them anymore.

When he had first gone to work for the Colts, the great question had been about the degree of his acceptance on the part of the players. He was younger than most of them, he had not attended a great football program, and he was not, on the Richter Scale of professional football, physically imposing. He came from outside the game as they knew it and judged it, and they saw themselves coming from inside it, because they judged the game, especially in terms of those their own age, only by who had played it. Yet he could not succeed unless he gained their respect and could impose his authority on them. Before he set foot on the field on the first day of practice, he had been somewhat apprehensive about this, more than a little anxious about any potential resistance to him. Could he, who had not been to a big-time football school, coach in a place as macho as the NFL? That was, he sensed, going to be the first big test. But he did know the world of football. He had seen it as a boy, and he had watched players and how they related to coaches, and the most important thing, he believed, the thing that in the end generated respect, was not necessarily a loud and commanding or threatening voice, but knowledge. Players respected coaches who could help them play better and who knew things that they didn't know. That, more than anything else, he believed, defined successful player-coach relationships. He had watched his father with the Navy players each Monday night, and he knew what they wanted. If you could go to these professionals each week and say that on Sunday the opposing team was going to run these particular plays out of this particular offense, and get it right, then you would gain their respect.

◆◆◆

The other thing that gave him confidence was that he was sure he knew more football than they did. In that sense he had a very high degree of self-confidence. In some ways he was entering what they thought was their world, but it was also to no small degree his world as well, because in the NFL, where the game was so much more complicated than in college, the hierarchy held and the power of the coaches was even greater than in college. Though he had gone to a small-time football college, he had mastered parts of the game that they had never needed to master. The fact that they had superior physical abilities was no longer going to be enough, because in the pros everyone had superior physical abilities. Yet he knew that in film there was power, and he was the man working the film, and he knew he was good at it. He had been taught by a man who was the best, but more important he had a gift for it himself. It came naturally to him, or at least to the degree that something that entailed so much grinding work could be natural, he was the natural.

When he really knew he had made it, that he was going to be all right and that he could coach in the NFL, was when the players started coming to him directly, without going through Baughan. Which was all right because Maxie was so overloaded. They needed the information and they did not want to waste time. That was when Belichick knew he would be able to have the career he hoped for, that his knowledge of the game was the critical part, not whether he had played at Notre Dame or Alabama. For him it was an epiphany, and it was a thrilling one. The first two players who came to him directly were Stan White, an immensely talented linebacker from Ohio State, three years in the League, and Bruce Laird, the gifted defensive back from American International. Belichick was damn good from day one, White thought, already better than the defensive line coach and the defensive safety coach, who were technically much senior to him. "You could tell he was going to be what I call a 'forever coach,' that is, a man who was going to coach forever, because he was so good at it, so natural," White said. But he was also trying to establish himself in a very tough world. Because of that, he was very brash and very cocky at first, instinctively territorial, and not all the players liked him, not by a long shot, at first. The punk, some of the players called him privately, especially the offensive players who were not getting that much value from him; they thought him a little too arrogant, a little too full of himself. He was not particularly lovable at that point. "He burned with his purpose, which was football, and he did not care about popularity," Laird said, "and football is not about popularity."

"Bad News Bill," some of the others called him, because he was also The Turk, the guy who had to go to the rooms of players who had just been cut and collect their playbooks. He was demanding their respect, and among the offensive players there was a feeling that he had yet to earn it. "There were a couple of players who wanted to clock him," White said. "Probably the only reason they didn't was because they were football players, and football players have been taught all their lives to respect authority, and he was a coach, so they had to respect that. But it was edgy. He was doing some special teams coaching, and he would be in their faces—I think some of our coaches had told him not to take any crap from the players. I think his attitude, because he was so young, was 'I'm not going to let you push me around because I'm so young, so I'm going to push you around first.' "

He was already very good at what they called tells. A tell was a tip-off or an unconscious sign from the other team—the way a halfback positioned his feet differently on a pass play than on a running play, or the way a tight end might line up and what it would say about the ensuing play. They were considered very valuable, those tells. "It was like having a great spy working for us," Laird said. He thought that Belichick, in concert with the other coaches, was empowering the players by giving them so much information, which allowed them to adapt game by game to what was coming. Not a lot of NFL coaches like to do that, Laird said. Most of them are wary of changing, and they like to stay with what they've always done, because change makes them nervous. What was interesting, he decided, was that watching Belichick was like watching a youthful George Allen because Allen always had so much information; he always wanted to know more than anyone else about what the other team might do. Allen, more than any coach Laird knew, believed in knowledge as a key to football; he wanted his players to know as much as they could, and he was always talking to them. "He always wanted to know not just if you knew what he had been talking about, but also if you *understood* what he had been talking about. And Bill, though he was just starting out, was much the same way."

To Belichick it all felt so natural, doing what he had been doing. "I never felt I had to reach or was in an alien profession. I knew I had a better instinct for it than some of the older coaches on the staff," he said. "What I didn't know, I could learn—one of the things I had working for me was that I knew how to learn. The things they asked me to do I could do faster and more cleanly than the other people there." That he did so well, and that the Colts did so well, going from 2–12 the year before to 10–4 that year, did not necessarily mean that he had a job there for very long. Whether they would pay him for a second year soon became a serious issue. "We'd love to keep you," Marchibroda told him after the season was over. "I'd love to stay here," Belichick answered, because he liked the situation and thought the future looked very bright for the team. But he wanted to be paid a real wage, and he asked for a car. He and Marchibroda discussed salary, and because he so loved what he was doing, and because he knew Thomas was not going to pay much, they agreed on $4000. That was a bargain basement price, because he already had a better offer in his pocket. The head coach in Detroit, Rick Forzano, was connected to his father, and the word was getting out that the Belichick kid was good, very much his father's son, that no one did film better. Forzano offered what seemed like a munificent deal, $10,000 a year and a car.

Joe Thomas was predictably negative. "No, no, no," he told Marchibroda when the idea was proposed. They did not need to pay some young kid a salary and give him a car as well. Around the same time, Thomas was having a meeting with the county executive in Baltimore about a new stadium, and the county executive was waiting in the outer office while Thomas argued with Marchibroda about Belichick, who was sitting next to him. "I really need him," Marchibroda said, but Thomas assured him that he did not, that he himself was living proof that great things had been done with a total of three coaches. Meanwhile, the county executive was waiting outside the office, wanting to talk about the new stadium, which was crucial to the future of the entire franchise. The meeting over an assistant coach and paying him $4000 went on for almost an hour. Marchibroda lost. "Billy, you see what I'm up against every day," an exhausted Marchibroda said afterward. "He's arguing with me about a $4000 job, and meanwhile he's keeping the county executive waiting an hour about a brand-new stadium." It was one of the most surreal scenes he would ever witness in the football world, Belichick later decided.

So Detroit it would be, not Baltimore. To Marchibroda, there was something symbolic about the rejection of so small a salary for so important a young coach, and it was the beginning of what would become a permanent rift between him and Thomas. "Is this the way it's going to be all season?" Marchibroda asked Thomas later that day. No, Thomas said; but it was, Marchibroda thought, it was.

◆◆◆

Rick Forzano badly wanted Belichick for the Lions. Forzano was part of the Paul Brown Club; he had coached high school ball at Akron, then at the College of Wooster in Ohio, then at Kent State, and finally as an assistant at the Naval Academy. As a boy, he had been partially blinded in one eye, but Brown told him to stay in coaching, that just because he could not play at a certain level did not mean that he could not coach there. When Forzano had arrived at the Naval Academy, Steve Belichick had taken him in and helped him adjust to the Academy's quite special culture. Forzano remembered his first dinner with Belichick, Dick Duden, another of the assistants, and Ernie Jorge, the line coach. They went to a fancy restaurant, and ate like kings, he thought; then they smoked big cigars. That had made him feel, for the first time in his career, that he was in the big time. Belichick was like the Godfather there; he knew everyone and knew how things worked, "a kind of permanent head coach," in Forzano's phrase, "not the head coach in name, but the head coach under the head coach, the guy everyone turned to on so many little things. He kept things together, never politicked—but he was the man everyone trusted."

Forzano was an assistant at Navy, then went on to the University of Connecticut, where he did well, returning to Annapolis as head coach. His years as head coach were hard ones; the recruiting had gotten harder, and Navy, like Army, was no longer able to compete with the top football teams (though it was still playing a tough schedule). It was not a time in America when talented young football players wanted to sign on for the toughest of academic programs, to be followed not by a professional football career, but more likely a tour of Vietnam. He resigned in 1972 after four frustrating years and soon ended up with the Lions. So when Bill Belichick, the same Bill Belichick who, when he was ten years old, had once helped Forzano break down film—"quiet as a church mouse, but a great brain that was like a sponge even then"—called asking for a job, Forzano was delighted. "I knew he had done well in Baltimore, and I knew they were not paying him anything, and I knew he was going to be very good. So I wanted him badly. Hey, back when he was about ten or eleven, I had told Steve that one day he was going to be a hell of a coach. I think that made Steve a little nervous, because he and Jeannette were not pushing him to be a coach, and Steve gave me one of those gruff answers, 'Yeah-yeah-yeah,' which meant maybe yes, maybe no, but we aren't pushing him. 'No,' I told him, 'he's really going to be a coach—I can tell.' And now here he was just starting out as a coach, so I wanted him. I knew what he could do. I think I was making about $50,000 in Detroit at the time, and I went to the general manager and said I had a chance at this great kid. So, of course, the first question from him is 'How much is it going to cost me?' 'Ten thousand dollars and a car,' I answered. 'Ten thousand dollars? How old is he?' 'Twenty-four years old,' I answered. 'Ten thousand dollars for a kid twenty-four years old? That's a lot of money.' 'He'll be worth it,' I said, 'he's a gem. We'll get our money's worth.' " Once he was hired, his acceptance came quickly. "I think," Forzano added, "it took about a day for the people who ran the team to find out how good he was."

So he became personal assistant to Forzano, and a film guy, and a tight end coach. Detroit was never in those days a strong organization; it was owned by William Clay Ford, a member of the Ford family, who was very rich but did not really have much to do with the making of cars, and who was always battling his own personal demons. Because of that, the team's managerial structure was traditionally weak. In some ways what happened in Detroit was a quick lesson in how tough the NFL can be, and how quickly any coach can fall. The team went 1–3 in its first four games, pressure soon came down from above, and Forzano resigned after the fourth game. Tommy Hudspeth, the player personnel chief, took over, and management hoped to get Chuck Knox the next year, but that didn't happen, so Hudspeth stayed a second year. Even so, the clock was ticking away. Floyd Reese, one of the assistants there, remembered one game—it happened to be the day his son was born—when they had run a fake field goal play and it had worked, and they had scored a touchdown instead. "The next day we read in the paper that if it hadn't worked, we were all going to be fired, but the play had saved us. We were all there on sufferance—there was no protection for us at all, no security," he said.

It was nonetheless, Belichick thought, a great place to learn.

Among those he learned the most from was Ken Shipp, the offensive coordinator, who had been with Joe Namath and the Jets in some of their glory years and was considered to be a very creative offensive coach. Shipp had no earthly idea who Belichick was—Forzano had simply mentioned that they were hiring a young man who he thought would do well with the film. When he first met Shipp, Belichick was properly modest in giving his background, and Shipp had come away with the idea that he had never done film before. For that reason Shipp thought they were on the brink of a disaster, but he gave Belichick the offensive playbook, told him to learn it, and that he would quiz him on it in two weeks. It was a complicated playbook, and Shipp doubted that Belichick would have even a novice's knowledge of it in two weeks, but when the appointed time was up, Belichick got a perfect score, and Shipp thought to himself, "Well, we won't have any problems doing the film." At the same time he made a note that he was dealing with what was probably the smartest young coach he had ever met.

There was a very good staff there: Fritz Schurmer, who ended up as the defensive coach of the Packers, and Jimmy Carr, an exceptional defensive coach. Joe Bugel, who coached the offensive line, was considered by many the best offensive line coach in the business, and Jerry Glanville, a very young coach then, was there doing special teams. Floyd Reese was only about five years older than the twenty-four-year-old Belichick, but he had already lost most of his hair, so he did not look so young, and he was spared the teasing that Belichick, as the youngest staff member, had to endure. There was a lot of teasing of Belichick as the boy wonder, because of the Steve Belichick–Rick Forzano connection: "Here's Bill Belichick, the child prodigy." "Here's the boy genius; let's just do what the kid tells us to do." "Bill Belichick, the wizard who broke down film when he was still in the cradle." There was, Belichick thought, a certain inevitability to it, and it was generally good-natured. He saw it as a kind of hazing you had to go through to get into the coaches' club.

But Belichick was ever more confident now that the only limits he faced in coaching were those he set himself. He was beginning a process typical of many talented young coaches: studying other programs, creating his own vision of the game, borrowing a piece here and a piece there, and talking football, or perhaps more accurately, talking coaching, all the time. The impression he made on his colleagues was almost universally favorable—open-minded, incredibly hardworking, absolutely committed to being a little better every day, and knowing a lot more than most other young coaches, a master at using film.

In Detroit, he befriended Reese, and because they lived only three blocks from each other, they went back and forth to work every day, talking football all the time. They had dinner together every night and became close in the way that young men filled with the same dreams and ambitions become close. What struck Reese then and later was the discipline, and the eagerness to learn. Belichick just worked harder than everyone else. "I think a lot of it came from the fact that he had not played big-time football and because of that he felt he had to work twice as hard as anyone else to prove himself, to prove his bona fides," Reese said. The work ethic, Reese said, was almost unique; everyone there worked hard, but Belichick seemed to work harder than the others. "He was someone who simply was not going to be denied. He was not very different back then when he was just starting out than he is as the coach of a team that has won three Super Bowls." If they went to a team meeting to discuss the team they were playing that Sunday, Reese might ask two or three questions, while Belichick would ask just one question, "but his question went far beyond what the rest of us could see and envision about what the other team was doing and why it was doing it. He had this rare ability to place himself in the other team's position. The boy genius," Reese said, "we loved calling him the boy genius, but it was done admiringly. The thing I worried about most was whether he was too smart for the game, whether there would be enough challenge for him in it, or whether he would leave the game and end up the CEO of some giant corporation instead."

Reese had been an All-American defensive lineman at UCLA, and then had played in Canada, and he seemed to Belichick unusually thoughtful and wise. After Canada, knowing his playing days were over, but wanting to stay in football, he had found a master's program as close to football as he could, in kinesiology. He was preparing himself to be a strength and conditioning coach. If the field of strength and conditioning was not exactly a virgin one at that time in the NFL, then it was a somewhat new one, an area which football coaches were only beginning to explore. But it was something that fascinated Reese and fascinated Belichick as well. Most other young coaches might not have been that eager to learn about something that was a bit arcane, but Belichick, Reese thought, knew from the start that the game was changing, and if the game was professional, that meant being professional about every aspect of it. As pro football was becoming ever more popular and affluent, with more money coming in from gate and television revenues, and more money going out to players, the value of each player was going to rise accordingly, and the ability to prevent or limit injuries was going to be more important. The world of pro football was in the process of dramatic change from the moment when he walked into his first locker room. Everyone then had been sitting around smoking cigarettes and drinking coffee—it had not been unlike, Reese thought, walking into a bar.

In those days, when the game was just becoming truly professional, no one arrived at camp in shape. The salaries were not that good, and most players had off-season jobs. "If someone ran a hundred yards during the off-season," as Reese said, "that was unusual."

The idea that the players would train during the summer and arrive at camp in good shape was still in the future. There was still a considerable suspicion of any kind of weight training, because of the fear that it would bulk a player up and cost him speed. That would soon change as people learned how to strengthen their bodies without sacrificing speed—indeed, they could work out and become faster. There were not many colleges back then paying attention to strength—Nebraska under a man named Boyd Epley was one of the first. What they were really trying to do, Reese thought, was figure out how to protect players from injuries. Some injuries were unavoidable, but others reflected the erosion or the fatigue of the body over a difficult, exhausting season—those injuries might be avoided if a player and the strength coach could build up the more vulnerable muscles, the ones that were in harm's way. Because of that, Detroit began an off-season weight-training program, one of the first in the League to do it. Reese felt he was something of a pioneer in this, and he was viewed with suspicion by some coaches, notably the older ones, because what he was doing was all new, and no one had done it before.

Belichick, though, was intrigued by it, and quick to absorb everything Reese said. But, as much as he was learning about strength and conditioning from Reese, he was also learning about being a coach from him. Reese was older, and he had a very good sense of how to relate to players—it seemed to come naturally to him, perhaps because he had played at a very high level, one just below the NFL. He had an intuitive sense of how the players thought and reacted. He was the same age as many of the players, and younger than some of them. "Do not," he warned Belichick, "try to be the players' pal. It won't work. They'll screw you every time. There are some young coaches who come in and make that mistake and think that's the ticket, and they're gone very soon. You're not here to be their pal. You're here to coach them, and that often means telling them things they don't want to hear about doing things they don't want to do. If they knew these things, if they had been taught them back in college, or wanted to do them, they wouldn't need you to teach it to them by the time they show up here. The more you can help them, the better, and they'll know it when it happens, and the other coaches will know it. But if you go out drinking with them—and a lot of young coaches do it, thinking it will prove to their bosses how well they can get on with the players—that will kill your authority. And authority is the only thing you have." Belichick had known some of that before, but hearing it from someone just a little older, who had played at a higher level than he had in college and thus had a better sense of the psyches and attitudes of the players, was both very valuable and reassuring.

One of his assignments—they were all being thrown in a little over their heads—was to coach the tight ends. He had two very good tight ends, Charlie Sanders, a high-level professional, and David Hill, a rookie who had been a second-round draft choice out of Texas A&I. Sanders, a Pro Bowl–level player, was very good to Belichick. He was an important player on that team, experienced and accomplished, and he could have destroyed a young coach very easily. But Belichick figured that Sanders had sized him up and somehow decided that he could learn something from him. "He was very good in the way he dealt with me. If he had a question, and I didn't have the answer, he didn't make fun of me, but waited until I did have the answer, instead of getting on my ass," said Belichick. "He could easily have been a jerk and undermined me. And instead he was very professional about it."

Belichick was also enormously impressed with Ken Shipp, who had a very original mind and was one of the best offensive coaches of the era, Belichick later decided. He was an open man, one easy to deal with. Though Belichick's instinct was to coach defense—it was where he was pulled as if by some kind of magnetic force—he was also beginning to understand that if you were going to coach defense, you had to master the offense as well, otherwise you were only half a coach. The more he knew about the offensive side and the way the people on the offensive side thought, the better prepared he would be coaching defense. And here was Shipp, who had come from a very sophisticated offense, one where the offensive players read the defenses very quickly and then reacted to them; it was as if Shipp, in Belichick's view, were running a clinic every day for his personal use. It was absolutely remarkable to see the game from his point of view, that of the offense, like being an American spy placed at the highest level of the Kremlin during the Cold War, Belichick thought, because you could learn so much from such an exceptional mind about the way the other half lived and thought.

Shipp was there for one year, and the next season under Hudspeth, they brought in Ed Hughes to run the offense. Hughes arrived from Dallas with the Dallas offensive system, which was very complicated and completely different from Shipp's system. It was probably much too complicated for the Detroit players to handle all at once; if it had been introduced incrementally, things might have worked out, but in its totality it overwhelmed the Detroit players. That was not an easy year; too many people had been fired and too many changes had been made in too short a time, and there was a feeling that Detroit, because of the ownership and the constant management crises, was almost permanently mired in difficulties. It was seen as a place where you went to coach only if there were no openings anywhere else, and then you hoped that the people in charge of hiring at the next station understood the current you had been going up against. At the end of the season everyone was let go. "Worst situation I ever coached in, a nightmare, nothing but surprises, and every single one of them a bad one, a great relief to get out of there," Shipp said years later. Belichick, his knowledge of the game greatly expanded, thereupon set out for Denver for the third act and fourth year of his apprenticeship. The head coach there was Red Miller, who had just come from New England. Ernie Adams, who was an assistant in New England at the time, had recommended Belichick to Miller, who brought him out to break down film for the defensive coach, Joe Collier. His pay was gradually going up. The second year in Detroit it had been around $15,000, and now it was going to be $20,000. He needed the money now. In 1977, after his second year of coaching, he had married his longtime girlfriend, Debby Clarke. They had gone to Annapolis together—she had been a cheerleader there—and then they had dated while he was at Wesleyan. She was, his friends thought, lovely and bright and, they hoped, well prepared for life with a man so completely obsessed with his work.

In Denver, Belichick became very close to an assistant coach named Richie McCabe, who was handling the secondary. McCabe was about forty at the time, and he had not yet moved his family to Denver, so he was living at the same hotel where Belichick was staying. As with Reese in Detroit, Belichick constantly talked football with McCabe, at breakfast together, driving to the practice field together, and then at dinner for two hours, talking football all the time, until it was time to go back to their rooms, at which point, as Belichick noted, "Richie would go back to his room, where he would sit around *thinking* football."

McCabe was an exuberant man who had come from the tough side of Pittsburgh and become a friend of some members of the Rooney family, who owned the Steelers. He played for the University of Pittsburgh and then had been drafted by the Steelers. If Joe Collier, McCabe's boss, was a little reserved, then that was not a problem with McCabe, who was talkative and a very good teacher. One of the most valuable things he taught Bill Belichick was about the Al Davis system in Oakland, where he had coached before coming to Denver. Davis was one of the most feared and quite possibly one of the most disliked owner-coaches in the League, a maverick who stood apart from many of the League's niceties and courtesies, but who beat other teams on the field, often with players they had just discarded. His teams seemed to play on the very edge of unnecessary roughness (and sometimes over it). He was shrewd and cunning, a hard man who pushed everyone around to the limit and often beyond, and he cared nothing about being a part of football's old boy fraternity. If other coaches (and owners) hated him, it was also possible that some of his own players hated him even more, and that some of his assistants hated him even more than that, because if you coached for him, you were never supposed to leave Oakland, even if it was for a better job. Al Davis wanted you for life, it was believed by his assistants. "He doesn't let you go," McCabe told his wife, Judy. "You come here to coach, and it's supposed to be for life, a kind of lifetime sentence." McCabe, after a few years in Oakland, had wanted out, and there was a good offer in Denver and one in Cleveland. He had wanted the one in Denver, but because Davis made such a fuss with the League's office, threatening tampering if McCabe went to Denver—it was in the same division—McCabe went to Cleveland first and only later to Denver. One of the first things that Rich McCabe said to Belichick was, "Al Davis hates me because I left—you're never supposed to leave him."

But there were important things that McCabe told Belichick about the Davis system that would one day serve Belichick well. The first thing was that Oakland looked only for size and speed. Their players had to be big and fast. That was a rule. If you weren't big and fast, Oakland wasn't interested. The other thing was about the constancy of player evaluation. Most coaches stopped serious evaluation of their personnel on draft day—they chose their people, and that was that. But Davis never stopped evaluating his people—what they could do, what you could teach them, and what you couldn't teach them. He made his coaches rate the players every day. Were they improving? Were they slipping? Who had practiced well? Who had gone ahead of whom in practice? The jobs the starters had were not held in perpetuity. They were not tenured professors. The coaches hated doing it, rating the players on their daily performances, because they knew Davis was rating them, the coaches, as well. But Davis knew that by doing this, they would have to challenge the players; in his system, McCabe said, everyone was supposed to stay on top of everyone else's ass. You had to look at your players and defend every player to the rest of the organization. If the coaches hated it, McCabe said, it had also worked, because no one could rest on what he had done in the past, even if the past was only a week ago; it made you know your own personnel better, something teams did not always do. You had to keep on top of the players. Davis believed, accurately enough, that you kept your players alert by keeping your coaches alert.

In Denver, Joe Collier played a three-four defense, three down linemen, four linebackers. It was a defense mandated not just by the material he was working with—he did not have a classic big front four; instead, he had smaller, quicker men, who could play better as linebackers—but also by the changing nature of the game, the fact that more and more offenses were driven by passing, and more and more, it was the job of the defense to stop the pass as well as the run. The three-four gave you more flexibility. Collier's was a good, imaginative defense, known as the Orange Crush, because of the team's orange uniforms; it was predicated more on speed than power and based very much on cohesiveness and execution. The four linebackers were Randy Gradishar, who made the Pro Bowl seven times; Tom Jackson; Joe Rizzo; and Bob Swenson. Of the four only Gradishar, at 233 pounds, seemed big enough to be a linebacker in that era. Jackson and Rizzo both weighed about 220, and Swenson was 215. But they were all fast and knew exactly what they were supposed to be doing. There were lessons to be learned working with that defensive team, and they would prove invaluable to Belichick for his later defenses, especially in

New England. Every player was supposed to know where he was on each play. Everyone was to be very disciplined. Football was not about being a big star; it was about fulfilling your assigned role. You were supposed to do the things you were assigned even if you did not get the glory. There were some very big names in that defense: Barney Chavous, Lyle Alzado, and Rubin Carter were the front three, and Chavous and Alzado were unusually well known, but it was very much the players whose names were not so well known—Carter, who was the nose tackle; Billy Thompson, the strong safety; and Swenson, the least well known of the linebackers—who were critical, because they were always where they were supposed to be, doing what they were supposed to do, often forcing the play toward their more celebrated teammates. They were the ones who made the better-known players look so good each Sunday. The fans loved the stars, whose heroics were so obvious, but often it was the lesser-known players whom the coaches loved best, the guys who, day after day, made the defense work.

It was the beginning of the kind of defense that Belichick would favor in New England, featuring players who knew their roles and understood that playing their role was more important than being a star. McCabe always knew who had come through for him, and he was very careful after a game to let those players know they were appreciated, that he knew Swenson had slowed up the tight end at the line of scrimmage, for instance. McCabe understood that the little things were not little things, because it was the accumulation of little things that made big things happen. "And I understood that in an age where there was so much ego, because of the camera, that it was very important to look for that kind of player," said Belichick years later.

It had been a great year, if somewhat unsatisfactory for Belichick in terms of the actual coaching. He wanted to move up just one more increment, and they wanted someone who only did the film and was happy to do it, and so at the end of the year it was time to go.

It was January 1979 when the job came to an end, and for a time he was again at loose ends, unsure of where his next job would be. Two offers to coach came from Canada, neither of which he was anxious to take. It seemed to him that a number of possibilities had closed out a little too soon for him. He talked with a young coach at the nearby Air Force Academy named Bill Parcells about going to work there as an assistant, and there seemed to be a real chance of it happening, but then he found it hard to reach Parcells, who had gradually become more cautious in his comments, and much slower to return calls. There were, Belichick remembered, about ten calls to Parcells at one point, but Belichick could never quite get a clear answer. The reason, he would learn soon enough, was that Parcells was unhappy with his situation at Air Force, and trying to get out himself, so he did not want to hire an assistant at that moment.

Nonetheless, even if a door did not open immediately, Belichick felt good about himself and his future as a coach. It had been a great learning curve, four years in three cities, and he had worked for a number of uncommonly talented men who had been wonderful teachers. That summer he came home and visited with his boyhood friend Mark Fredland and told him he had found the key to success: It was in being organized; the more organized you were at all times, the more you knew at every minute what you were doing and why you were doing it, the less time you wasted and the better a coach you were.

CHAPTER EIGHT

It was Ray Perkins who brought him to the Giants. Perkins had been prompted by, of all people, Ernie Adams. Perkins and Adams made an unlikely pairing, since Perkins was as hard and tough a man as football produced, while Adams was one of its most genteel citizens, quiet, thoughtful, and cerebral. But Perkins had come to understand Adams's great value to a head coach. The two men had worked together in New England for two years, in 1976 and 1977, and Perkins had been greatly impressed by Adams's ability with film, the originality of his mind, and his superior overall knowledge of football. "He was the smartest young coach you could imagine," Perkins said. "He had a genuine photographic memory—if you showed him a piece of paper, you only had to do it once. You'd give him this immensely complicated playbook, and three days later he wouldn't need it, because it was all photographed and all filed away in his mind. He was breaking down the film on both offense and defense, and no one was better at it. And it wasn't just one of those trick minds where he could store it away, but didn't really know what it meant. He had great analytical abilities; he knew what all of it meant, the plays and the context in which they had been used."

Adams had seemed a bit of an anomaly at first in New England, Perkins remembered, "someone who was different from other coaches because he seemed to want different things from life than most coaches." He was, much more than most of them, a man who could have intellectual interests outside of football, even while excelling as a coach. But he was accepted quickly by the others. There were some very good coaches there—about eight of them, Perkins recalled, went on to be head coaches—and they were all quite amazed by Adams. As Perkins said, "It became clear after a while that he was somebody very special, a football mind that was almost apart from other football minds, that he had a very rare gift of being able to look at film, to understand it all, being able to dissect it, store it away, and then be able to call it up whenever he needed it. He was a kind of football genius."

In 1978, Perkins had left New England and gone to San Diego as offensive coordinator; then, the next year, he was given the New York Giants head coaching job. He immediately hired Adams, giving him the job of quarterback coach. "Jesus Christ," said Steve Belichick, when he heard the news, echoing the view of most of the coaching fraternity. "Here's a guy who's never taken a snap from center—and now he's a quarterback coach in the NFL! That's a reach!" When Adams got there, the first thing that he told Perkins was that he ought to hire his brilliant young friend who had been working in Denver; he was very good at film, too, but was going to be a very good, very complete coach. What Adams said dovetailed with what Perkins was hearing from another source, Floyd Reese. Perkins had also called

Reese to offer him a job, but Reese had already been offered a job with Minnesota. Since the Giant front office at that moment seemed in turmoil, he decided in favor of the Vikings job. But he told Perkins that if he wanted a talented young coach, someone who was quite possibly smarter than anyone around, that he ought to meet with Belichick. "If you just meet him and visit with him," Reese said, "you'll know how good he is." That meant Belichick had two exceptional recommendations; it was a sign that his four-year apprenticeship was coming to an end.

Belichick flew out to San Diego to meet Perkins at an airport hotel. Perkins was immediately impressed. "He knew a lot for someone so young," Perkins said years later, "and it was obvious that he burned to learn more—I didn't worry much about both of them, Bill and Ernie, being so young. I was young myself, only thirty-seven. What I liked about him was his passion for the game—that was what I looked for more than anything else, and that was what he had." Perkins hired him to coach the special teams, among other duties. Belichick was a bit restless at that time; he felt that he had become so good at the relatively narrow assignments he had been given—working with film and doing special teams—that he was in danger of being pigeonholed as a specialist. He was sure he could be a very good defensive coach, and he asked Perkins if he could work not just with the special teams, but also with the linebackers. Perkins said that was fine with him, as long as he cleared it with the linebackers' coach.

So in February 1979, when he was about to be twenty-seven, Belichick boarded a plane from Denver to New York. By chance, Bill Parcells was on the same plane, having just been hired by Perkins as his linebacker coach. Now for the first time Parcells was able to explain to Belichick why he had been so slow in returning calls and so indirect in his answers—he had planned on getting out of the Air Force job. In New York Belichick was going to be paid a reasonably good wage: $36,000 a year. All in all, it was a great offer, the situation more important than the money, but it was going to be a very tough job for all of them; the Giants, one of the league's premier franchises, had been in a very bad stretch, in which divided ownership, weak management, appalling draft choices, and poor teams had resulted in a long series of losing seasons. In the previous six seasons their record was 23–62–1; their best season had been 6–10.

It had been, Perkins noted, eighteen years since they had gone to the playoffs. "It was like F Troop there, absolutely out of control," remembered Ernie Adams of those early days when they first arrived. Or, as Ray Perkins said, "There was a very negative culture. They had a loser's mentality. The first thing you had to do was change the attitude, which is very hard to do. You have to find out what the source of it is, get rid of the players who cause the defeatist undertow, get a lot of new players, and get them to put out their best. Because when we got there, there were a handful of players who were leading in the wrong direction and you had to put a stop to that. And do it quickly." Perkins's marching orders, which allegedly came from George Young, who had been put in through the League's connivance in order to end the family bickering and bring some kind of order out of the chaos, were relatively simple: I want the kind of coach who's going to make the players uncomfortable when they lose. If those were the orders, then they had chosen the right man in Ray Perkins, a hard man who had been produced by a hard program in Alabama that was run by someone who by reputation was the hardest of all football men—Bear Bryant.

The kindest thing you could say about the Giants in 1979 was that it was a very soft team. If there was ever a coach born to rectify a situation like that, it was Ray Perkins. He was old-fashioned and, to use a favorite football term, hard-nosed. "The stamp of Bear Bryant was really on him," Belichick remembered. "He was not in the business of cutting people slack. Cutting people slack was for other professions. In football, cutting people slack got you beat. He had that hard, chiseled face. Looked like he could have been on a poster recruiting men for the Confederate side in the Civil War. All in all, a very, very tough man. You could almost physically feel his toughness. There was no bend in it at all, no give to him."

The picnic in New York was over. Everyone had to work hard. He did allow water on brutally hot days, unlike Bryant in his early days at Texas A&M, but he made clear to the players that actually drinking the water was perilously close to being a sign of weakness. He did not seem to believe in injuries; if players were hurt in practices, unless it involved a broken bone and an emergency trip to the hospital in an ambulance, he regarded the injury as an interruption of his timetable and, if at all possible, not to be taken too seriously. It was more important to keep the drill going. Some of the players never knew what hit them. "The hours were long, and the practices were grueling under Ray," Belichick remembered. "He was very demanding, and they badly needed those demands. There were a few good players—Harry Carson, who had arrived in 1976—and a situation like that was hard on him, very damaging." Or, as Carson himself once said, "After a loss I would be depressed for days. It's not a depression where you want to kill yourself. You just want to go into a hole. You don't want to go out of the house. At the market, the cashier looks at you kind of funny—you loser."

With Perkins any privilege would have to be earned, and earned by hard work. Soft players and dissident players were to depart, the sooner the better. If they were going to lose, they were going to lose playing hard. The practices were not only going to be long, there were going to be a lot of them, and if the weather was unbearably hot and muggy, with no breeze, why, there might be an additional practice or a longer one. On one very hot day the players were exhausted, and they were dragging. They finally gathered together and sent Jim Clack, the center, a player whom everyone respected (even, it was hoped, the coaches), to meet with Perkins and ask for mercy. Clack returned all too soon, shaking his head, followed very soon by Perkins himself, who gave them the iciest of glances and told them, "I'm not going to listen to you. It's not going to get easier. In fact it's going to get harder—it's going to get a lot worse before it gets better."

Indeed it did. That year they played one of their preseason games in Denver, and they fell down very poorly on a goal-line defense. Perkins was furious, and he had worked them so hard the following Monday that it seemed like an all-out war, the offense and defense going at it forty plays in a row, with no break. Players seemed to be dying on the field, with Perkins watching it all, saying nothing, with no change in expression, until he turned to several of the assistants and said, almost amused, as if talking to himself, "Think they're all going to quit?" How tough he was that year was something of a legend. That was the same year the Iranians took members of the American embassy hostage, and the New York tabloids soon began calling Perkins the Ayatollah Perkins. A few weeks later, as they were all boarding the bus for their first game against Philadelphia, Perkins, seated at the front of the bus, signaled to Ernie Adams that he wanted Adams to sit next to him. Adams took his seat, and Perkins leaned over. "What's an Ayatollah?" he asked. That, thought Adams, is truly a man of tunnel vision.

The NFL is a very tough, very Darwinian place. For a coach, as Ernie Adams says, "it is a little like being in a high-wire act, with no net underneath you." Everyone else seems to want what everyone else has, often quite nakedly, and they want to take it away through the use of brute force. It is about people who, all their lives, have used power and muscularity to have their way, and whose success has always been dependent on, more than anything else, their strength.

That strength tends to produce a very strong macho culture. All professional sports locker rooms have a certain macho culture: Basketball players, for example, are often very macho, but there is a certain delicacy and balance built into the bodies of many of them, and therefore it's a slightly different strain of macho. But football is different. It is more about pure size and strength than other sports: The players are all macho guys who've graduated from programs at schools where everyone on campus knows how strong and tough you are. Football players are always testing people on their own scale of willpower to see who is tougher—opponents, teammates, and, of course, coaches. The coaches in turn often feel they need to bend the players to their will, before the players can bend them. Thus, the balance in authority can be surprisingly delicate, and a team can slip away from even a good coach very quickly. Al Groh, one of the assistants who worked with Belichick when they were with the Giants and who is now the coach of Virginia, liked to talk about the divisions between the world of coaches and the world of the players, whether people were OOU or OOT, one of us or one of them. Or, as someone added, the guards or the inmates.

During those same years the coach of the Patriots was a man named Ron Meyer, and the players had decided he was too tough, so they went after him. He was fired in the middle of the 1984 season and replaced by Raymond Berry, the former great receiver, but a gentler man as coach. When the Cowboys played the Giants, Tom Landry, the Cowboys coach, stopped to talk to Bill Parcells, right before the game. The first thing they talked about was what had happened at New England, because it was the kind of thing that all coaches monitor all the time; any challenge to any coach was viewed as a challenge to all coaches. "That's what happens when the players are calling the shots," Landry said very simply.

In an odd way, what had happened in New York was not even

that personal a struggle: Rather, it was more like something out of *Lord of the Flies*. But it was viewed as a kind of football nightmare for a coach. Formidable, strong football players had landed at a franchise where the traditional sense of purpose, of winning, had long ago been lost, and in the struggle that ensued, the players had somehow taken power, not because they wanted to do anything with it, but because it was there and because it was easier to do things their way and to be in charge, rather than do the difficult things a series of coaches asked them to do. "If you couldn't deal with the school bully when you were back in high school, it's going to be very hard in the NFL," as Ernie Adams noted. A coach's respect and authority were always at stake, and when Ray Perkins and his assistants took over in New York, the Giants were exhibit A of a team where the players seemed to be undermining the coaches. "The players had come to believe," Perkins said, "that if a coach came in, they could beat the coach."

There was an early confrontation between Belichick and a player named Gary Jeter. Jeter was an important player on the team, a star defensive lineman, and all too representative, Belichick believed, of what was wrong with the team. A talented player, Jeter was also an underachiever and a locker room dissident, a man who helped drive what the coaches considered to be the negative undertow of the team. He had been a very high draft choice only two years earlier and was taken not merely in the first round, but as number five overall. He had been a two-time All-American at USC; he was handsome and he had the body, as Belichick said, of an Adonis. He was, it appeared, perfectly built for the job: six-four, 262 pounds, with a body, the *New York Times* once wrote, "that Muhammad Ali would like to borrow." If expectations for his career had been very high when he first arrived, he would end up being something of a disappointment to those who drafted him—good, not great, the coaches thought. There were too many injuries perhaps, and somehow in his New York years he did not maximize his immense raw talent. He showed moments of greatness, but there was never the consistency that great players have. There was a feeling among the coaches that it had all come too easily for him, and that because of his natural gifts and because the USC program was so strong, so flooded with talent, he had never been forced to learn technique. Once he reached the pros, it was hard for him to change, because he had already been so handsomely rewarded.

He lasted five seasons with the Giants, was eventually traded to the Rams, and would later talk about being immature in those early years. "I was a little arrogant, pretty cocky. That was my style then. I was leading cheers and playing on a team that was going noplace. It was like I was trying to get personal attention," he said. Given his size and good looks, he was the kind of guy who was very big in the locker room. There his nickname was Hollywood. "He was also," Belichick recalled, "a very easy guy for a coach to get tired of—there was always an undertow there."

That year, at the first special teams meeting, Jeter challenged Bill Belichick. They had all filed into the team meeting room, the entire team there for special teams, before separating for offensive and defensive unit meetings. Everyone sat down, and Belichick started the meeting. But there was Gary Jeter, talking and laughing, very deliberately not paying attention and very deliberately not paying attention in a way that the entire team could witness; he was trying to pull the other players with him and very obviously mocking the coach. Belichick looked over at him very deliberately, as if the look would then end it, and Jeter kept right on talking and laughing. At that point, it became a crucial challenge to a young coach with the whole team watching. It was, Belichick believed, as basic as it gets. In his mind Jeter had looked at him and seen just another young coach, someone who was going to be there a year or two and then get fired. It was, Belichick was sure, a defining moment, if not for Jeter, then certainly for him. If Jeter wanted a confrontation, then Belichick would grant him his wish.

"Hey, Jeter," he said, "one of the reasons you fucking guys were 5–11 last year was because your special teams stunk, and so if you want to laugh about it, and you think it's a joke, you can get the hell out of here. So shut the hell up or get the hell out of the room, right now!" Jeter did not say anything, but his private conversation ended. Afterward, Ray Perkins had been pleased. "Hey, that was good—that was the way to handle him," he told Belichick. "I was close to stepping in myself, and then you did it, and I want you to know I'll back you all the way."

◆◆◆

That summer Perkins, Bill Parcells, and Bill Belichick stayed at the same hotel near the Giants compound. There was some talk of Belichick eventually helping out Parcells on the defense. But then, one day, Parcells asked Belichick to drive him to the airport because, as he said, things weren't working out. He was going back to Colorado. He had, he said, become too much of a football gypsy over the previous fifteen years, had made too many moves in too short a time, and his wife and daughters were objecting. They did not want to be uprooted again; they loved living in Colorado Springs; his daughters liked the schools there, and they did not want to move east. Parcells lived in Colorado for a year, mostly out of the game. He was so miserable and so willing to share his misery with the rest of his family that Judy Parcells eventually surrendered; one more move was better than a husband that unhappy, and she said she would move east. With that he returned to coaching.

The turnaround of the Giants took seven years, and by the time it happened Bill Parcells had become the head coach, and Ray Perkins had gone back to Alabama to take the one job that would lure him away from the Giants: replacing Bear Bryant at Alabama. The one former Alabama player who seemed more than any other to reflect Bryant's singular toughness in this new era was Perkins. There had been a moment early on in his Giant years when he had invited several of the beat reporters to his home, and Dave Klein of the *Newark Star-Ledger* had asked him, What would happen if the Alabama job became open in a few years, and they called you and offered it to you? He had answered, "I'd walk to Tuscaloosa for it."

CHAPTER NINE

Their names were linked together for a decade at the Giants, and then later, over a span of some two decades, with New England and the Jets: Parcells and Belichick. The Bills, they were called, and those on the outside presumed they were good friends, which they were not. They were close associates who worked extremely well together for a common cause; their skills and talents blended uncommonly well, and, in the beginning at least, each needed the other. Both of them were very smart, but they were far too different in style and manner to really be friends. Parcells was physically bigger, and he seemed much more like what a football coach should be. If a stranger who knew almost nothing about football went into a room of twenty men and was told to pick out the one who was a football coach, it was an almost sure thing that he would pick Parcells. He was volatile and wore his emotions close to the surface. He found that it worked for him, that he could use his emotions as an instrument of coaching. He had a sharp, sardonic wit and a very considerable skill with words; he could taunt a player, sometimes with cruel humor, and in the one-way coach-to-player relationship, the player dared not answer back. Even his very best players and his assistant coaches feared his tongue. He knew the game and had a very good feel for the game and for the mood of his team, but he was never an Xs and Os man, like his junior partner.

No one in that era, it seemed, was better at challenging his players to reach for more, and Parcells had the rare ability to make it seem like a question of their very manhood. His great edge as a coach came from getting into the heads of his players. Starting in the mid-eighties and -nineties, he became the lineal descendant of Vince Lombardi, coaching as Lombardi might have, with a great hold on the emotions of his players, and doing it in an era that was far less congenial to such techniques than when Lombardi had ruled the coaching world. After all, once, when one player had sent his agent in to negotiate a better contract with Lombardi, the coach had simply picked up the phone and traded the player to another team. That kind of unchallenged authority no longer existed, not in an age of agents and free agency. Parcells's manner seemed to shout that he was a tough guy, that he was not to be crossed, and that those who failed him failed because they were too soft. He could be quite sophisticated when he wanted to be, but he cultivated the public image—and it was not a badly contrived image—as the prototype of the blue-collar, local guy, a man of old-fashioned loyalties and simple tastes, meat and potatoes, and maybe a draft beer at the neighborhood bar. He came across as someone who might well have been driving a truck had he not just by chance found his calling as a football coach. In that incarnation he was very simply a Jersey Guy.

Belichick was very different. He was driven by his brain power, and by his fascination with the challenge that professional football represented to the mind of the coach as well as the bodies of the players. He could not lightly shed Andover and Wesleyan; nor did he try to. He was much less skilled than Parcells at reaching his players emotionally and thereby challenging them to do more. This never came naturally to him; it was not who he was. In addition he thought it was the wrong way to go, that it was too short-range, and that in the end you could only go to that emotional well so often, and then it went dry. What did fit his personality was the sum of his knowledge, being the best-prepared coach on the field. Players would do what he asked not because he was their pal, but because he could help them win and they came to believe in his abilities. If Bill Parcells's strength came from being the coach who believed that everyone had a button to push, and that he was the man who knew how to push each and every button, then Bill Belichick's strength was to be the coach as the ultimate rational man, surrounding himself with players who wanted to learn his system, who would buy in because his skills always prepared them so superbly.

In the beginning Parcells's and Belichick's relationship was a mutually advantageous one, and both men knew it. Each had strengths the other lacked, and they made a formidable combination in that first decade—Parcells, the head coach, the motivator, a man putting together a team of excellent assistants, of whom certainly the most talented was Belichick, who started as a linebacker coach and in time became the defensive coordinator. Building on what Ray Perkins had started, Parcells began to turn the Giants' program around, and by the middle of the decade they were once again a feared team. Anyone who played them had to pay a price, and even if you won, the victory tended to be Pyrrhic. They played in the NFC East, where the football was not always fancy, and at a time when the Redskins, Eagles, Cowboys, and Giants competed for hegemony. It was very physical football, with plenty of outdoor games late in the season in what would surely be cold, windy, perhaps even snowy weather. Both of them, Parcells and Belichick, coached through their defense. They did not want to put their defense in a bad situation, and they did not want to wear it out. They did not like to go three and out—that is, three plays, no first down, and have to kick. They preferred to grind out first downs and wear the opposing defense down. When Parcells got the team in late 1982, he told Belichick that he wanted him to be the defensive coordinator the next year, but that he was not going to give him the title yet, because he did not want to put too much pressure on him. So at first there was no defensive coordinator, although Belichick handled the defensive team meetings.

As Parcells and Belichick were never destined to be real pals, the Parcells regime made genuine friendship difficult. It was always an edgy place, deliberately so. There were always going to be zingers, one-way zingers, for in the Parcells world, the head man zinged but others did not zing back. Many of the zingers were aimed at the better players, in order to show that there were no immunities; there were plenty of jabs at Phil Simms and Jeff Hostetler, the quarterbacks, just to let all the players know that no one was safe from Parcells's tongue. ("I have nothing but great things to say about the man as a coach," Hostetler once told Bill Gutman, who wrote a biography of Parcells, "but I didn't enjoy a minute of my time around him. I know that sounds strange, but that's how it is when you're around Bill Parcells.") In the same way, Parcells often used his sarcasm against some of his better assistant coaches, perhaps because he knew they were the ones who could take it. To be successful, an assistant had to be able to stand up to the head coach, and the good ones did, though that did not mean they liked the ground rules, the kind of hazing that went with the job.

The rules were very simple. There was one head coach, and that was Bill Parcells, and he gave all the interviews and met with the press, and unless otherwise instructed, the other coaches worked in semi-anonymity. That did not mean that serious fans, those watching the Giants as they began to emerge into greatness, did not understand that there was, hidden away there, an exceptional young assistant coach named Belichick, his emotionless face, on occasion, flashing across the television screen, and the network announcers would sometimes make references to Bill Belichick's extremely creative defenses.

Bill Parcells's journey to the Giants job had been a long and hard one, harder than that of Bill Belichick, because Belichick had started out with the connections that came through his father. Parcells grew up in New Jersey, a good if not especially great high school player, went off to Colgate, a very good small college, but one with a small-time program, not that different, in fact, from Wesleyan. He soon decided it was too small a football platform and transferred to Wichita State, where he played linebacker and was picked in the seventh round by the Detroit Lions. He went to their camp, but lasted only two weeks there; the players were already getting bigger and faster, and his future in football, if he wanted one—and he badly wanted one—would have to be as a coach, not a player. He needed a job—he was already married and the father of a daughter—but the doors of coaching did not open that readily for him. Luckily, one of the Wichita State assistant coaches had taken a job at Hastings College in Nebraska, and he offered Parcells a job as a defensive coach. It was 1964, and his salary was $1750 a year. Included among his duties was lining the field before practice, he later said, and washing the uniforms afterward. He and his wife and baby daughter lived in a small one-bedroom apartment above a dentist's office for $62.50 a month. He coached there for a year and then went back to Wichita State as a defensive line and linebackers coach. Hastings, in the coaching world, had been a step down, and this was a step back up. He spent two years coaching at Wichita, and then the head coach was fired, and he was out of a job. This time his luck was a little better. His high school coach, Tom Cahill, was coaching at West Point by then—so, finally, in terms of the larger coaching fraternity, there was a connection and a break, and in 1967 he went to Army.

He spent three years at West Point, critical years for a young coach, for they were when you looked to establish more connections, tried to meet more people, tried to find out who was on the ascent and who had the feel of a winner. From West Point, he went to Florida State, where Steve Sloan, a former Alabama quarterback, was already marked as one of the rising talents, coaching on the offensive side of the ball. Sloan liked Parcells. He thought he had an unusually good way with the players; his style was an interesting combination of being gruff and yet oddly human.

Sloan went from Florida State to Georgia Tech, where he did well, and when word began to get around that he might be offered the head coaching job at Vanderbilt, Parcells called and said he would like to come along. In fact, Sloan had already penciled him in as his first choice to become defensive coordinator. In 1973 the Vanderbilt job came through. At Vanderbilt, Sloan and Parcells did well enough to go to one Bowl game, the Peach Bowl, but the problems that had bedeviled Bill Edwards and Steve Belichick twenty years earlier were now greater than ever, as the SEC had become quite possibly the toughest conference in the country. They were soon both frustrated there, and Sloan wanted out. He took a job at Texas Tech, the team he had tied in the Peach Bowl. Sloan again offered Parcells the job as his top defensive assistant, but he also told the Vanderbilt officials that Parcells was the best person to succeed him. Vanderbilt thereupon offered Parcells the head coaching job. It was the ultimate coach's dilemma. He was thirty-four, and like every young coach who had taken such a hard road, he dreamed of only one thing, of being a head coach. But he had also been fighting the Vanderbilt system for some time from the inside, and he knew the only way to go was down. By this time Vanderbilt simply could not compete on the SEC level. He could see season after season of 3–8 and 4–7 records just ahead. When they failed yet again, it was not the chancellor they would fire, but the coach. So he took the Texas Tech job instead. He did well at Texas Tech, and that was where he learned the uses of sarcasm and how to challenge the players. He liked to tell the story about a halftime speech he gave in one game when his defense was not playing well, and he had gone out into the hall and brought in one of those huge industrial garbage cans, and there, in front of his team, he had dumped the entire garbage can on the floor, telling them, "That's all you are, you're garbage."

Three years later he was offered the Air Force Academy job. Since 1964, as Bill Gutman wrote, Parcells had been "a Bronco, a Shocker, a Cadet, a Seminole, a Commodore, and a Red Raider. Now he was about to become a Falcon." More importantly, he was finally about to become a head coach. But he did not like coaching at Air Force. It took only three months for him to realize that he had made a mistake. In his first season there he was 4–7. The situation was not unlike the one at Vanderbilt. Any coach there had to struggle with tough academic entrance requirements and, in addition, accept the primacy of military rules—and the politics that went with them. But then in 1979, Ray Perkins, whom Parcells had once met through Sloan (the Alabama connection), asked him to become the linebacker coach in New York. That was his seventh job in fourteen years. No wonder that when the Giants called, Judy Parcells had no taste for moving yet again.

If Bill Belichick had done a serious apprenticeship, four years at a relatively low level in three different systems, it had not been that difficult. From the start he had been in the *NFL,* surrounded by mostly big-time assistants, experienced professionals who were going places, and living in big cities. By contrast, Parcells had been working for much of that time on the fringe, in tiny towns, not all of them easy for a Jersey Guy. As Parcells himself once wrote about Lubbock, Texas, where Texas Tech is located, the only thing you could do was "watch the wind blow [as you're] wondering where the next city was exactly." Coming to New York and New Jersey, then, was even sweeter for him than it was for Belichick.

If any coach had ever paid his dues on the way to getting the job he wanted, it was Bill Parcells. But his first year as head coach was hard; they went 3–12–1. Phil Simms, who they hoped would be the quarterback of the future, was injured once again; if anything the team seemed to be slipping. George Young, the Giants general manager, who had given Parcells the job, covertly offered it to his old friend Howard Schnellenberger, then in the process of coaching some great University of Miami teams. A decade earlier they had both been in Baltimore, where Schnellenberger was head coach and Young his offensive coordinator. Young never confirmed that he tried to replace Parcells, but there was no doubt that the offer had been made, and there was also no doubt, among the people who knew and liked Bill Parcells, that his personality seemed to change after that. He became, they believed, harder-edged, more cynical about it all, less trusting of anyone and everything. Here, after all, was the man who had hired him, barely giving him a chance, and, without talking to him, going out and looking for a successor. It was a reminder of how tenuous your job was in the world of coaching and that no matter how hard you had worked for it, they could and would take it all away so quickly. It was not a place for the tenderhearted.

There was a lesson there for Parcells: You had to take care of yourself—at the expense of others, if need be. If you had to be tougher on the players than you had been in the past, so be it. If you had to be tougher on your assistants, then so be it. Everyone, after all, was out to screw everyone else, and George Young had just proved it.

Parcells, with his own job in jeopardy, warned Bill Belichick that he might not be able to protect him, because he could not even protect himself. "George Young is trying to screw me, and we might all be gone," Parcells said. "So if you want to go, and you get the right offer, you ought to go." They had just had a terrible year, Belichick thought, and one more like that, and they would all have been gone for sure. Belichick had been asked to come out to Minnesota by his old friend Floyd Reese, who had taken a job as defensive coordinator and who offered him a job with the Vikings as a kind of deputy, handling the defensive backs. Les Steckel, a tough, hard-line kind of coach, was about to replace Bud Grant, who was considered to be one of the last of the laid-back coaches. Steckel was not in any way laid back, he was an ex-Marine and an Ironman competitor, and he was going to run a very different kind of team. Belichick had flown out and talked with Reese and Steckel, and the pay was very good for that period—$60,000 a year plus bonuses. He had come very close to taking the job, so close that it had even been announced on the local Minnesota television stations on the late night news.

But at the last minute he had pulled back. There were too many things that bothered him—a new head coach, a large part of the coaching staff left over from his predecessor, an uncertainty as to whether he would fit in well with the group other than with Reese. The next morning Reese came by to pick him up and Belichick said he couldn't do it. For all the things that were wrong with the New York situation—the second-rate practice facilities, the uncertainty at the top—he was happier than he had realized back East, not at all sure of how well he would do in the Midwest. He liked the East Coast and had fallen in love with Nantucket, the island off Cape Cod, and hoped to build a house there. He was not sure he would fit in well under Steckel, who did not work out well in Minnesota and was gone in a year. But the very sense that he had a choice made him feel better, indeed liberated him. He was not locked into one venue, and he returned from Minnesota happier than when he had gone out, because he had chosen his job, and the job had not entirely chosen him.

He also thought there was a good chance that the Giants' situation would get better.

It did. If 1983 was a terrible year, then very quickly the program began to turn around: 9–7 in 1984, 10–6 in 1985, and then 14–2 in 1986. Parcells ran the Giants very well in those years. He was a smart football man and had a natural feel for the moods and needs of his players. Having coached in so many different places, he had a solid sense of how to put an organization together. If he was a lot tougher than some of the coaches the players had dealt with, he still gained in comparison with the unbending Perkins. Amid all of that, Parcells and Belichick would emerge as two of the League's signature coaches of the era, both of them talented, both of them for a time content to work together in a partnership; it was fascinating, because it involved two very different human beings, each representing a very different side of football's human equation—one primarily its emotions, the other primarily its strategy. But, caught in all that, was something that weighed on each man, as Parcells reached higher and higher plateaus of success (almost always with Belichick at his side). There was the question of whether Parcells could do it without his supremely gifted assistant—was he not merely dependent on Belichick, but perhaps too dependent on him? (Were Jersey guys ever dependent on anything or anyone else?) But a comparable question surrounded Belichick as he gained more and more recognition: whether he could do as well as a head coach—did he have what was then considered to be the right personality or did he have a charisma deficit? Was he the kind of man you wanted next to you in a foxhole?—a saying used almost always by men who had never been in foxholes about other men who had never been in foxholes either.

Parcells dealt with his assistants by challenging them, and the challenges often came in the form of second guesses. It was your job to answer the challenge, to defend your idea, but because of the way his advice was proffered, he was always the winner: If the play worked, everyone was a winner, and if it didn't, then it was your fault, not his. "That blitz won't work," he might say to Belichick. "Do you want me to throw it out?" Belichick would respond. "No," he would answer, "but it won't work."

Once they played Detroit when Barry Sanders was at the height of his game. Sanders was the most artistic of running backs, an absolute joy to watch, unless you were assigned to stop him; he was a runner with power and speed, and wonderful moves. No one in the game could hesitate and then move to full speed—often, it seemed, in a completely different direction—like Sanders. Belichick had prepared an unusual defense, one designed for Sanders's speed and agility. It featured only two down linemen, four linebackers, and five defensive backs. In that sense, it was something of a forerunner of the defense he would eventually use, a few years later, against Marshall Faulk and the Rams. "What the hell is this?" asked Parcells, who always favored the three-four. "Well," Belichick answered, "we're up against a run and shoot, and we need as much speed in there as we can get." Parcells did not agree. "Don't you think we need to be more physical?" he asked. Belichick said no. Then Parcells slammed his fist down on the table. "Why the hell don't you just put Stephen Baker in there—he'll give you the speed," he said, referring to a wide receiver who, at 155 pounds, was the smallest, lightest player on the team. From then on, whenever Belichick drew up a comparable defense, he would tell Parcells, "And we're going to put Stephen Baker in on this particular defense. . . ."

Parcells loved to create intrigue among his coaching staff. One of the things he would do was tell one coach what was bothering him about another coach, so that the message would be delivered, without it coming directly from the head coach. He also, Belichick thought, had a shrewd way of putting the burden on the assistants; it was as if there was the general implication that everyone was always trying to screw him. Here in Belichick's case he had given him these great linebackers, and all this freedom, and what was Belichick going to do with them? Was he maximizing their abilities? *I'm giving them to you, and if you don't lead the league in defense, then something's wrong. So don't screw it up,* he seemed to be saying.

Sometimes he would get on Belichick during a game. For instance, if Belichick had put something extra in on the defense, an extra wrinkle or variation, he would hear, "What the hell was that? That wasn't in the game plan. That was dumb as shit." Later, he might apologize—he hadn't really meant it, he wasn't really like that, they were all a team here. It was a complicated relationship with benefits for both men, and yet with feelings that were never entirely reconciled. It probably, as these things do, tended to work better and more harmoniously when they were all on the ascent, when everything was yet to be achieved, than when they reached the higher plateaus, when the scrutiny of the media and public became infinitely greater and the rewards for the success were to be divvied up. The egos of everyone tended to be suppressed on the ascent—subservient to the great task ahead, when a team begins to win—and much more of a problem once a championship had been attained. In truth, Parcells did give Belichick magnificent players and essentially a free hand to use them as he wanted. They had poured most of their top draft choices into defense rather than offense, and they had put together a great defense, a good if not dominant front three (or four, or even two), a good if patched secondary, and a great, essentially world-class group of linebackers. A good many talented men make their way through the portals of the NFL as defensive coaches without the good fortune to handle such extraordinary players. They would form the critical core of two Super Bowl championship teams and make the Giants, for much of the eighties, a joy to watch, not merely for its own regional fans, but also for any football fans who liked the tempo of a game to be set by the pure physicality and intelligence of the defense. There was no doubt that this was a marvelous opportunity for Belichick.

◆ ◆ ◆

When Belichick arrived to help coach the Giants, his old friend Ernie Adams was on a very different kind of coaching track. Quite content to be a sort of resident intellectual and theoretician of the staff, he was immediately aware of the changes that had taken place in his friend during the four-year apprenticeship. He had already put it all together, Adams thought. He might have a preference to coach the defense, but he understood what was happening with the offense equally well. What was wonderful about his apprenticeship, Belichick would say, was that he had been given so many different jobs and forced to learn things that he might not have bothered to learn otherwise. When he first got together with Adams on the Giants, the two of them would often run laps around the field after practice, and he would tell Adams that he did not understand how some of the other coaches in the League had decided they were only going to understand one side of the ball—offensive specialists who did not master the defensive side, and defensive coaches who seemed to have equally little interest in the offense. That absolutely amazed him. He had made it his business to know both.

That totality of his knowledge, the great depth of it, would manifest itself, Adams came to believe, in his being so good a game coach; he excelled not just in preparation before a game, but also while the game was actually going on. He was much more analytical than most other coaches, and he never lost that analytical ability, not even in the most tense moments of a game. Knowledge about both teams was stored away and ready to be used at all times. With the Giants he was already very good at doing his game plan in the days before a game, but what was even more remarkable, Adams believed, was that during the game, as the other team began to make its adjustments against his defenses and began to enjoy a greater measure of success, he was just as good. With the game on the line and thousands of people screaming away, often in hostile venues, Belichick did not lose his cool; he could always somehow manage to step back and take a cold look at what the other team was doing and what his own team had tried, and then figure out what he needed to do in terms of instant adjustments. That, Adams believed, became a kind of Belichick trademark: the ability to adapt his game plan even as the game was being played out, and not to be sucked in by the emotions of it, or to be a prisoner of what he had decided to do beforehand. In Adams's words, that was "the rarest kind of ability—the ability to see the game as if it were over, even as it was being played out." It would not do very much good, Belichick would often say, to do a brilliant analysis on Monday.

All of that, Adams believed, came together in his other trademark: He was an outstanding situational coach, a man who could get his team to adapt week after week in order to respond to the strengths and weaknesses of any particular team they would be playing. Most of the other teams were much more predictable; each Sunday the same team with essentially the same defense would show up. But his teams were always a bit different, always adapting to the needs of that week and that particular opposition. This was never more in evidence than during the extraordinary run the Patriots made during the 2004 playoffs, as they defeated the Colts, the Steelers, and finally the Eagles—three very exceptional and very different teams—with a dazzling display of defensive artistry, but different artistry each week. What was particularly interesting, Adams believed, was that Belichick already had much of that ability when he joined the Giants in 1979; it was just a matter of letting it flower.

Adams had always known where Belichick intended to go, how

successful he wanted to be, and by 1979 he believed that his friend had already reached the point where all his talents were in play, and that others soon would see it as well. What Belichick had felt somewhat tentatively four years earlier when he had first arrived in Baltimore had crystallized into a hard-edged confidence. Then he had needed, at least in his own mind, to prove to himself and to the players that he could coach them, that he had the ability to get them to do the things they were supposed to do. For four years he had been in the process of becoming the Bill Belichick of the NFL who would finally surface in the media: serious, ultra-studious, not much downtime, and not much laughter there. He did not have a light touch, especially with the general public; he was there to know the answers, often before the players had the questions. That persona—the Belichick who had never been young—was one he had either created for the NFL or had evolved because of the game's needs. Part of the design was more or less deliberate, and part of it was who he was. For when he had first entered the League, he had been a young man teaching older men, and he had needed to prove to them he was an authority figure. Thus, he believed, he had been forced to be more aloof and more authoritarian than most coaches or teachers working their first jobs. In physical terms he was not imposing, so he would have to make up for it by dint of willpower. A stern game face did not hurt. But it was also how he was most comfortable—being serious and completely disciplined. That did not mean he was not close to other coaches his own age and did not socialize with them, but it meant that the more human Belichick, the Belichick who laughed and relaxed, was someone his players could only wonder about.

He was not one of the League's hard-ass coaches, one of those men who deliberately came up with rules almost for the sake of rules, as if the more rules there were, the stronger the hierarchy. But he was tough, and he always knew what point he wanted to make. Pepper Johnson, the linebacker who was drafted out of Ohio State in 1986 and who became one of his favorite players, remembered the difficulty of dealing with him when Johnson was a rookie. Once there was a preseason rookie scrimmage against the Cleveland Browns, in which the Giants were on defense and the Browns were driving, getting five yards per carry on each play. One of the reasons for their success—and it seemed to be an afternoon given over to a successful Cleveland running game—was that the Giants had the wrong defense in there, a defense especially designed to stop the pass.

As the afternoon went on, Johnson, who was calling defensive signals, kept looking over to the sideline, where Belichick was standing, to let him know that they had to make an adjustment, so they could stop the run. It seemed as if Belichick was intentionally looking away. Finally, Johnson did catch his eye, and the coach's face seemed to be framed in anger; that anger seemed to be directed, as best Johnson could tell, at him personally, as if all of this were Pepper Johnson's fault, because he was the highest draft choice on the field. Finally, the Giants made the defensive stop. As they came to the sidelines, totally exhausted, they expected to hear some words of praise. Not on this day, for on this day a lesson was being taught. Suddenly, Belichick's voice seemed to lash out at them: *You're with the New York Giants now! I don't care what you did in college. I don't care whether you were All-American!* (That zinger was aimed directly at Johnson, who had made some All-American teams.) *Here you stop the run! I do not care what defense you're caught in! You stop the run! They don't run against us! They never run against the Giants! And they never, never run against us up the middle! If we can't stop them any other way, we stop them with pure physical ability!*

And that, thought Johnson, was the lesson for today and for every day as long as they played for the Giants: You began with a physical game, and you stopped the run first and foremost.

Much of the Giants' sustained success was attributable to their greatest player, Lawrence Taylor, who was also quite possibly the best defensive player in the League in that era. They had drafted Taylor from North Carolina in 1981, and he joined the talented Harry Carson as a linebacker. It was the beginning of something very special. In 1984, the Giants added Carl Banks, a great linebacker from Michigan State, and then, in 1986, Pepper Johnson from Ohio State. With that, and with Gary Reasons, the Giants had one of the most exceptional groups of linebackers in pro football history, and the core defensive team that would help to win two Super Bowls.

All four were different, Belichick thought. Taylor was the kind of player you got once in a lifetime, unbelievably strong and quick, with astonishing instincts for the game and for the ball. Parcells, Belichick thought, wanted to hold Taylor out a bit as a rookie, but Belichick told Perkins that Taylor had to be on the field, and he got permission to use Taylor from the start on special teams. He just splattered opposing players, and soon the coaches began to enjoy watching the film of the special teams, watching certain opposing players deliberately try to get out of Taylor's way—if need be, slipping a little to the other side of the field as he approached. Taylor was one of the smartest players Belichick had ever coached; he not only knew his own role, but the role of every other player on the defense. When Belichick gave the linebackers tests, Taylor was always the first to finish; the others needed to study hard the night before, but he never did. He was also stronger than almost anyone else on the team. He weighed about 250 pounds, but he could power rush better than players fifty pounds heavier. His power resided mostly in his lower body, from his knees to his butt, and his thighs, in particular, were so powerful that he was incredibly explosive. No tight end in the League could really handle him. "I'd watch him, and it was fascinating," Belichick said years later. "He'd be fighting off the tight end with one hand, checking out the way the play was going, and then he would make his move, and it always seemed so easy for him."

Taylor's feel for a given game, Belichick thought, was just phenomenal, and it gave him the rare ability to lift his teammates, and if they were playing at home, the crowd, as well. He did not always go all out, at one hundred miles an hour, Belichick thought, but he had a great feel for the hinge plays—that is, the plays on which the game turned—and he would rise to them. When the other team was moving the ball late in a game, if he was not that keyed to second and eight, "then when it was third and four, he was a lion." There were days when he simply soared above the level of everyone else on the field, and he would not let anything interfere—and days when he played and played brilliantly when any other player would have sat it out. There had been a day in practice—Belichick thought it was during the 1986 season—when he had rolled his ankle in practice and everyone was sure he would be out for one or two weeks, the ankle was a truly gruesome sight. So on his own, without telling the coaches, he went to a nearby racetrack and somehow managed to find someone there who was an expert in horse medicine, who had some kind of pill—a horse pill—and he took it and played well. Belichick had been told about the pill later, and absolutely believed the story. They could motivate him by saying someone was better than he. In the 1981 draft George Rogers had been taken ahead of him, so when they were going to play New Orleans, Belichick, in the defense team meetings, would talk about what a great runner Rogers was, how powerful he was, how hard to stop, knowing it was like throwing gasoline on a fire. He did the same when they played Tampa Bay, talking about what a great defensive lineman Hugh Green was, taken number seven in the country, five places after Taylor, and he lovingly showed film that highlighted Green's best plays. "Look what Green did there—now that's a great play," he would say, until Taylor would shout out that if they liked the fucking guy so much, they should have drafted him.

Banks was different, a tough player with exceptional technique and, like Taylor, a great team player. He always understood that what he was doing demanded sacrificing for the team, so that, more often than not, Taylor could be showcased. At first, Banks was not that strong in pass coverage, but he worked at it, and he became better every year. Because Banks was so good, the defenses could not load up against Taylor, as they might have otherwise. If he did not have the pure physical ability of Taylor—and no one did—he made up for it by working harder. At the end of a game, his teammates knew, he would have left everything he had on the field. In those days the Giants also had Mark Bavaro, who was quite possibly the best tight end in the League, or certainly one of the two or three best ones, and Steve Belichick, who occasionally dropped by the practices, noticed that Parcells never became so animated and interested as when they were doing drills that pitted Banks against Bavaro. It was great fun to watch for everyone, the best against the best.

Harry Carson had been there before the others, and he had suffered through many bad years, a fine football player waiting for the rest of the team to catch up with him. He was a man of uncommon integrity, as good a man, those around him believed, as he was a football player. Greatly respected by his teammates for his willingness to accept responsibility, he was the son of a railroad worker and a domestic. He burned with the belief that he had not gotten the respect and acclaim that should properly have been his, because he had gone to a predominantly black college, South Carolina State, in an era when black athletes no longer had to do that. Thus, there had been a not-so-subtle downgrading of his career. He was taken by the Giants in the fourth round of the 1976 draft—and had he played for a white college, he might have gone much higher. That made him the kind of man, Belichick thought, who always had a little more to prove and always managed to prove it, a man with a chip on his shoulder, albeit a good chip. All those losing years in New York had been very hard on him. He had once tried to give back a week's salary because he felt he had not played well, and a few years later, when Ray Perkins arrived, he tried to quit, because the team had started the 1980 season 1–5. Only the combination of Perkins and Willie Jeffries, his college coach, managed to talk him into staying.

He was, Belichick thought, a very good athlete, not quite as fast as Taylor, but very strong, a player who might seem faster than he was because he made such quick reads. His body was a little different from the others; he had shorter legs, a long torso, and thus a lower center of gravity. But, with Carson, so much of it was about instincts, almost beyond what a coach could teach him. "I would ask him," Belichick once said, "Harry, how did you know that was the trap and not the trap pass, because they look exactly alike." He couldn't really explain it, Belichick remembered, but it had something to do with the tempo of the play.

Pepper Johnson came later to the group, but he ended up staying with Belichick for much of his career, and in 2005 was still working for him as a coach. Johnson was quick—he had longer legs, and a shorter torso than Carson—and he was good on pass coverage. He was a very smart, almost bubbly player, who got on well with his teammates.

Suddenly it was as if Belichick had nothing less than the best job in professional football; he was working with great players who had a wonderful sense of one another, and there was wildly intense competition from other teams in the NFL—most notably from the Eagles, the Cowboys, and the Redskins, and eventually, at playoff time, from the Forty-Niners. Every game was a challenge, but a challenge you went into with confidence. He was in his mid-thirties when that run began and he was very aware of his good fortune the entire time, that something like this might not happen again, that it was best to take the pleasure from it while it was there. He could not believe his good luck in his choice of professions. It was almost a decade since he had first entered the League, and getting to work each morning was still thrilling.

In 1986 the Giants finally made it to the Super Bowl, which was always the main objective. "In this league the only thing that matters is the jewelry," as Parcells once said, referring to Super Bowl rings. The road to the Super Bowl in those days was a great deal harder in the National Conference than in the American Conference, because of the sheer physicality of the dominant teams. That year the Giants manhandled San Francisco in a playoff game, 49–3. Just before that game, Parcells had walked into the offensive line meeting and asked, "Is this the meeting of Club 13?" *What was Club 13?* one of the linemen wanted to know. The number of yards the Giants had been able to get on the ground against San Francisco the last time they had played, he answered—thirteen yards on nineteen rushing plays. They could, he added, have gained more yards just calling nineteen quarterback sneaks.

Then they played Washington in the Conference championship game. If anything, some of the New York coaches thought, the real championship game that season was not the Super Bowl, but the conference title game against the Redskins. The Redskins were very good that year, but because the Giants had been better during the regular season, beating them twice, the game was at Giants Stadium. The Washington games in those years were small wars, a great traditional rivalry upgraded in its modern incarnation because both teams were very good and played exceptional defense. The thing that Belichick knew was that the Redskins were a very different team if you were ahead of them in the second half, than if they had the lead. For a variety of reasons they were not nearly as good a team at coming from behind. He had forgotten the precise statistic, but it was something like twenty-six wins and one defeat when they entered the fourth quarter with a lead back then. They were primarily a running team, and when Jay Schroeder passed, it was often a play action pass, that is, a pass disguised within a seeming run formation. At the same time they had a ferocious pass rush, with two of the best rushers in the league, Dexter Manley and Charles Mann, and thus their ability to put pressure on your passer—if you were behind—was lethal.

It was perfect, late-season weather—in a reverse sense: very cold, with winds up to thirty-five miles an hour, the kind of weather that mandated the kind of defense the Giants played so well. That day they just shut down the Redskins, leading 17–0 at halftime, and their defense permitted Washington nothing in the second half. The Redskins got off thirty-seven plays in the second half, thirty-four passes, two would-be passes that ended in sacks, and one run. The Giants' Phil Simms, content to sit on his lead, had thrown the ball only twice during the entire second half. The most impressive statistic of all was what they had done to the Redskins on third and fourth downs: Washington was 0 for 14 on third down, and 0 for 4 on fourth down, which meant they were 0 for 18 on the biggest plays of any drive. The Redskins had won twenty-six games in a row in which they had gained one hundred yards on the ground. No coach, drawing up defensive assignments, could have expected them to be carried out so completely. That day, George Rogers, one of the best backs in the League, ran nine times for fifteen yards, and Kelvin Bryant did only a little better, carrying the ball six times for twenty-five yards. That was the day the players carried Bill Belichick off the field on their shoulders—something very rare for an assistant coach.

There were, Belichick thought, four or five moments in an entire coaching career when all the hard work was validated, and one of them had come after that game. It came not as he was being carried off the field by his defensive players, though that was sweet, but later in the locker room. There was jubilation in the locker room, not just because of the thrill of victory, but because now they were going to the Super Bowl. Carl Banks lay down in front of his locker, unable to join the celebration at first because he was so tired. For a moment Belichick was worried. "Carl, are you okay—is anything wrong?" he asked Banks. "No, I'm just totally exhausted," Banks said, and Belichick thought to himself, what an extraordinary moment for a coach, to witness a great athlete who had played so hard and given so much right to the very last play that he could not join the celebration.

Based on that performance against so physical a Washington team, the Giants did not think Denver could stay with them. They simply did not believe the Broncos had comparable physical power. In the regular season they had played Denver in late November, and it had been, in the minds of the Giants coaches, a surprisingly close game. Raul Allegre had kicked four field goals, and George Martin, the big defensive end, had intercepted a pass and returned it, running it back seventy-eight yards, as Frank Litsky of the *New York Times* noted, as if in slow motion. The final score had been Giants, 19–16. John Elway had played well, completing twenty-nine of forty-seven passes for 336 yards, but there was a one-dimensional quality to the Denver offense at that point, which was made to order for someone like Belichick.

But the regular-season game had given the Broncos a sense that they might be physically close to the Giants. To Belichick the job was a relatively simple one, given that New York had such a significant physical advantage. The main job was to keep John Elway from scrambling, because if he got outside the pocket, he instantly became far more dangerous.

In the Super Bowl the Giants were able to do that with a reasonable amount of success. Belichick did not think that New York played that well in the first half. There were a couple of dumb penalties. But with Denver leading 10–7 and driving near the end of the half, with a chance to open an even larger lead, the Giants made a goal-line stand and Denver missed the field goal. Then, just before the half, George Martin sacked Elway in the end zone, and the score was 10–9.

At halftime Belichick told the defensive players that they were overreaching, trying to do too much, and that each player did not have to make every play; all they had to do was carry out their assignments, and it would work out. They were so keyed up, he thought, he needed to rein them in. And then in the second half they completely wore the Broncos down, scoring the first four times they touched the ball. Phil Simms had one of his great days, twenty-two of twenty-five when it was over, and they won Super Bowl XXI, 39–20.

◆◆◆

The competition in the National Conference in those days was unsparing. Starting with the victory of the Forty-Niners in Super Bowl XIX, the Chicago Bears won once, the Giants twice, the Redskins twice, the Niners three more times, and the Cowboys, a new emerging dynasty, three times over a dozen years. The Eagles, an equally punishing team, seemed to be slotted in the bridesmaid role. Getting to the Super Bowl was difficult enough; repeating was much harder. Certainly, no one thought the Giants were easy to play, but it took four years for them to get back to the Super Bowl. Even then it was a hard go. They won their first ten games, then stumbled, and lost three of their last four games, including a tough, very physical one against San Francisco, 7–3. But then, when the playoffs started, Carl Banks finally returned from an injury and that significantly strengthened the defense. The National Conference Championship game, played in San Francisco, pitted the favored Niners (14–2 in the regular season, going in) against the Giants (13–3, going in). It promised to be uncommonly physical, featuring two great teams with superb defenses; one, the Niners, probably had the better offense. It was also a collision of two teams which, because of the competition, though they inhabited different coasts, knew each other very well. George Seifert had been an exceptional defensive coordinator, and he had been studying and admiring the handiwork of Belichick since the latter had coached the Giant special teams. To someone like Seifert, the talents and drive of the young man back east were obvious—great intensity, well above the norm, and exceptional originality. The defensive coverage that Belichick had created for the regular season game was infinitely more sophisticated than anything San Francisco had faced all season, and had kept the Niners off balance for much of the game. Thus before the game there had been a lot of talk among the San Francisco coaches about opening the game up more and taking the initiative more—not so much reacting to the Giant defensive set and not letting them dictate the play calling and the tempo, but making them react to the Niners offense, something they would find, during the game, easier said than done. To say that it was physical was an understatement—both quarterbacks were racked up that day, Jeff Hostetler, starting for the Giants on a hard hit by Jim Burt (though able to come back), and Montana, trying to elude Lawrence Taylor, creamed by George Martin on a clean hit from the blind side in the fourth quarter.

It had been a very close game, and the Giant defense had once again done an exceptionally good job of limiting Montana and making him throw short, taking away the things he wanted to do. Banks had pounded Jones all day long, and the corners had worked hard on slowing down the wide receivers. Montana would end the day completing eighteen of twenty-six passes, good for only (for him) 190 yards. There had been just one big offensive play, a 61-yard third-quarter pass from Montana to John Taylor, which had given San

Francisco a 13–6 lead. That meant the other seventeen completions brought the Niners a total of only 129 yards. The first six Giant points had come from two Matt Bahr field goals.

As such the Giants had managed to keep it close, and they had added two more field goals. After Bahr's fourth field goal, San Francisco led 13–12. The Niners got the ball back with only 5:47 left in the game. They seemed at that moment very much in control, moving down the field comfortably on a drive that appeared likely to give them not merely a critical field goal, and thus a decisive lead in a game that was so much about defense, but would allow them to hand the ball over to the Giants with precious little time left on the clock. "We were on the drive to ice the game," Seifert said, "and everything was going exactly the way it should have gone." They had reached the Giant 30-yard line. All they needed was one more first down, Seifert remembered. Then they called a running play, Roger Craig carrying the ball, part of the attempt to get the first down and burn the clock, when Erik Howard, the Giant nose tackle, broke through, smashed Craig hard in the midsection, and knocked the ball loose. Lawrence Taylor recovered it. It was, Seifert decided later, poor play calling on his part, a coaching mistake. It was too much of a finesse play, with the guard pulling, and when the guard had pulled it had meant that there was more in the way of opportunity for the defense to penetrate and a lot less protection for Craig when he was most vulnerable. The Giants had taken over the ball on their own 43 with 2:36 left, and they finally drove to the San Francisco 24, where, with four seconds left, Bahr kicked his fifth field goal for the two-point New York victory, 15–13. A kick that just barely made it through, Seifert remembered. That was something for the Giant defense to be proud of, two games in the same season against the great Montana, the most resourceful and agile quarterback of an era, a player who had always seemed able to outwit even the best defenses, 120 minutes against him and only two touchdowns and a total of 23 points given up. It had been two great defensive teams playing at a superlative level, one touchdown allowed in the entire game. Seifert was more impressed than ever by Belichick. As for himself, coaches live in a world where the possibilities for regret, even over just one play, are boundless, and George Seifert thought he had coached poorly not in that game, but for one play, and though he went on to a career of continued excellence, that decision on occasion gnawed at him, and sometimes when he was out on his boat fishing, fifteen years after the fact, he thought of the moment, under three minutes on the clock, and how he had failed to make the more conservative call, and they had lost the chance for the only three-peat in Super Bowl history. The victory gave the Giants the Conference championship and the right to play Buffalo in the Super Bowl in Tampa.

Buffalo was probably, Belichick thought, a better team than the Giants, with more weapons, because they were so good on offense. They were seemingly without weaknesses. On their way to the Super Bowl they had scored 44 points against Miami and then destroyed a good Raider team, 51–3. Buffalo was certainly the most explosive team the Giants had seen all season. Their offensive coordinator was Belichick's old friend and first boss, Ted Marchibroda. No one did the offensive part of the game better in that era than Marchibroda, unless it was Bill Walsh. A year earlier Marchibroda had invented what was called the no-huddle offense: Designed for maximum speed, it was supposed to confuse the defense, to keep it from being set and prepared, and finally to exhaust it. Essentially, it was the two-minute drill—the kind of super-speed offense normally used only at the end of the game when you were behind.

In fact, that was how Marchibroda had discovered it; the previous year when the Bills had fallen behind the Houston Oilers late in a game, the Bills had gone to their two-minute drill, in which the offensive team needed to run a maximum number of plays in the shortest time possible in order to score more than once. That worked so well against the Oilers, Marchibroda suddenly thought, why not use it throughout the game, why not confuse them and wear them down earlier? So the Bills started running it, more and more often, and they enjoyed great success with it. What made them particularly successful was that their offense was perfectly tailored for it—some very good receivers, a talented quarterback, and a running back, Thurman Thomas, who was also an excellent receiver. It put enormous pressure on a defense that had a hard time getting set and adjusting to all the weapons that might be used against it.

Marchibroda, however, was idiosyncratic in one way: He was fifty-eight years old at the time, and he did not like to call the plays himself. In that sense he was old-fashioned. He wanted his quarterback to do the play calling, because the quarterback was the one out there on the field, and he was not merely seeing the defense, but feeling it as well. That was the way it had been done when Marchibroda was a young quarterback, breaking in more than three decades earlier, and it was the way he had always coached: You prepared your quarterback, and then let him call his game. Belichick remembered a moment in his first season with the Colts, back in 1975, when he was working as a young assistant for Marchibroda; Bert Jones, their quarterback, had come to the sideline on a critical third and short play and asked Marchibroda for a play, and Marchibroda gave him four plays. Jones, a bit flustered, asked the coach *which one* he wanted, and Marchibroda told him to make the choice himself. Now, with Kelly at quarterback, Belichick thought, that might prove a small advantage. Belichick, who had given hours and hours of his life over to the study of Jim Kelly during the past two seasons, on the theory that they were fated to meet him in a big game like this, did not think that Jim Kelly read defenses as well as some other quarterbacks in the League.

But the Bills were quick, and they had a lot of tools. They came up to the line of scrimmage in the no-huddle offense and simply exploded at you. The defense had barely set up, it sometimes seemed, and the Bills had already called their play and moved the ball. After just four or five plays in a row from the no-huddle, the defensive linemen seemed to be dragging and seemed to get no chance between plays to catch their breath. The system, if nothing else, gave the offense far greater control over the tempo of a game. Perhaps, people thought, watching the Bills, it was one of those moments when the offenses in the NFL were so good, the players so fast, the possibilities on each play so varied, that the offenses in pro football had finally and definitively gone beyond the capacity of defenses. The challenge for a defensive coach in dealing with them was obvious: Try to slow down the Buffalo offense and change the tempo. They had already beaten the Giants in Giants Stadium during the regular season, and their victories in the playoff games implied that they were getting better each week. There was one break for the Giants—when they played in Tampa it would be on grass, not turf. One of the things they ought to do if at all possible, Belichick told his players, was accidentally kick the ball after the referees took it from the huddle and set it up; they could also disentangle themselves more slowly from piles after the play, just to slow down the Bills. In addition, if they were injured when the Bills were running the no-huddle, they were not to limp off—because the Bills could easily run a play. Instead they were to stay where they were, and let the trainer come out to them.

If there was any vulnerability to Buffalo, Belichick decided, it was going to have to be Jim Kelly, and the fact (or the hope) that he did not read the defense as well as some other elite quarterbacks, most notably Montana and, later, Belichick's own Tom Brady. As expected, Kelly was calling all the plays that day, and Belichick thought he had a tendency to look at a defense, see it and freeze it in his mind, and not understand the variations the defensive players might run off of it. Thus Kelly might not react well to what seemed to be the same defense, but which in reality disguised quite different ones. He would, when a series of offensive downs was over, Belichick believed, come to the sidelines, ask his coaches what the defense had been doing, and take it back with him for the next offensive series. Thus Belichick thought that his defense had a good chance to be a step ahead of Kelly all day long. Time of possession, he and the other Giant coaches thought, would also be very important; the longer the Buffalo defense was on the field, given the explosiveness of the Buffalo offense, the better for the Giants.

In the first half, he believed, the Bills would try to show speed and depend on their passing attack. All week he tried to prepare his defense for the speed of the Buffalo offense. The Giant defense would line up, and, as quickly as possible, the scout team would run its plays—quick, quick, quicker—in order to key the team to a much faster tempo than they were accustomed to. Belichick also thought that the Bills would not be able to run the ball consistently against them, not when it really mattered and when the Giants wanted to stop the run. Not many teams could. So he decided to let Buffalo run it a bit, giving them a little more mileage on their runs than he usually did. He did not want Jim Kelly throwing on every down. The Bills were less dangerous, he thought, given the superb abilities of the New York defense, if they went to their running game, which also had the advantage of taking more time off the clock. He thought the Giants could stop Thurman Thomas, even though he was an exceptional back, if and when they needed to, because they were so good against the run. Maybe on a drive Buffalo would get three first downs, but the Giants could stop them on a fourth one. So he told the defensive team that he did not care if Thurman Thomas gained a hundred yards on them that day. Better, he said, that Thurman Thomas gained a hundred yards, and Kelly passed for a hundred fifty, than Thomas be shut down completely, because then Buffalo, frustrated on the ground, would go to the air, and Kelly might pass for three hundred fifty. What Belichick really hoped was, in effect, to tease Kelly, to offer him the running game in the second half and then at critical moments take it away from him.

Thinking that way, that they should cut Thurman Thomas some slack, and selling it to his players were two different things. If there was one thing that Giant defense prided itself on that season it was the ability to stop the run, to shut down the League's star running backs. It was a point of pride with them that they did not readily give up hundred-yard games to opposing runners; only Gerald Riggs of the Redskins and Johnny Johnson of the Cardinals had done it in the last two seasons. Every week that season, when Belichick met with the defense and pointed out their goals for Sunday, the first thing he spoke about was keeping the other team's top rusher under a hundred yards. That was what Giants football was all about. But now he was saying he wanted to change that for the Super Bowl. "You guys have to believe me," he kept saying. "If Thomas runs for a hundred yards, we win this game." The defensive players were appalled. They were in no mood on the eve of their biggest game in four years to change their MO and become so generous. Preventing Thomas from running was virtually built into their manhood. Belichick asked them for a show of hands—who in the group wanted to be the MVP of the Super Bowl. At first no hands went up. "Don't be shy," he said and gradually a great many hands went up—Pepper Johnson, always ebullient, put up both hands. "Then let Thomas run," he told them.

What followed was as good a Super Bowl as had ever been played. Who would win the game would be whoever had the lead when the clock ran out. In the first half, the Giants showed what looked like a three-four defense, although whether it actually was represented a very good question. Essentially it called for two down linemen, traditionally heavier and slower, in the front three (in this case Leonard Marshall and Erik Howard), along with Lawrence Taylor, who was normally a linebacker and was a man so fast as to be impossible to categorize, and then went to the four linebackers. But the four linebackers who represented the four part of the three-four were not really linebackers. Only two were: Pepper Johnson, very quick, very versatile in what he could do and exceptionally good at pass coverage, and Carl Banks, a great linebacker against the run and constantly improving against the pass. The outside linebackers were safeties, Greg Jackson and Reyna Thompson. That meant that with the other two safeties and the two cornerbacks, there were six defensive backs on the field, and if you counted Taylor and Johnson as men who played almost as if they were defensive backs, it was almost like eight. Sometimes in that half they also went to a two-three-six, that is, two defensive ends, three linebackers, and six defensive backs. Occasionally, though, they would show the same formation, but change it enough to make it heavier, by bringing in different players, more true linebackers. Sometimes, for a few snaps, they played a two-man front with four linebackers (Taylor a linebacker now) and five defensive backs.

It was a very tight first half, 12–10 Bills, with the Buffalo offense largely held down. The Giants were surprisingly confident at halftime that they could move the ball on the Bills. Belichick thought that the Bills, given the defenses New York had used in the first half, would try to run more in the second half, and that he could vary his defense, without showing all the variations of it when they lined up. He thought Kelly would have difficulty in deciphering their changing defensive look. He believed that the Bills, having seen so small a New York defense, would think that they could run on the Giants in the second half. So the Giants got a little bigger in the second half, and they went to four linebackers, instead of using the two defensive backs as linebackers. In a way, it was a tease defense, egging on Buffalo to do the things you wanted them to do, rather than the things that came more naturally to them. If the defense was imperfect in the second half, if Belichick got angry over a couple of missed coverages and blown plays, they nonetheless kept the Bills from the most important objective of all—setting the tempo of the game—and they kept Buffalo slightly confused, always a bit behind.

It more or less worked. It worked because the Giants won, and because, among other critical things, their offensive line won the battle with the Buffalo defense in the second half, when they were able to go on two very long drives that took a huge amount of time off the clock. One drive, which opened the second half with a touchdown, took fourteen plays and lasted for 9 minutes and 29 seconds, and the other, in the fourth quarter, yielded only a field goal, but took 7:24 off the clock. The Giants ended up dominating the time of possession for the game: 40:33 minutes to 19:27 for the Bills.

But it was still close. With four seconds left and the ball on the Giant 29, the Bills sent their placekicker, Scott Norwood, in, and his kick went wide right. If the Bills had gone to Thurman Thomas more at the very end, Belichick thought, they might have gotten their kicker a little closer to the goal line, and the kick would have been easier, and they might have won. At the end of the game, Marv Levy, the Buffalo coach, told reporters, "We just didn't have enough time to move the ball." Belichick believed, after the game was over, that his sense of Kelly had been accurate.

Thurman Thomas ran for 135 yards, a little more than Belichick had in mind. His own Giant players had not entirely believed Belichick's scheme before the game, but they had gone along with it because they believed in him; he almost always got these things right, and this time he had done it again. After the game, in the locker room, Carl Banks turned to Pepper Johnson and said, "Man, did Bill call that game, or did he call that game?"

CHAPTER TEN

The reward for the Super Bowl victory against so powerful and talented a Buffalo team was that he was finally out of Parcells's shadow. More and more, the announcers on television and the print reporters were mentioning Bill Belichick's defensive schemes, the operative words being "brilliant" and "original." In concrete terms what the Super Bowl brought was an offer to be head coach at Cleveland and perhaps at Tampa. Cleveland was the hard offer, and it would turn out to be a dubious reward.

It started with the highest hopes, with one of the youngest head coaches in NFL history, a man of certifiable major talent and credentials, arriving in a citadel of pro football, but it ended a few years later in unparalleled bitterness in mid-season when the owner announced that he was leaving the city and taking the team with him to Baltimore. To Browns fans, among the most passionate in the League, there were only two villains: Art Modell, the owner, and Bill Belichick, the coach. Cleveland ended with thundering choruses from the fans of "Bill Must Go" and bumper stickers that said "Belichick Is an Idiot." Debby Belichick was forced to take their kids off the school bus and send them to school by car, because the taunting had gotten so cruel and personal. Police had to be stationed near their house, on occasion, because of death threats. "Butch Davis quit during the 2004 season," said Casey Coleman, a radio broadcaster in Cleveland, about one of Belichick's successors, "saying he couldn't take the vilification anymore—the vilification of him was nothing compared to what went on for Bill. Now, *that* was real vilification." At one point during the height of the anti-Belichick tide, Coleman, who did the radio broadcasts of the games and was known as being a friend of Belichick's, needed cops stationed at *his* house because of threats against him. Years later, when Belichick had made his remarkable coaching run in New England, a local paper did a piece praising Coleman for his restraint in not gloating that he had been proven right about his friend.

When it started, in 1990, it seemed like a healthy marriage. The people of Cleveland were desperate to win; they had come close to going to the Super Bowl three times in the mid- and late eighties, and here was this exceptionally thoughtful, careful, disciplined young man, about whom everyone spoke in such superlatives, arriving just in time to take them the final step. Nothing in his world seemed to take place by accident, and everything always seemed to be part of a larger plan. Here was an owner, Art Modell, now sixty-five, desperate to go to the Super Bowl. And here was the young coach, Belichick, just thirty-eight, who seemed to know the way there.

When he showed up for his job interview, Belichick, disciplined and well prepared as ever, had arrived with everything in binders, including a year-by-year plan. It told how they would start with a certain number of players in the three-to-seven-year category in terms of experience, players who were right at the Pro Bowl level; from this they would form the core of their team, so that the other younger players could learn from them. Everything was laid out step by step, where they would be after the first year, and then the second year, and the third year. There was no doubt that, more than any other candidate, Belichick had thought it out. Moreover, as Kevin Byrne, the Browns' media man, pointed out, the plan was tough-minded and detailed, and it wasn't based on hope. It was "not an I-want-to-win-and-go-to-the-Super-Bowl wishful presentation, but how we can win, all laid out," he said. There were others in Cleveland who were supposed to be in on the decision-making, but by the time they met Belichick it was a done deal. Modell was sold on him, as was Pat Modell, the owner's wife, who was duly impressed at how organized he was.

Seemingly, it was the ideal job: a talented young man, just reaching his full potential, taking over the position once held by one of the gods of football coaching, especially a god in the Belichick household—Paul Brown. That meant that someone who was, in effect, a child of the great Ohio football coaching dynasty, the Paul Brown dynasty, was returning to Cleveland, one of the great professional football cities in the country. It was a city where the game was a genuine passion, but where the fans were feeling increasingly frustrated, because there had been no championship since the days of Paul Brown, more than thirty years earlier. If there is a cruel joke in all this, in what happened there and in the success that eventually came to Bill Belichick in New England, it is a joke on the Cleveland fans, so starved for victory and championship—for they had gotten the right coach, and with a break or two he would have coached the kind of football they understood and loved, with his brilliant defenses.

To say that the stars were not aligned properly is an understatement of considerable magnitude. The only law that seemed to apply to Cleveland was Murphy's Law: Everything that could go wrong did go wrong. The coach and the owner were ill-suited to each other. The coach was the ultimate anti-celebrity figure, and by contrast, the owner was a product of the marketing world, and he loved the spotlight. His ego fed on it, especially his association with the team's star players. He liked having the media around all the time and loved talking to its members, and he often blurted out to them what the coach thought were secrets. In his relationships with the players, he sometimes seemed to be offering an alternative to the only relationship that the coach thought they should have, a dependency upon him and his rules. Moreover, in contrast to most NFL owners, Art Modell not only lacked even a semblance of wealth, he was the rarest of things—a relatively poor NFL owner—and he was annually facing a much more difficult challenge than most of his peers, who began their seasons with sold-out, or nearly sold-out, stadiums. Modell was barely above 50 percent in terms of season ticket sales, one of the lowest season ticket bases of any owner in the League. Thus there was a tendency on his part and on the part of some of the people working for him to project a certain optimism about the season ahead, not always justified, thereby raising expectations that the coach was not sure the team could meet. The owner, said one man who knew both men very well, was in the sizzle business, and Belichick was not only in the steak business, he had contempt for sizzle. Modell was flamboyant, volatile, and emotional; he had arrived in Cleveland from the world of New York marketing and television rather than from coaching, starting back in the sixties, when marketing, soon to be one of the great growth areas of the NFL (and the American economy), was a small part of the package, and when producing things was more important than marketing and selling them.

In January 1963, the unthinkable had happened, in Paul Brown's eyes at least, since, in his mind, he *was* the Cleveland Browns: Art Modell, who in Brown's opinion knew nothing about football, had fired him, Paul Brown, the greatest football innovator of an era. His accomplishments ranged from using flankers, to inventing the helmet face bar to protect the players' faces (a great invention shrewdly patented so that Brown got a royalty on the bar on each face mask). He was the man after whom the team had been named, a man who thought—and not without some justification—that he had invented the modern game of professional football. But I have eight years left on my contract, Brown protested, so Modell said that he would be paid for all eight years, and with that, Paul Brown was gone, left to play golf (the only man being paid more to play golf at that moment in America, he once noted, was Arnold Palmer). If he was gone, he was never, in the minds of many Browns fans who thought of those as the glory years, forgotten. In time, Paul Brown got another team, the expansion Cincinnati Bengals. (What happened in Cleveland, he decided, was never going to happen again, certainly not with the Bengals. Once in a preseason team meeting in Cincinnati, he asked the team owner, John Sawyer, to stand up. Sawyer did so. Then Brown said, "Sit down," and Sawyer sat down. The lesson, said one of his players, Pat Matson, was clear—this was not Cleveland with the intrusive Art Modell. Here there was no one else to go to.)

Then there was the media, which Belichick had never dealt with before, that being a Parcells rule—the assistant coaches did not deal with the media. Nor was it something that came naturally to Belichick. His instinct was to draw back from it. What some media people often wanted to talk about seemed either frivolous, or invasive, and they soon tired of hearing him answer, when they asked about an injured player, that he was not a doctor. The lines were drawn very early on. He did not handle it well, modeling himself on Parcells, which was a mistake. Parcells, after all, was singularly skilled, as if he had been born to do this and nothing else, conducting an amazingly combative one-sided dialogue with the media. He might have had a brilliant career on Madison Avenue had he not become a football coach (he once nicknamed one of his defensive backs Toast, explaining that the player had earned the name because he got burned so often). Parcells managed to get away with it because although he was gruff and threatening, able to stiff-arm the media, he was almost always quotable. Many television people did not mind his put-downs, as long as they could get the sound bite, and no one did sound bites better than Parcells. But Belichick was no Parcells. He was not physically intimidating, so the tough-guy manner did not suit him particularly well. He also failed to remember that Parcells was allowed the macho frontal assault on reporters (giving answers which implied that their otherwise legitimate questions were flat-out stupid and an unwelcome imposition on a busy man) only after he had won. There are two sets of standards for the media in the world of sports, and the first rule is that a coach or player can get away with almost anything if he is winning.

Belichick wanted to control the media from the first, to set new rules about where they could go and, more important, where they could *not* go. In Cleveland, though, the media had long enjoyed unusual freedom because of Art Modell, who liked to hang out with reporters, liked in no small part seeing his name in the newspapers and his face on television, and who also needed to sell a lot of tickets. There would be Modell, showing up at practice, talking freely with reporters, telling Mary Kay Cabot, a beat reporter for the *Cleveland Plain Dealer,* one Friday that Michael Jackson, one of their best receivers, had gotten dinged up and would not play, and she ran with it. Belichick, who normally got on well with her, was furious, waking her up at 7 A.M. to complain, because she had given away information, he believed, that would help the opposing coaches. She was, she tried to tell him, just doing her job, just as he was trying to do his.

In the past, Cleveland reporters had enjoyed a freedom of access rarely available in the modern NFL; reporters could walk into the locker room anytime they wanted and talk to whomever they wanted. Belichick ended that immediately. There was a critical moment at his first meeting with the media, when Belichick outlined his new Parcellian rules for the media: far more limited access to the locker room, no talking to assistant coaches, and no talking to the trainer. With the announcement of each additional rule, the mood in the room turned more sullen. What were considered historic privileges were being taken away. About one minute into his presentation, Casey Coleman, one of the team's radio broadcasters, turned to Kevin Byrne, the Browns media man, and said, "The honeymoon didn't last very long, did it?" Worse, this was coming from someone judged to be an outsider (he might have had Ohio roots, but not in the eyes of most Browns fans; they saw him as someone imported from New York). That was not surprising. Art Modell had been in Cleveland for some thirty years or more, and had tried to be a major civic figure and philanthropist (his philanthropy had been limited by the fact that he had very little wealth of his own; he was a man getting by, to use Arthur Miller's phrase, on a shoeshine and a smile), but he was still considered an outsider, no matter how many professions of loyalty to Cleveland he made.

◆◆◆

It was an old team, the oldest team in the NFL, and though it had recently competed at a very high level—with only John Elway, the Broncos quarterback, standing between it and a Conference championship,

Cleveland fans thought—it was aging. The skills of many of the players—favorite players to the fans, because they had been there a long time and had brought the team so close to a championship—were eroding. This erosion was visible to the new Cleveland coaches and to opposing coaches and opposing quarterbacks, if not necessarily to Cleveland fans. The team was increasingly predictable in its offense; its quarterback, Bernie Kosar, never mobile, was more and more vulnerable to good defenses.

Belichick, who was particularly skilled at seeing the weaknesses of the opposing offense and the vulnerability of opposing quarterbacks, understood all too well how the better defenses in the League now saw his own quarterback and offense. He thought almost everything about the Browns needed to be changed, as quickly as possible. The team looked good on paper, if you did not look too closely, and it had been in a Conference championship game three out of the last four years, in 1986, 1987, and 1989, but it had not won any of them. Teams in the NFL, Belichick knew all too well, can age almost overnight.

The team's more recent drafts had not been good, and so there was not a core of good younger players coming up. There was a lack of toughness to the team, both physical and mental, Belichick believed. The contrast between the sheer strength and the attitude of the Giants, who had played at such a ferocious physical level over the last few years, and that of the Cleveland team shocked Belichick. But to the fans, the future—that is the championship—was still just around the corner. Thus the prisms through which the coach saw the team and the one through which fans and many people in the media saw the same team were completely different.

He was always cautious in talking about what the team could do. "The voice of doom," Mary Kay Cabot once called him. (Years later there would be a grudging acceptance on the part of some of the same media people who had been so hard on Belichick, that he had been more right than wrong and that most of the things he had tried to do were the right ones.) If he was not really a pessimist, he was a realist, stoic, buttoned-up, and, in that situation at least, guarded. He was also singularly uneasy playing the role of the public figure that the world of fans now demanded their coach be. This caused in him a good deal of grief in Cleveland, and might have caused him grief in New England had he not won so quickly there. That the people of Cleveland probably were more interested in his private life than they were in the private life of their mayor, he did not consider a plus. He did not have the chiseled good looks that seemed to say his character was so strong that his teams would surely win. He was neither funny nor good at one-liners in his public appearances, as fans might have hoped, and as Art Modell might have wanted. He was funny only in private.

He was a workaholic's workaholic, but then so was almost everyone else at his level in the NFL, for these were killer jobs; there was no choice but to work those hours, because everyone else was always coming after you, all of them just as hardworking and all of them wanting what you had. Sometimes it seemed that Belichick had invented his own coaching persona; he affected a fixed, rather wary face, generally seen as dour and stern in Cleveland, where he lost, and aloof and stoic in New England, where he won. It was a face that his college fraternity brothers at Wesleyan, who had elected him president, would not have recognized. The professional face was the one that he had acquired when he had first entered the League as a kid just out of college, determined to prove that he belonged there, that he was someone not to be trifled with. He tried to make his face an extension of the authority he hoped to exercise. What he had always wanted, he would say later, from the moment he had entered the League, was respect, and he had been aware how hard it was for someone so young to gain it.

As he grew older, and respect had come his way—a great deal of respect—the face had stayed much the same, however. It seemed to reflect a certain wariness that both came with the man and went with the job, the face of someone on guard. The face seemed to reflect a belief that if you relaxed too much, someone—owner, player, reporter, stranger—would take advantage of you. Unveiling your emotions might be seen as a weakness.

Behind that face, however, was another face, which appeared when he was with family and old friends and he could relax. But he was reluctant to let people from the professional world into the private one. He became angry once in Cleveland when a reporter asked a rather mild question about a tonsillectomy one of his children was undergoing; he thought it an intrusion into his family's privacy, and he brushed off the question with considerable irritation. There was, in fact, a sense of humor there—an ironic, skeptical one, to be sure—but he saw no upside in displaying it publicly; if fact, he was sure that if he did it would come back to bite him.

In Cleveland, his manner lacked any sense of the emotions required for the special relationship of the team to the city. When *Sports Illustrated* wrote a wrap-up article about Belichick's image problems in Cleveland, the writer, Ned Zeman, as if speaking to Belichick personally, made reference to "the incessant droning about how you never lighten up, about how you have all the panache of a toaster oven, about how you're not, as they say in the NFL, 'a player's coach.' "

◆ ◆ ◆

Perhaps he never had a chance in Cleveland, given the pressures and the need to win quickly. Perhaps the difference between his reality and the owner's reality was from the start too great, and so many other things would flow from that. Ernie Adams, who had, it seemed, read every book on professional football and remembered every page of every book, told his friend when he accepted the Cleveland job to be sure and put in his traveling bag a book called *PB,* which was the memoir of Paul Brown, and of which a mere twenty-three pages are devoted to how much Paul Brown hated Art Modell, and the varying sins committed by that same Modell against the coaches of the world, or at least their designated representative, Paul Brown. (Modell considered the book libelous, but did not sue.) "Don't say you weren't warned," Adams noted. "It's all spelled out." Of course, Paul Brown was not an easy man to share the stage with if you were an owner, since he had an almost pathological dislike of sharing either control or credit. Modell, newly arrived in Cleveland, was duly warned by Brown, then at the zenith of his power and reputation, not to drop in casually on the coach, that if he wanted to see him, to make an appointment. Modell failed to observe these rules. "Art was not a football person at all," Brown once said with obvious contempt. "He was from a PR firm in New York." And so Modell is depicted as constantly caught meddling, buying the players drinks, taking them to dinner, and worst of all, asking them if Paul Brown was treating them right, and, by the way, did they think that perhaps, just perhaps, Paul Brown was over the hill, that the game had passed him by. This was every coach's nightmare: the players judging the coach as opposed to the coach judging the players; the inmates running the asylum; authority based not on how well the players had played, but on whether they were pals of Modell. "I'm just a fan," Modell would say when Brown brought this up, and Brown would say, No, you're not just a fan, you're an owner. You're an owner, and you have to conduct yourself differently in public, especially with the press.

When it turned dark in Belichick's tour, and eventually it turned very dark, it was over a question of a quarterback. That, as much as anything else, did Belichick in, and used up so much of his limited power. Bernie Kosar, the quarterback, was a huge local celebrity, a kind of Mr. Cleveland. He was from Boardman, Ohio, only ninety miles away (ironically, very close to Struthers, where the Belichicks first settled), and he was seen as a hometown boy. A great college star at the University of Miami, Kosar had worked the NFL's draft regulations so that he would graduate in three years, and thus place himself in the supplemental draft. The Buffalo Bills had the first choice there, but they were willing to part with it for a mere two first-round picks, as well as a third and a sixth—a fairly handsome penalty, but one the Browns were more than eager to pay and for which they got good value. The problem was that by the time Belichick arrived, Bernie Kosar was growing old, and he had taken a terrible pounding over the years. Archie Manning, the longtime quarterback for the New Orleans Saints, who had taken a terrible pounding himself, even spoke publicly of his concerns for Kosar. The poundings that Kosar was taking, Manning said, were even worse than the ones he had taken, because the defensive players were so much bigger and faster. Even when Kosar was young, he had never been mobile, and now there was a noticeable decline in that mobility and in his arm strength, as well. If this was as yet undetected by most of the fans, it was not by Belichick and other coaches around the country.

For almost a decade Kosar had been the signature sports figure in a sports-crazed city, a much-loved figure in a community that badly needed any success in sports to compensate for a profound economic and social decline; the city was becoming something of a national joke (the Cuyahoga River was so polluted that it actually caught fire) used by comics on late night television. Kosar, shy and standoffish at first, had slowly reached out to the local media, warming to them as they warmed to him, making himself available to them in the locker room, and sometimes after work for a beer or two. In an age when tensions between athletes and reporters were growing ever sharper, a comfortable relationship with journalists could make life significantly easier—the good days on the field enhanced by that kinship, and the bad days softened. As he was good with the media, he was also good with the fans, and there were more than enough heroics on the field over the years to guarantee their admiration for not merely his considerable skills but his sheer toughness. Only an unjust fate, in the incarnation of John Elway, had deprived the Browns of a chance to play in three Super Bowls, especially in 1986. That year Kosar passed for 3854 yards and the Browns finished with a 12–4 record; they defeated the Jets, 23–20, in a double overtime divisional playoff game, one in which Kosar had passed for a playoff record of 489 yards. That brought them to the AFC championship game against the Denver Broncos, and with victory seemingly guaranteed, Cleveland had scored, and Denver had the ball on its 2-yard line with five minutes left. The weather was terrible, very windy, and seemed to favor the defense, but Elway, in one of the most famous finishes in NFL history, took the Broncos ninety-eight yards (in front of Cleveland, not Denver, fans), a drive that included three third-down plays, one of them being a third and eighteen. It was known thereafter simply as The Drive. The Browns lost and Denver went to the Super Bowl, where it was outmuscled by the powerful Giant defense, coached by this same Bill Belichick. Whatever had been wrong with Cleveland and the Cleveland Browns in recent years, it was not, in the minds of the fans, Bernie Kosar.

He seemed also, as Mary Kay Cabot said, to represent the tough, enduring blue-collar values of the city. His values were their values, and the values of their parents and grandparents, as well. He was *of* Cleveland as neither Art Modell nor Bill Belichick could ever be. Some reporters thought Kosar so popular that he might even have political ambitions—certainly he was someone that no Cleveland politician in his right mind wanted to run against. And in a certain way, although no elective office was at stake, just the right to define professional football success in that city at that time, Bill Belichick ended up running against him. Just before Belichick had taken the job, Rod Woodson, the cornerback of the archrival Pittsburgh Steelers, had said publicly of Kosar, "He's not mobile at all. Now when you look at them on your schedule, you're putting a W down before you play, because you think their offense isn't that mobile either." Probably, the Cleveland fans, or at least some of them, could have seen it, too, had they chosen to look hard enough. Unfortunately, Kosar, like so many great athletes nearing the end, was loath to admit his waning abilities; he, too, had an ego, and he felt his grasp on the team, and perhaps the city as well, threatened by this new coach who was not that much older than he was.

In the view of Belichick and his staff, there had been too many times when a receiver was open for just a brief instant and Kosar had not thrown; he had either held the ball and taken the sack or thrown elsewhere, and when he came back to the sidelines, he would say something like "I didn't think he was really open." Ernie Adams thought that meant that he knew he no longer had the necessary arm strength to fire it in there. The coaches had not been pleased with such excuses, and they felt that every defensive coordinator in the League would soon see the vulnerability. Moreover, he seemed to be challenging Belichick, or at least Belichick thought he was—going away from the game plan, not calling the plays the coach wanted, doing audibles at the line of scrimmage, so that there were occasions when as he came off the field, Belichick would be screaming at him to run the goddamn play.

Obviously there was a serious confrontation on the way. In a way, each man was challenging the other. Kosar thought Belichick was a threat to his control of the team, which had been absolute, and Belichick thought Kosar could not do the job, or at least could not do it as he wanted, and thus was a threat to his control of the team, which needed to be absolute. As things stood, he could not put together the program he wanted, the one he had promised the owner. So Belichick brought in Vinny Testaverde (ironically, the quarterback who had replaced Kosar at Miami) in 1993 before the season started, as an alternative at quarterback. Testaverde, who was the same age as Kosar (in fact, he was twelve days older), was one of the strongest and most durable quarterbacks in football, and though there might have been some grumbling among Kosar loyalists, it was seen as a legitimate coaching decision. And Testaverde started well in Cleveland, but then he injured his shoulder, and they had to go back to Kosar.

Years later, it struck Belichick that he and Kosar met at the wrong moments in each other's life, and that what happened, the confrontation, might have been avoided with a little bit of luck. If Testaverde had not gotten injured, he might have bought Belichick time to put his system in place, and a graceful passage might have been arranged for Kosar. With a break or two, Belichick might have avoided the ultimate confrontation with Kosar that cost him his acceptance there and so damaged his reputation at the critical mid-career point.

In the end he handled the fall of an icon in what was judged to be a harsh, unsentimental, and uncaring manner, as if it were nothing more than a business decision. There was one terrible moment when it finally exploded, on November 7, 1993, in a game at home against Denver. The final straw was a pass that Kosar had drawn up in the huddle and thrown to Michael Jackson for a touchdown. Afterward, in his postgame interview, Kosar took pleasure in saying that he had drawn the play up in the dirt, which was a deliberate insult to Belichick. With that, Belichick demanded the right to release him. Modell, who loved Kosar, and who had spoken of him as being like a son, reluctantly went along with it, pushed by Jim Brown, the former

Cleveland running back, who was by then a consultant to the team. Modell attended the press conference where the announcement was made, though he told Kevin Byrne, his media guy, "I know a lot of owners who would be in the south of France today."

On Monday, November 8, they cut him, and they did it with a certain brutality, as Belichick spoke of Kosar's diminished skills. For Cleveland the unthinkable had happened. He had cut their favorite son. It was huge news, the most unpopular of men had fired the most popular of men, and in some ways Belichick was probably finished in Cleveland then and there. The next morning Modell called Byrne to ask how he would characterize the *Plain Dealer* coverage. "It's JAPAN SURRENDERS," said Byrne. It was possible that that was an understatement, there being twenty-three separate stories, nine photos, including an eighteen-inch photo of Kosar on page one, and a cartoon. The headline said: "SACKED BROWNS BOUNCE BERNIE/ HE'S LOSING IT, BELICHICK SAYS/I HAVE NOT, KOSAR INSISTS/FANS IN A FRENZY."

You can be right, but sometimes when you are right you are wrong, too, which is what happened in Cleveland. There was no doubt that Belichick was right, that Kosar had essentially come to the end of his career, and that in any big game, a skilled defensive coach with a competent team could feast off Kosar's weaknesses. But the brutality of the way it was done was unacceptable. Years later, Belichick faulted himself on the way he had handled it. He left those passionate local fans who might have agreed with him no place to go. He thought he was just doing his job, but he had been mistaken; he had defined his job too narrowly.

So it was a Pyrrhic victory, at least in Cleveland. Belichick had never intended to be popular—a successful coach was not necessarily popular, and a good coach always had to do a lot of unpleasant things that worked against his popularity, especially in an age of free agency—but the savagery of the response was beyond anyone's expectations. The media by and large took Kosar's side. That began the "Bill Must Go" chants, which rained down, not just during the games, but afterward, outside the trailer from which he broadcast his postgame show, near the locker room. The fans would gather there, shouting that he had to go, and sometimes they even beat against the trailer itself in a sort of Bill-Must-Go rhythm, so that it seemed as though the trailer were under siege.

Belichick was stoic, and he did not give in to the pressure, did not even admit it was there. His response, typically Belichickian, was just to work harder. Some of the Cleveland reporters, watching this man under such unbearable pressure, without, it seemed, any kind of safety valves of his own, wondered what would happen if he ever had to face the pressure of a Super Bowl, and they concluded he would implode under the relentless pressure of that event. "And of course we were completely wrong," said Tony Grossi, who wrote for the *Plain Dealer*. "When it came time, and he went there, he handled it perfectly, and more important, so did his teams."

It was almost like a football lynching, and it became uncommonly personal; in the media the fans criticized his looks, his dress, his overall manner. It was so toxic that it seemed he had tapped into something deep and dark and angry in this city (and America as well; Cleveland, one had to know, might be different, but it was not that different from the rest of the country), little of it probably in the long run about football. Rather, it was the product of myriad other disappointments, personal and economic and social, but, somehow, the continued failure of a not very good football team, a group of strangers who were not viewed as strangers, became the focal point for so much rage; the alternative, one assistant coach privately noted, was probably to beat your wife. What was ironic about the 1993 season, which they finished 7–9, was that they had actually started at 5–2 before Testaverde went down. In 1994, they did better, finishing 11–5, and went to the playoffs, but it was too late. Art Modell was in financial trouble and was fast approaching bankruptcy; in 1995, when he moved during the season, the team collapsed.

◆◆◆

If there was one great lesson Belichick learned in this era, it was one that was primarily about the players. It could be called the Lawrence Taylor Lesson, and it had begun in New York and finished in Cleveland. Lawrence Taylor, the great Giant linebacker, was arguably the greatest football player of his era. He played fearlessly, indeed recklessly, with little concern for his own physical safety. It was around him that the great Giant linebacker core had been built, and it was around the great linebacker core that the magnificent Giant defenses were created, upon which so much of the Giants' success of the late eighties and early nineties depended. His ability, the fact that he played at a level above everyone else, was obvious from the start. Bob Schnelker, the Green Bay Packers' offensive coach, told his players before a game in Taylor's rookie season, "Guys, let me tell you. I've seen Butkus. I've seen Nitschke. I've seen 'em all. He's better than all of 'em."

But, if getting a player of Taylor's magnitude was the rarest thing for any coach, let alone a young assistant coach, it also presented a dilemma. For if he played on the edge, beyond the capabilities of other players, he lived over the edge; he broke team rules, he drank excessively, he did increasingly dangerous amounts of drugs, and he womanized openly and increasingly carelessly. What players did with women was their business, it was believed in the NFL, but Taylor's womanizing began to interfere with his work; there was one memorable episode, which he described in his autobiography, when he had shared an evening with a woman who somehow managed to place him in handcuffs and then left their hotel room, taking the key with her. The next day, still handcuffed, and wearing a loose sweater to hide the cuffs, he walked into the team meeting before the game. "What kind of bracelets you wearing?" a puzzled Carl Banks had asked him that morning, hearing an unusually noisy rattle coming from his wrists.

His drug habit was costing $600 and $700 a pop, several times a week, but he believed he could handle it. "Taylor controls the drugs, the drugs don't control Taylor," he would tell worried friends. He had teammates who were squeaky clean, such as Butch Woolfolk, take the periodic urine tests for him, and he would often show up for meetings, after a one-night stand, reeking of alcohol, despite having just swallowed a bottle of Scope. For the Giant coaches the dilemma was a serious one: There was one set of rules for the other players and another set for Lawrence Taylor. He did not study the playbook, but he did not have to—it all seemed to come to him intuitively; he showed up at meetings, sometimes still drunk, or hungover at the very least, wearing dark glasses and a hat pulled down over his face; on occasion he slept through defensive-team meetings.

That there were two sets of rules bothered the coaches, because it undermined their authority; it meant they were being bent by his sheer talent. But they accepted him for what he was, and the players accepted him, too—any dissent from them was a light murmur of protest, and there was a consensus that because he was the great LT, and because the team needed him so badly, and because he played so hard on Sunday and was in many ways such a good teammate, they were all willing to make an exception. A coach would tamper with him at his own risk.

They were all aware that Taylor was different, that he played with such recklessness you could not expect him to do the mundane things that other players had to do; it was part of his special quality that you had to let him be himself, that the man who played a free-spirited game on Sunday could do it only because he was a free spirit during the week. To come down too heavily on him might cause him to lose his instinct for the game, or perhaps even his love of it, which was equally important. He played well beyond the normal limits of pain, and after he retired, when someone asked him if he missed the game, he said that the one thing he did not miss was his body sounding like popcorn when he got up in the morning and walked to the bathroom.

If Taylor's relationship with Parcells was exceptionally good—it was as if the head coach knew exactly how to motivate him—then his relationship with Belichick was less successful. To Taylor, Belichick was a ball-buster, a little guy from some place called Wesleyan, who had never played a down of real football and who held all these meetings telling him how to do things that Taylor did by instinct. It was not an easy job to try and discipline Taylor, Belichick thought; everyone else applauded him and had always applauded his on-field heroics, first in college, and now in the pros—the fans, the media, the coaches, and of course his teammates. But while his teammates applauded, they were also uneasy with the double standard that existed in terms of player behavior. Taylor would attend the meetings during the week, but he was often not really there, not really paying attention. There was in fact a small inner coach-player war going on, Taylor on occasion sleeping during a defensive team meeting, waking up to see Belichick staring at him, and Taylor sometimes stomping out, saying memorably, "You either get me on Thursday or you get me on Sunday." Then, on Sunday, when the Giants went through their pregame drills, he would, as Ernie Adams loved to note, "sit there in the locker room as Bill went through this detailed game plan, always so brilliant, of course, always so prescient: They do such and such on first down, and such and such on second down. He'd have all their tendencies down pat, and of course, he'd have them better than anyone in the League. Then they would go out on the field for their pregame warm-up, and then as they came off the field for one last session in the locker room, Taylor would amble over to Belichick and say, 'Hey Bill, now tell me, what the fuck these guys run off of? And what the fuck are we going to do to stop them?' " You would not know, thought Adams, whether it was true that LT did not really know the game plan or whether he was just zinging the coach.

Belichick would sometimes say of Taylor that the only time he was fun to coach was on Sunday, when he was magnificent. Taylor was always looking for an edge, Adams thought, even with his own coach—perhaps especially with his own coach. The byplay between the two was great fun to watch, thought Adams, probably for everyone but Belichick, but it was also in the end a game, and there were two givens to it: Belichick knew that Taylor was going to play his best (except in his drug-diminished period when he was on occasion not the player he was supposed to be), and Taylor knew that Belichick was going to come up with a game plan that gave him an edge.

But Belichick was bothered by it all, especially as Taylor began to spin out of control with greater and greater drug use; he thought the team ought to do something, if only for Taylor's sake. But he had been waved off by Parcells, who had a special relationship with Taylor, and Belichick knew that it was the head coach's decision to make. Even though he was aware there would be a price to be paid someday, he went along with it. And there was a price to be paid: In 1986 Taylor's world collapsed because of his drug use, and he had to check himself into a clinic to get clean. Later, after Taylor's years in the NFL were over, Belichick thought there were three separate Taylor careers: 1981, when he was brilliant; 1982–87, when he was brilliant but erratic; and after 1987, when he was completely in control of his almost unparalleled natural abilities.

At Cleveland, Belichick had inherited some veteran players who wanted to bend the rules just a little. Because he had been softened slightly by the Taylor experience, he allowed them to do it. The difference was with Taylor you always got something back, more often than not an inspired game; it was different in Cleveland, where what you got back was players who found that they could bend the rules only to show the other players that the rules could be bent. What Belichick decided after he left Cleveland was that if he ever got another head coaching job, there would be one set of rules for everyone, that he would go for players who had both talent and character, and if there was a great player like Taylor, a unique player who created a unique problem, he would deal with it sooner, rather than later.

Cleveland had ended badly; when Modell announced the move to Baltimore early in the season, the team virtually gave up. Belichick watched from the sidelines during one of the games that followed and turned to an assistant and said, "We don't really have a team out there anymore." In the final game there, against Cincinnati, the fans sitting in what was called the Dog Pound—fans often spoken of by commentators as being among the most passionate in pro football—started throwing things on the field, not as one might expect, paper and plastic cups, but heavy things, even the seats they had been sitting in, which they had somehow gotten loose—apparently they had ingeniously brought their own wrenches to the stadium.

But the Cleveland years would turn out to be invaluable. In fact, they were the foundation of Belichick's future success. He had started there virtually alone—none of the New York people had gone with him—so he had had to bring his own people in. Out of that came

Belichick University, the young men he had spotted and brought in and tutored and who came to see the game as he saw it and who became the core of his system. They were mostly like him: Not-great players from less famous schools, they were hungry now to be a part of the game at a level that had somehow eluded them as boys. Their love of the game equaled his, and they were willing to put aside their egos—that was rule number one—as he put aside his.

Cleveland was wounding and disappointing, but it did not change him. He might adapt, but he would not change. He was, his friends thought, quite sure he would get another head coaching job—he had done too well for so long not to get another chance. He was too confident of his abilities to think he would get only one shot. Certainly, anyone examining the Cleveland record would decide that whatever the reasons for failure there, it was hardly a final judgment against him as a coach. But if he was going to get another chance, his friends thought, he would surely want it to be in a situation where he felt comfortable with the owner and where he had a fair shot at developing his own program in an acceptable time frame. He did not want to be known merely as a defensive genius, a brilliant coordinator, who somehow lacked the human skills to be a head coach. If he failed a second time—and whatever his sense of the forces that worked against him in Cleveland, he had failed there—then he would have to succeed the next time, or he would be consigned to a life as a permanent coordinator; that, or be offered head coaching jobs in horrendous situations where he could not possibly win.

◆◆◆

Years later, after one of his Super Bowl wins, a reporter asked Belichick what he had learned in Cleveland. "Not to move your team to another city in the middle of a season," he answered.

CHAPTER ELEVEN

Cleveland done with, Bill Belichick went back to working with Bill Parcells in New England, this time as assistant head coach. For all the tensions simmering just underneath the surface, they still needed each other. Parcells, who had been flirting with Tampa Bay, among other teams, at the end of his New York tour, ended up taking over a weak New England team, which had gone 2–14 the year before he arrived. There he had quickly begun to work his specialty: the quick rehabilitation of teams embedded near the bottom of the standings. In 1993, New England went to 5–11, and in 1994, 10–6. In those years for the first time, a Parcells-coached team, New England, had played a Belichick team, Cleveland. They split four games 2–2 but in the one that mattered the most, a 1994 playoff game (called by some the Bill Bowl, since aficionados were well aware of the complex relationship between the two coaches), the Browns won, 20–13. The

Cleveland defense shut down the Patriot running game, limiting them to fifty-seven yards on the ground, and then forced Drew Bledsoe, appearing in his first playoff game, to throw far more than any Parcells quarterback was normally allowed to—fifty times, for a total of only 235 yards, an average gain of 4.7 yards per pass; the afternoon had yielded him one touchdown and three interceptions. The next year the Patriots slipped back to 6 and 10. In 1996, with Belichick out of work, and Parcells needing a great assistant, Belichick joined his former boss in New England.

He did so with a certain misgiving. He knew better than anyone what it was like to work for Bill Parcells, and he knew there was a roller coaster quality to it. Good days were followed by bad days, when he was very tough on you; his tongue could sting you in front of others, even if it was followed by some form of muted apology. The problem was never his football intelligence, which was very high, but the changing moods and the way he treated underlings. But the tour turned out to be the easiest of their three shared coaching experiences. They got on very well, and there was less bark to Parcells, possibly, Belichick thought, because his 6–10 record the previous season had underscored his need for his old partner.

The only difficult part was an escalating battle between the New England owner, Bob Kraft, and Parcells. Thus, Belichick often found himself if not exactly the mediator, then certainly the messenger between two men who had come to despise each other. But that Patriot team did exceptionally well, going 11–5 in the regular season, before beating a strong Pittsburgh team, 28–3, and the Jacksonville Jaguars, 20–6, in the AFC championship game. In the Jacksonville game they limited the Jaguars' running game and forced two interceptions from Mark Brunell. The Super Bowl week was something of a zoo, filled with rumors that Parcells was about to leave and go to another team, most likely the ever-floundering New York Jets. A very strong Green

Bay team, with Brett Favre at the absolute height of his abilities, beat them 35–21, and Parcells did not fly back to Boston on the team plane.

Parcells then left for New York in what was a comedy of charges and countercharges over the legality of his departure. There ensued a bitter struggle between the Jets and the Patriots, and the arrival on the scene of what seemed like platoons of lawyers, and in time, compensation to the Patriots, of a goodly number of Jet draft choices. Belichick decided to follow Parcells to New York, though he had gotten on rather well with Kraft, who he thought was an astute businessman eager to learn about football. Belichick understood that no matter how decent a personal relationship he had formed with the owner and no matter how badly he wanted the job that year, the tensions with Parcells had been so great that Kraft wanted the entire Parcells team gone, in order to make a fresh start. In the brief period that the League, the Jets, and the Patriots were working out the compensation that would free Parcells from his New England contract, Belichick was actually the Jets head coach, and he got the equivalent of a coach's contract.

If things had worked well between the two men in New England, that would not be the case with their third partnership, in New York with the often woebegone Jets. This time the relationship was more difficult than ever. Parcells's tongue was sharper than ever. There was talk about the Cleveland Mafia, that is, Belichick and the people who had been close to him in Cleveland, most notably Eric Mangini, a young defensive coach whom Belichick had reached out for, and Scott Pioli, the aspiring player personnel man (who was, ironically enough, starting to date Parcells's daughter, Dallas, in those days, thus a man caught in a doubly difficult position). There were Parcells guys as well, including Dan Henning, a quarterback coach. Lines were drawn between the two camps. One young assistant from the Parcells side was told he was spending too much time with the Cleveland Mafia.

There was one terrible moment, during a game, when Belichick called a blitz, and Parcells seemed to oppose it. They went ahead with it and the blitz worked—the other team did what Belichick had expected, not what Parcells had—but Parcells was furious, and over the open microphones in the middle of a game, he let go: "Yeah, you're a genius, everyone knows it, a goddamn genius, but that's why you failed as a head coach—that's why you'll never be a head coach . . . some genius." It was deeply shocking to everyone who heard it; they were the cruelest words imaginable.

When they were both there, the Jets improved, going 9–7 in 1997, 12–4 in 1998 to win their division, but then slipping to 8–8 in 1999. Then it all came to a head. Leon Hess, the owner of the Jets, had died, and the team was for sale. There was great uncertainty over the future and what Parcells's role was going to be. In New England, Kraft was disenchanted with his coach Pete Carroll (who would soon coach a series of national champion college teams at USC), and he let it be known that he wanted to hire Belichick as his head coach, saying in passing that he never should have let him go in the first place.

◆ ◆ ◆

Bob Kraft was arguably one of the smartest new owners in the League, a very skillful businessman who had taken a successful but relatively small paper company owned by his wife's family and turned it into one of the most important paper companies in the country. He was also football obsessed, having played for Columbia on its lightweight teams as a college student, and having been a longtime Patriots season ticket holder. He was one of several suitors for the Patriot franchise when it was being sold back and forth in the late eighties, and managed to become the owner by shrewdly buying the stadium itself. He had started out rather typically as the fan as owner, somewhat of an innocent at first, but he was also an acute businessman who always sought value for his money. If his status in the Boston community was greatly enhanced by dint of owning a football team (most very successful businessmen are reasonably anonymous—and their faces, unlike those of people in the worlds of sports and entertainment, are rarely their signatures), he nonetheless intended to be successful at it, both in terms of games won and in the game's finances as well.

He might unconsciously at first make more of an emotional commitment to some of the players than he later thought was wise (notably to Drew Bledsoe), but in the end he intended to run the team as a business. His questions were often quite searching, and what he did not know at the start was not going to be a problem for very long, because he was an exceptionally quick study. His relationship with his first coach, Bill Parcells (he had not chosen Parcells as a coach and Parcells had not chosen him as an owner), was an absolute disaster.

By contrast Kraft and Belichick got on quite well—Kraft thought that Belichick was helpful with a novice owner, a good teacher as it were, and found that he could learn a great deal about the game from Belichick, and Belichick considered Kraft a shrewd and thoughtful businessman. One of the areas where they discovered that their attitudes intersected was on the concept of value required for a given player in the era of both salary cap and free agency. The salary cap was very important in the way Kraft looked at the game—it was a ceiling that all owners, the very, very rich and the merely very rich, had to live with. Kraft had become an owner only after the salary cap was imposed; if there had been no salary cap, he would not have bought in, because then it would have been a question of which owner could pay the most for the largest number of players, a competition among the super rich he wanted no part of.

One of the things that impressed him in his early talks with Belichick, when the latter was an assistant head coach in New England, was that Belichick seemed to think much the same way, and could break the team down, player by player, and give a knowing estimate of the value received for each player. Belichick had come up with his own philosophy of how to operate in the current NFL; he seemed wary of throwing big money at available superstar players. A truly great player, one who completely altered a given game, a Lawrence Taylor, he said, came along very rarely. The right model was to scout well, both in the draft and free agency, and create a team with a lot of good players, in effect a team with a significant amount of depth and as many interchangeable parts as possible. It was important to figure out how much a player—or a position—was worth in the contemporary game, because each salary potentially subtracted from every other salary. That view made Belichick a coach who was far ahead of the curve, Kraft decided. He had already checked around the League and decided that most other coaches wanted all the star players they could get, and wanted them on the roster immediately. The mantra of the coaches, always so close to being fired, was *I've got to have him . . . and I've got to have him now . . .*

Years later Kraft, who by then had become a good deal more expert about the League, would decide that Belichick was very different from most other coaches, first because he made it his business to know as much as he could about the cap, and second, because unlike most head coaches, who felt enormous pressure to win and win quickly, he did not instinctively want to pour all his resources into his team as quickly as he could, and did not think that the future was now, and took care not to become, as the phrase went, capped out, trading the future for the present. Instead he understood that the way to deal with the cap was to create a system and to play for the future as well as the present. He was the rare coach who understood that in order to succeed as a coach you had to be a businessman as well and know the cap and its long-range consequences. He did not want to throw money at seemingly dazzling players who might bring a team a quick fix and then a long downward descent, but who might also regard their big-ticket free-agent salary as a reward long due them, while at the same time throwing your own team's salary structure—and emotional balance—out of whack. Pro football had never been a place for coaches who were sentimental; in the era of the salary cap sentiment became even more of a weakness.

When Kraft and Parcells parted in uncommon acrimony, Kraft had a sense that Belichick badly wanted the head coaching job. But Kraft's animosity toward Parcells was so great that it affected Belichick as well—guilt by association, Kraft would say later. He did not know how complicated the internal dynamic between Parcells and Belichick was, but he was sure that he did not want to hire a man who could have worked with Bill Parcells so closely for so long. Later he faulted himself for not knowing that the coach he would eventually want was the one who was already working for him. Kraft knew there was a certain back-channel word about Belichick, which was that he was a brilliant coordinator but doomed to be that and nothing more. (Belichick hated that, and hated the fact that George Young, when he was the general manager of the Giants, had bad-mouthed him when jobs as a head coach opened up.) Kraft decided to hire Belichick.

◆◆◆

With New England coming after Belichick, Parcells decided to make Belichick the head coach. But Belichick was not entirely comfortable with the game plan: Would he coach in the shadow of Parcells? Would someone like Parcells, so driven and active, ever really decide to retire? Who would really be in charge of football operations? How much freedom would a head coach under Parcells have? In addition, who would the owner be? The choice seemed to be between a wealthy man named Robert Wood Johnson IV, an heir to a medical supply company, and the Dolan family, who ran the New York cable business and would go on to do a horrendous job with the New York basketball and hockey teams, both famous for inflated payrolls and poor performances. Neither potential owner impressed Belichick. Parcells, having resigned, now said his resignation had preempted New England's right to talk to Belichick. For his deputy to leave, Parcells said, it would take some kind of trade—that is, draft choices. It was all beginning to turn into a bad soap opera.

Belichick was aware that this was a critical career moment. He was no longer a boy wonder; he was forty-seven, and all of his dues in the League had been paid and then some. It was critical, in his mind, that he not fail, for if he failed a second time, no matter whose fault, no matter how extenuating the circumstances, he was likely to be typecast as a permanent number two—a defensive coordinator for life.

The contracts Belichick and Parcells had with the Jets were unclear—both of them, it seemed, had the right to run the team. Belichick was supposed to take over if Parcells left, but now Parcells was both leaving and staying. Belichick wanted badly to succeed on his own, and if he had to fail, he wanted to do that on his own; he did not want to fail because he was blocked in doing the things he wanted by other men. What followed was a strange episode that reflected many of the complicated undercurrents in the convoluted Belichick-Parcells relationship. Having been named head coach one day (a job most of the media thought he would jump at), Belichick held a crowded press conference the next day to announce, in a fifty-five-minute performance, which was judged a bit bizarre, that he had turned the job down. Parcells, now apparently the general manager, demanded compensation from the Patriots. For a time it seemed to be a hopeless tangle of interests and emotions. Then Parcells placed a call to Kraft, his archenemy, saying that it was Darth Vader calling, and he broke the logjam on compensation, with the Jets getting three draft choices, including a first-round draft choice for 2000.

With that Parcells and Belichick finally parted. Theirs had been an immensely complicated relationship, beneficial but difficult for both men. It went on in different forms and in three separate venues for some two decades, never easy, despite the exceptional rewards. In the end, the more successful the relationship was professionally, the more that both men, in different ways, felt prisoners of it; finally less was resolved between them than at the beginning and it was mutually diminishing.

CHAPTER TWELVE

When he got the New England job in time for the 2000 season, Bill Belichick was well aware that this might be the last best chance for him. Therefore he was determined to do it right and to learn from Cleveland. Someone once asked Mary Kay Cabot, the football beat reporter for the *Cleveland Plain Dealer,* what had happened in Cleveland compared to what had happened in New England, and she answered, "He got to make all his mistakes here and to learn from them there." There was a fair amount of truth in that.

In New England the first thing he was determined to do was place his own people in all the critical positions. This time he wanted Scott Pioli to handle player personnel. Pioli was probably the first truly certified graduate of Belichick University, a young man who had learned football entirely through Belichick's prism. When Belichick had coached in Cleveland, Pioli was just a notch above an intern, running off to the airport to pick up film or a visiting free agent, but he had impressed everyone around him with his talent and energy.

Pioli and Belichick first connected in 1987, right after the first Giants Super Bowl victory. Pioli was from Washingtonville, New York, near West Point, and when the two men met, he was a player himself, at Central Connecticut, not exactly one of the mightiest of the region's football teams. Though Belichick was not yet technically famous, he was famous in certain circles, among other NFL coaches and scouts and people who were passionate Giant fans. Pioli was working evenings back then, but during the summer he started commuting to the Giant practices every day, just to watch; the round-trip drive totaled three and sometimes four hours a day. He was twenty-one at the time, with one year of college left, and he was not, even in his own estimation, a particularly good player. All he had was a love of the game. By chance, a young woman he knew worked in security for the Giants and was a friend of Belichick's, so one day she introduced Pioli to Belichick, who was thirty-five at the time. As they talked, Belichick sensed the young man's passion for the game, and on the spur of the moment, he suggested that Pioli come stay with Belichick and Al Groh, another assistant coach, in the tiny dorm room they were sharing at Fairleigh Dickinson College, where the practices were being held. Pioli could sleep on the couch. Why he had made that offer, Pioli never knew; nor for that matter did Belichick, although, as he noted, when he looked at Pioli, it was a little like looking at himself twelve years earlier.

That was a great summer for Pioli; he absorbed more football from two very good coaches than he could ever have imagined, and it made him more determined than ever to become a coach when he graduated from college. This was not entirely welcome news in the Pioli home; his mother wanted him to become an accountant, and she burst into tears when she heard the news, while his father, who worked for the telephone company installing phone lines—often a hard, unpleasant job that he hated—was thrilled, because he wanted his son to find a job that gave him the kind of pleasure he himself had never found in work. Pioli went from college to Syracuse, where he became a graduate assistant, doing some scouting (and running into Steve Belichick, whom he considered by far the best prepared scout he had ever met on the road). He kept in touch with Belichick, but was careful not to exploit their still-new friendship. In time, he found a job at Murray State University in Kentucky. He did two years at Murray State, long enough to convince himself that his talent lay in recruiting and player personnel work. He was anxious to get back into the professional game, and he wrote a bunch of letters (none to Belichick) looking for work, and, in time, he was offered a job scouting in San Francisco by the Forty-Niners. This was in 1992. Belichick, by then at Cleveland, heard about the San Francisco job, and told Pioli to fly out to Cleveland, where he would have a job. Pioli said he could not do that, that he had accepted the job with the Forty-Niners and that he had pushed them very hard for it—the San Francisco job was for $24,000. Pioli then flew to Cleveland, where he and Belichick had dinner at a restaurant. Art Modell was at a nearby table. "I don't know what the job is yet, but I'm offering you one," Belichick said. The salary, and Belichick never overpaid, for part of the challenge he liked to give young, would-be assistants was an austerity test, was $16,000 a year, $8,000 less than the San Francisco offer. Pioli chose Cleveland over San Francisco. Pioli started to thank him, but Belichick brushed away the thanks. "Thank me by doing a good job," he said. Then he added what might well be the motto of Belichick University: "The more you can do, the more you can do," which meant that if you did well, you would be rewarded with a good deal more work.

Pioli was thus witness to the difficulties and eventual failure of the Belichick team in Cleveland; a lot of it had not been their fault, he believed, but some of it was, especially in terms of player personnel—they were saying one thing in terms of the kind of players they wanted, but, because of the intense pressure to win and win quickly, they were choosing players who were very different. That was true, he thought, with some of their draft choices and their free agent selections. Free agency was a new and important part of the game; it relieved a coach of depending totally upon the draft, but it also made a successful team's roster vulnerable, and it was soon coupled with something else new: a salary cap. The cap bound every player personnel decision to every other one—what you paid Peter took away from Paul. A decade later, Bill Belichick (along with Scott Pioli, by then his player personnel man, and Bob Kraft, the New England owner) headed a team that handled player personnel and the salary cap with exceptional shrewdness, perhaps the best at it in the League.

That had not been true in Cleveland. Then it had been too much like recruiting in college, Pioli thought. The free agent would be flown in, always first class. He would be met at the airport by a limo and taken to the best hotel in town. Then they would wine and dine him at a steak house that night. Pioli decided that the wrong signals were being given. "You're not going to treat them with limos once they've signed," he once told Belichick. "Why wine them and dine them at fancy places, when we're really meat and potatoes?" They should want to come to Cleveland to play football under the Belichick system, not for these artificial trappings. Belichick had been thinking much the same way and immediately agreed with Pioli. They both decided they had been going after the wrong players in the wrong way, and it was time to stop. In the future, they decided, they would not blow any smoke, and it would either work or not work, but character and a willingness to fit into the system would be of the essence, not just ability. Thank Cleveland for that lesson.

When Belichick took the New England job, one of the first things he did was to move Scott Pioli into player personnel. Both he and Belichick arrived in February 2000, in time for the 2000 draft. There were still some holdovers from the old regime working in Foxboro, Massachusetts, including Bobby Grier, who had done player personnel and who had famously tangled with Bill Parcells over a wide receiver named Terry Glenn, a player Grier had wanted who had caused no amount of coaching heartache when he finally arrived. At first, under the new regime, Grier was the chief player personnel man, and Pioli was listed as his assistant. But it was an uncomfortable situation, made more difficult by the fact that the Patriots already had their draft board up, with their likely choices circled; unfortunately, the scouts were those of the old regime, men who did not know what type of player Belichick and Pioli wanted.

Belichick soon discovered that the team he was taking over was not in good shape. He was, in fact, shocked at how much it had deteriorated in such a short time. There was, as he had found at Cleveland, a lack of mental and physical toughness. He knew he had to change that, but this time he was not as hard on the players as he had been in Cleveland. He had learned to show more patience in a difficult situation. As in Cleveland, some of the good players were getting too old. In addition, the players they had gotten in recent drafts were not very good. The cap situation was bad, seriously bloated. The new owner, Bob Kraft, was still learning, and right before the season started, he asked Ernie Adams, "Don't you think we have a good team, and we can go to the playoffs?" Adams was torn whether to tell the truth at once, or let him find it out over a sixteen-game schedule; he opted for the cold-shower truth. "No, no we don't—we don't have the players," he said. It was probably, Adams later decided, a little worse than that. The opening game with Tampa Bay was a kind of slaughter, and no one seemed to be able, or perhaps to want, to block defensive tackle Warren Sapp.

If there was even the slightest sign of a turnaround in that first season, it came during a practice before the fourth game. They were using a defensive end named Bobby Hamilton, who had been a reserve on the Jets, and there was a crack-back block on him, a receiver coming over and getting him when he was effectively blind to where the blocker had come from. It was the responsibility of the defensive back to warn Hamilton, but he didn't, so Hamilton completely lost control, wanting to kill the defensive back. It was a wild scene, but the coaches saw it as a healthy one—the first sign of a pulse, the first sign that they might have real football players. It was the day, one of the other coaches noted, that Belichick smiled for the first time all season. The season ended 5–11, which was not good; it was the same record the Belichick team had posted in his farewell season in Cleveland.

The next year, 2001, the draft was better. They picked Richard Seymour, a defensive lineman from Georgia, a great player, the sixth pick overall, and Matt Light, an offensive lineman from Purdue. The best moment in the draft, Ernie Adams thought, came when Belichick offered to explain to Kraft why he was picking both Seymour and Light, and the owner waved him off. "Bill, I just want you to do what you think is right," Kraft said. That kind of confidence, voiced by the owner, was a big plus. There were, in addition, some good free-agent pickups, players who were not necessarily great on their own, and whose original teams had lost interest in them, but who might be perfect for Belichick's system: Mike Vrabel, a linebacker from Ohio State who had originally been drafted by the Steelers; David Patten, a wide receiver who seemed better than his statistics suggested, and who had once played for the Giants; and Joe Andruzzi, an offensive lineman who had never quite made it, but had been on the Green Bay Packer roster.

That draft would turn out to be good for the Belichick system, producing the kind of players both Pioli and Belichick had talked about. In 2000, they had not been ready, and the one bright spot, their pick of Tom Brady in the sixth round, had been a fluke. At least that had shown they were lucky. That mattered. To win in the National Football League you had to be good, but you also had to be lucky. Picking Brady was, in no small part, Pioli's decision, and it showed his willingness to take a chance. The Patriots had picked Brady in the sixth round, and he soon turned out to be one of the two or three best quarterbacks in the League, and absolutely perfect for the Belichick system and for the team's offense. So, as the team continued to make a series of very good calls on other player personnel choices, there was a general tendency to talk about how brilliant Pioli and Belichick were, and to regard Pioli as the best young player personnel man in the League. Just to remind himself not to believe all the hype and that he could readily have screwed up on that draft, Pioli kept on his desk a photo of Brady, along with a photo of the team's fifth-round draft choice, the man whom he had taken ahead of Brady: Dave Stachelski. He was a tight end from Boise State who never played a down for New England. Stachelski was taken with the 141st pick, Brady with the 199th one. "If I was so smart," Pioli liked to say, "I wouldn't have risked an entire round of the draft in picking Brady."

Tom Brady was absolute proof of the sheer mystery involved in scouting in the NFL. He had arrived at Michigan from San Mateo, California. In his first two years he had been beaten out by two very good college quarterbacks, Scott Dreisbach and Brian Griese. As a result, he felt very frustrated, and became, in his own words, "a whiner. Nothing was my fault, and finally I told Coach [Lloyd] Carr that I wanted to transfer to Cal. He said, 'Put everything out of your mind and worry about making yourself better.' " Brady became the starter at Michigan in his sophomore year (but his third year in school), and he did very well, leading the Wolverines to a 10–3 record, a share of the Big Ten title, and a victory over Arkansas in the Citrus Bowl. That was good at Michigan, but perhaps not good enough, because the next year, when he was a junior, his job was once again in jeopardy. One of the most highly recruited athletes in the country, a Michigan boy named Drew Henson, had chosen Michigan. Henson was far more celebrated than Brady, and it was believed by many Michigan fans, even before he entered college, that he was the vastly superior player, a kind of poster boy for the future of the Michigan program. *Sports Illustrated* had already written a five-page, 2800-word article on how good he was at both football and baseball, the headline of which was "Golden Boy." ("Michigan-bound quarterback and Yankee bonus baby Drew Henson—who also averaged 22 points in basketball and 4.0 in the classroom—is almost too good to be true," read the subhead.) Every college in the country, it seemed, had gone after Henson and as the *Sports Illustrated* piece noted, Bobby Bowden at Florida State, the coach of one of the country's ranking football powers, had gone so far as to promise not to recruit another quarterback for two years if Henson chose the Seminoles. He was an icon before he threw his first college pass.

The object of all that attention was all of eighteen years old at the time, but already, as the *Sports Illustrated* writer, Leigh Montville, noted, if you typed out his name on Yahoo!, there were 161,256 matches for him. Whether this kind of hype was good for Henson, a young man whose full athletic gifts had obviously accrued at a startlingly young age, well ahead of most of his peers, was one question, and whether it was good for the incumbent quarterback, Tom Brady, was quite another, and an equally obvious one. Almost immediately, even before the season began, the question of whether Brady could or should be allowed to hold his job was hotly debated by serious football fans throughout the state, all of whom seemed to know that Henson was better, that he was more mobile, and had a better arm. Lloyd Carr, the Michigan coach, seemed to stir the competition a bit by saying of Henson, before the season even started, "Without doubt, he's the most talented quarterback I've ever been around." But, somehow, Brady managed to hold his job, though for a time the coaches rotated them—Brady would start and, as Belichick later noted, "He'd do well, and get them a lead, and then he'd be replaced by Henson, who didn't do as well, and then they'd bring back Brady and he'd do well again. It was as if he was doing well but even so they didn't want him."

It was not easy. Even if Brady did well in a game, when Henson came in for him there were thundering cheers, not in appreciation of Brady, but because the real quarterback was now on the field. Brady ended up playing out his final year somewhat in Henson's shadow, as if no matter what he achieved, Henson could have done it better. To much of the public he was something of an interloper, a nice young man who was holding back the real star. There was already an assumption that Henson was the player the pros really wanted, and there was some talk, when Henson finally got the job and did quite well, that he would go in the top five and quite possibly be the top pick overall when he finished college and entered the draft. That was something that never happened, because he chose to play baseball in the Yankee organization after his junior year, making some $5 million in a prolonged minor league career, before deciding that baseball was not his sport and turning back to football.

Since the fuss over Henson had obscured Brady's own fine performance at Michigan, no one, including the people in the Patriots office who finally drafted him, had any idea of the exceptional qualities that set him apart, of his uncommon character, his fierce determination to excel, his high intelligence, and his rare inner toughness. Instead, they knew that he was quite tall, which was good because size was important, was obviously intelligent, though how intelligent they were still to find out, and that his teammates responded to his leadership. There were certain questions about him—his mechanics were a bit flawed, and he was a little skinny, for he had not built his body up. His arm strength was thought to be acceptable but not exceptional, and both his footwork and his overall speed left something to be desired. Then there were the doubts that had been created by the fact that he split time with Henson—had he really been good enough to be the quarterback on his own college team?

In truth, some of the Michigan players actually preferred Brady, as did some of the coaches, who were not sure, for all the hype and his superior athletic skills, that Henson was the better football player. Dick Rehbein, the quarterback coach, had gone out to Ann Arbor and had spent some time with Brady and had quite liked him. For Belichick, there was one tantalizing statistic about him: In the two years when he had started, his record as a starter was 20–5, and he was playing most of those games in one of the toughest conferences in the country. In addition, there was a second Bowl game victory in there, this time against Alabama in the Orange Bowl, which Michigan had won. His arm might not be what the pros hoped for, but there was something hidden away there that was of immense value: his game-time judgment. Somehow, once a game was under way, his game was better than his body; he made good decisions on the field under pressure, and his touchdown-to-interception ratio was admirable, better in his last year than the previous one. That led to an interesting judgment about Brady's character: Here was a young man who had been caught in an extremely difficult situation, knowing that he had a job that he could easily lose, and yet he had handled the situation with savvy and maturity that went well beyond his years; he had not cracked under pressure, but rather rose to meet the challenge.

◆◆◆

On the second day of the draft, when they did the fourth, fifth, and sixth rounds, his name was still on their board, and though they were already carrying three quarterbacks, including Drew Bledsoe, the team's star, they decided Brady simply represented too much value to pass up. Still, there was no sign of the greatness to come, or that a little more than a year later serious football people would be comparing him to Joe Montana. "If anyone from this office tells you that, that he spotted back then what Tom was going to be," Pioli said, "he's simply lying."

Brady himself had expected to go in the fourth round—going in the sixth stunned him—and he took it as a personal challenge and became even more determined to turn himself into a quality NFL quarterback. No one, he decided, was going to work harder. That was what surprised us the most, Ernie Adams said, and it was there from the very start. It would have been very easy for a player who had already done well in college but who was now listed as the number four quarterback to lose heart. Adams and the other coaches had all seen young quarterbacks, accustomed to being at the center of things and hearing the cheers, emotionally disappear on them when they found themselves very much off to the side. But here was Brady during his off hours behaving as if there were no off hours; he was always sitting in a small room, studying film, comparing it with the playbook, which he had already mastered. He did it in an interesting way, Adams thought; some players might have done it noisily to show how hard they were working, but Brady was as unobtrusive as possible, as if this were a private thing; he was doing it as quietly as possible, sneaking into a tiny office and burying himself in front of the film.

Then, when everyone else was gone for the day, he would go out and practice, using some of the receivers from the taxi squad, most notably a young man named Chris Eitzmann, a tight end who had just graduated from Harvard and signed as a free agent. Some members of the custodial staff were a little uneasy—did this young man have permission to do this, and keep them from closing up—but Pioli and Adams assured them that it was perfectly all right. What impressed Pioli and Adams, both of whom liked to slip down and watch these workouts, was how disciplined Brady was and how exceptional his work ethic was. What he was doing in those extra practices set him apart. He was not just telling the receivers, let's run a down and out, or a square in, but he was calling plays as if they were in the playbook and as if the players were in a pressurized, game-time situation. He would use the playbook terminology and call the requisite play. He was taking the theory of the playbook, Adams realized, and making it a reality, so he could understand it in a game situation, in case he was ever sent in.

The other thing he was doing was cajoling the receivers to work with him—pushing them to do more, telling them that it was the only way they were going to make it. He was a fourth-string quarterback behaving like a coach. He was also working out every day in the weight room, building his body up, and working on drills to improve his agility. "I remember one night it was late on a Friday, and everyone had gone home, but the light was on in the bubble, so I sneaked over, and there he was working with the wide receivers, using the playbook as if it were a game-time situation," said Pioli. "It was absolutely Belichickian."

Ray Perkins, the toughest man he had ever met in football, Adams thought, would have really liked Brady, because Perkins believed that the quarterback had to be the hardest working, mentally toughest man on the team, the one player who pushed himself hard when things were not going well, and there were early signs that Brady had those qualities.

By the end of the first year they knew they had something. How much, they did not yet know. But some of it was coming together.

His confidence had grown. The questions he asked the coaches in meetings were very good ones, and they were the questions that only smart players asked, players who were already in command of the game. It was during the preseason camp of 2001 when they really saw how much he had improved. The previous year he had been behind Bledsoe; Damon Huard, the backup, a competent player who had been in the Miami Dolphins organization; and Michael Bishop, the nominal third string, who had played at Kansas State and later in Europe. By the end of the preseason Brady had beat out Huard to be the backup.

He had mastered the playbook, added about twenty pounds of muscle to his body, and worked seriously on his mechanics. He understood the Patriots' system, one in which it was critically important to make good reads, and he knew how to operate in it. Comparing him to Phil Simms, who had been so valuable on those Giant teams, Belichick thought that Simms might have a little more arm strength and certainly came in as a more accurate passer, but he thought Brady might have at an earlier point in his career a better sense of clock management. He threw a very catchable ball, a ball that the receivers liked. About his ability to read what was happening on the field, that is, field intelligence, Belichick was pleased. The ability to make those reads on the defense was a hard thing to measure, as football intelligence was always hard to measure. There were some quarterbacks who were very smart, who knew the playbook cold, but who were not kinetic wonders, and could not make the instantaneous read. That was the rarest of abilities, the so-called Montana Factor: the eye perceiving, and then even as the eye perceives, transferring the signal, eye to brain, and then in the same instant, making the additional transfer from brain to the requisite muscles. The NFL was filled with coaches with weak arms themselves, who could see things quickly on the field but who were doomed to work with quarterbacks who had great arms, but whose ability to read the defense was less impressive. What Brady might have, they began to suspect, was that marvelous ability that sets the truly great athletes apart from the very good ones. Or as one of the assistants said, it was like having Belichick himself out there if only Belichick had had a great arm. In the 2001 training camp Brady would come off the field after an offensive series, and Belichick would question him about each play, and it was quite remarkable: Brady would be able to tell his coach what every receiver was doing on each play, what the defensive backs were doing, and explain why he had chosen to throw where he had. It was as if there were a camera secreted away in his brain. Afterward, Belichick would go back and run the film on those same plays and would find that everything Brady had said was borne out by the film.

Technically, the Patriots did not have a quarterback problem. The quarterback, Drew Bledsoe, was the star of the team, its signature player, the man the organization had used to sell tickets. The son of a coach and a teacher, Bledsoe was big and strong and had a formidable arm, and he had brought the team to great heights, including a visit to the Super Bowl. In the 2001 press booklet for the Patriots, he was on the cover, and the guide devoted twenty-five pages to his records and accomplishments. Articulate and thoughtful, he was a great favorite of the Kraft family, being, as someone said, so close as to be a kind of fifth son. He seemed to have a natural charm when he did interviews, and he was one of those talented young athletes who, in addition to performing heroics on the field, becomes something of a community figure who goes beyond sports, always available for important fundraisers and always gracious at them. He had been for almost a decade the face of the franchise—in good years and not so good years, especially in years when the offensive line was unacceptably weak; that face had been a very attractive one.

Bledsoe had been the first pick—number one in the entire

country—in the 1993 draft. He had had a difficult time with Bill Parcells, his first coach, who turned his sharp tongue on him from the start. Before he was drafted, Bledsoe had heard how much Parcells liked him; but after he flew east with his agent, Leigh Steinberg, to meet with the coach, the hazing had started immediately. A lot of people in the League, Parcells told them, think that Rick Mirer (the other top quarterback prospect in the country) is better than you are. "Bill was arrogant, challenging, insulting," Steinberg later said. "I wish I could convey to you the tone of his voice, the tone of disinterest. It was almost like: *Why are you here?*" ("It wasn't my job to impress him," Parcells later said. "It was his job to impress me.")

The hazing was hard during his rookie year, and there were constant suggestions from Parcells that he might well lose his job the following year when the top college quarterback, a player named Heath Shuler at Tennessee, turned pro. At one point during the hazing years, Bledsoe's mother voiced to journalists her lack of appreciation for the way Parcells was treating her son. Tell her to watch fewer games, the coach told reporters when they mentioned her unhappiness. Bledsoe survived all that and appeared to be at the height of his game as the 2001 season was about to start. He had played eight full seasons in the League. Of the quarterbacks in the game, only Brett Favre, of Green Bay, had played in more games since Bledsoe had entered the League. At the time he was ranked fourth among the active NFL quarterbacks, and he was a kind of walking New England Patriots record book: most yards gained, most passes thrown, most completions (but not most touchdowns; Steve Grogan owned that one, 182 to 164). He was twentieth in the history of the entire League in terms of total completions, and Phil Simms of the Giants was only seventy-three ahead of him; thus he seemed sure to move up to nineteenth by the fourth or fifth game of the season. Iconic status beckoned, if it had not already been achieved. He had been to the Pro Bowl three times in the mid-nineties, the first time when he was only twenty-two. He was the kind of player that fans absolutely loved, and sometimes his beautiful soaring passes were the only redeeming part of a Patriots game.

But the story was more complicated, at least in the view of the coaches. Bledsoe had played with some teams that were not very good and some offensive lines that leaked. Some damage had been done. Belichick and his assistants, who had their own view of the role of a quarterback and their own private evaluation of Bledsoe, had their quiet doubts. Bledsoe had never been especially mobile, and as he got older and had been hit repeatedly, he seemed even less mobile. Because of the increasing speed of the defenders, mobility on the part of the quarterback was becoming ever more important. Another worry was that he held the ball a little long, that his arm strength and the offensive sets from which he operated had taught him to look downfield hoping for the big play, rather than to take the quick square-in that the defense had given and that his current coaches wanted him to take.

Such doubts were magnified with Belichick, who had specialized in one thing for almost twenty-five years: discovering and exploiting the weaknesses of opposing quarterbacks. Because he had coached against Bledsoe, and coached with him, he felt he knew the quarterback's strengths and weaknesses exceptionally well. Most quarterbacks dislike rushes and blitzes from the outside because they usually came from their blind side. But against Bledsoe, because he was so tall and needed so much space to set up, the inside rush was unusually effective, bothersome to the quarterback himself, and resulted in, among other things, a surprising number of tipped balls. The other thing that Belichick was aware of was that Bledsoe, who was right handed, was much more accurate throwing to his right than to his left. It was surely about mechanics and the way he planted his feet, but in Belichick's view he was not as supple as he needed to be in adjusting his mechanics. Chris Palmer, who had been the quarterback coach when Belichick arrived in New England, had worked hard trying to improve those mechanics when Bledsoe threw to his left, but there was a feeling in 2000, when Belichick got there, that it was still a serious problem, and it allowed defenses to cheat on the quarterback.

If Belichick saw the weaknesses in Bledsoe, he knew all too well how other good defensive coaches would pick up on the same weaknesses. Could you disguise deep coverages on him and then trick him into throwing into them? Was his arm as accurate as that of, say, Vinny Testaverde? The salary cap had made the position ever more important—a very good quarterback made something like 14 percent of the entire cap—so if the quarterback was not producing, if he was the wrong man, then it was a very high price to pay. "We had played against him for three seasons in a row and we knew his weaknesses when we arrived," one of the coaches said. "Our eyes were open when we got here." Bledsoe had not done particularly well against Belichick-coached teams, 4–6 overall, 2–2 versus those struggling Cleveland teams, and worse, 2–4 against his not always brilliant Jets teams.

More than most coaches, Belichick knew the importance of Bledsoe's weaknesses. He had been taken down in his previous incarnation in Cleveland by a quarterback dilemma, and he did not intend to have it happen again. So the question beginning to surface in his mind, which he would talk about quietly with his other coaches, was a serious one: How far can Bledsoe take us? Are the skills, no matter how much he's meant to the franchise in the past, receding? Is the rest of the League on to him, or at least are the better teams, the playoff teams, on to him? Did he merely look like a great quarterback a couple of times a game, when he connected on the long ball, or was he still actually a great quarterback? Had his mobility, never great, slipped? It was hard for an offensive line to protect a quarterback in the NFL under the best of conditions, but it was harder still, they said among themselves, to protect a statue. Did Bledsoe play the game fast enough—for the game was getting faster every year—or was there now a critical split-second differential in what he saw and what was happening, a differential that was the difference between victory and defeat?

The question of what Bledsoe's place was in the Patriot universe was further complicated by the fact that the team was building a brand-new stadium in Foxboro, one ready to be opened in 2002. In order to draw fans, they needed a star, and Kraft (the coaches were more than a little underwhelmed by the decision) had just signed Bledsoe to a handsome ten-year, $100 million contract. He did that even though Bledsoe had two years remaining on his existing contract. Then late in the second game of the 2001 season, against the Jets, Bledsoe, trying to scramble, took a very hard hit from Mo Lewis, a Jet linebacker, a clean but violent tackle. It was so hard a hit that it sheared a blood vessel in Bledsoe's chest, and blood poured into his chest cavity. The coaches had not been happy with Bledsoe's play earlier that day, not so much his passing as what they saw as his poor clock management and mental mistakes on the field: If they had graded him that day, it would have been the grade of a player who was in jeopardy of losing his job.

After he went down, Brady took over. The Patriots lost that game, 10–3, making them 0–2 for the season. Then they beat Indianapolis, but lost to the Dolphins in Miami in a blowout, 30–10. That made their record 1–3. The turning point came in the fifth game, against San Diego. That was when Brady first showed he might have something special. The Patriots were down by 10 points, 26–16, with under nine minutes on the clock, and Brady started to connect. With 3:31 left, the Patriots got a field goal, and that made it 26–19. Then, with thirty-six seconds left, they scored the tying touchdown, and won in overtime.

They were 2–3 instead of the 1–4 they would have carried had they lost. It had been a breathtaking game for Brady; he had thrown for 364 yards, two touchdowns, no interceptions, and completed thirty-three of fifty-four pass attempts. What the coaches and his teammates had most liked about his performance was how cool he had remained under maximum San Diego pressure. A couple of key plays had come from two audibles called at the line of scrimmage, with the Chargers showing blitz, calls that a rookie normally would not have been able to make. San Diego liked to blitz, and twice in that game, at critical moments, they came to the line of scrimmage showing blitz, and Brady had been very calm and handled it well. The first was in the second quarter, when they were on their own 23; with twenty-three seconds left, Brady had adjusted quickly and thrown a short out pass to Troy Brown that was good for 23 yards. That had not gotten them a score—a subsequent field goal had been missed—but it showed that Brady had read the defense as if he had been doing it all his life and this was just one more unforeseen interruption in an otherwise ordinary day at the office. Cool as he could be, Belichick thought. Then later, during the overtime, again back on his 23, San Diego had shown blitz again. They had already agreed that if it happened again, Brady would call the same audible, as if to hit Brown in the same place, but instead run a different play, a longer pass route to the center of the field. He did and they fooled San Diego and got a big gain of thirty-seven yards off a pass interference call. That drive culminated in the winning field goal. What was exciting for them was how professionally Brady had handled it all.

They had not only won, they had won smart, which was exhilarating. It was not just Brady's coaches who were thrilled, but his teammates as well, because they sensed that he could read the game and quite possibly manage the direction and rhythm of it. They felt like a different team after that game, Belichick thought, as if life had been pumped back into them; they were going to be all right. Belichick was not sure that Bledsoe would have made the same calls—it was not something he thought was the older player's strength. No one was thinking Super Bowl, or maybe even playoffs at that point, but they knew they had a player who would not pull the team down. And then, gradually, expectations began to rise, because it became clearer and clearer he was authentic, the real thing, and that the team liked playing under him. The coaches sensed that it was easier for the offensive line with him in because he did not hold the ball as long as Bledsoe did. With that, the season began to change. So did Bill Belichick's coaching status. He started to become the winner of New England, instead of the loser of Cleveland. Or, as his friend Ernie Adams said, "The number one criteria for being a genius in this business is to have a great quarterback, and in New England he had one, and in Cleveland he did not."

You could win with Brady, and he was getting better by the week. It was all happening very fast. Others saw it, too—his cognitive abilities, the way he would go to his third and sometimes fourth receiver, the way he knew how to take what the defense left them and not try to reach and take too much. The name Montana was now being said in the same sentence with Brady's on occasion. The knowledge he had gotten from the film and the playbook, all that hard work, had become so much a part of him that the comparison seemed valid; he might not have Montana's sheer natural ability in making reads, but he had driven himself so hard that superior preparation and superior instincts now were blended together; he saw a lot and saw it quickly. Bill Walsh, who had coached Montana in San Francisco, noticed this sooner than most. Brady, he decided, was more like Montana than any other quarterback he had seen since Montana retired. Montana might have had slightly quicker reflexes, but Brady was very, very good; he had qualities that only great players bring to the table, qualities that are beyond what coaches can help develop. He had, Walsh thought, that rarest of gifts for a quarterback, a great football intuition.

Seven weeks later, before the regular season game with the St. Louis Rams, Drew Bledsoe was cleared by the medical staff to practice and to play. That week, he and Brady shared the snaps in practice, in part because Belichick wanted to evaluate Bledsoe, who had been out for nearly two months. Brady was 5–2 as a starter, including winning four of his last five. The St. Louis game with Brady as quarterback turned out to be a disaster, mostly because the defense was not prepared for the high-speed Ram offense. But Belichick also thought that having the quarterbacks share the practice snaps had affected the team negatively and had probably caused Brady to fall a little out of his rhythm. It was at that point that Belichick had to make what was probably the most critical decision of the season: Bledsoe or Brady—the experienced veteran, who owned almost every record in the team's book, or the virtual rookie. Belichick also had to assume that it was not just the most important call of the season but of his career as well, for if he was wrong, and the team did not do well, the decision would surely haunt him and quite possibly drive him from his job.

This decision was all his. It was what he got paid so handsomely to do, the kind of call that coaches had to make, and finally had to make on their own, and then had to live with. So he decided that Brady was the quarterback and would take most of the snaps during practice. He called Bledsoe in and told him that they could not go on sharing snaps, that the practice snaps had to go to the starting quarterback, and right now that was Tom Brady. Bledsoe was furious with his decision and went to Bob Kraft and said that Belichick had lied to him and had promised that he would have an even chance to compete to get his job back and would share the snaps.

Belichick did not think it had been that hard a decision, or that he had lied. He had been appalled at the beginning of that first season in New England by how many starting players could not finish their conditioning drills—say twenty sprints of forty yards for some positions, done within a certain time limit—and had simply collapsed on the field and did not even try to get up and finish them; worse, they did not think it was that important. There had been an attitude among all too many players, he had decided, that *I'm a starter, I own my job, and you can't bench me or even rotate me.* In every sense that went against Belichick's concept of what a real team was like; on a real team, the kind of team he intended to create, the more senior, more experienced players enforced the coach's concept of team by setting a certain example, working harder at practice and in the weight room than anyone else. The younger players thus came to understand that this was what the NFL was all about, that the better you were, the harder you worked. To him, everything had to be earned and earned again and again; nothing was a given. He had learned that years earlier talking to Rich McCabe back in Denver, when he had described how Al Davis went about his business.

In Belichick's view Bledsoe's attitude reflected that same sense of entitlement. The question was not what was best for Bledsoe, Belichick thought, or what the team owed Bledsoe, after all those years of service on weak Patriot teams; the only question was which player was the better quarterback, better able to lead the team at that moment. And that made the call easy. They were in the middle of a season, and the season was very much on the line; they were 5–5 after the St. Louis game. So it was not, he later thought, a very hard call, but neither was it a popular one, either with the media or the fans. Then they went and won the last six games of the season and made the playoffs, which made the call a little more popular. Brady had been 11–3 as a starter, the team 11–5. Brady, Belichick decided, had kept on improving and by the latter part of the 2001 season was simply a better quarterback than Bledsoe had been in 2000. Despite the public perception of Bledsoe's greatly superior arm strength, the physical abilities were surprisingly similar in sheer arm strength, the coach believed. Bledsoe was like a javelin thrower, formidable when his feet were perfectly set, something that did not happen too often in the NFL, but Brady was a little quicker in the pocket, with considerably greater pocket awareness of the rush. Sometimes Brady played as if he came equipped with one of those modern motion detectors attached to the entire pocket which signaled to him what was happening on his blind side. Brady's ability to feel the rush fascinated Adams, and after the 2004 season he sat down and went through some 600 plays where there had been fairly serious pressure on his quarterback and he was amazed by Brady's feel for it, and his ability to escape what appeared to be sure hits at the very last sliver of a second. In that sense Brady passed an early Bill Walsh test, for Walsh was always telling coaches at his clinics that the one thing your quarterback cannot be is a wildebeest, naming an uncommonly vulnerable African animal, which when it sees the killer lion approach, completely freezes.

But the tensions between Belichick and Bledsoe did not abate. Near the end of the season Bledsoe went to Belichick and told him that he thought the team needed an experienced quarterback for the playoffs, that they could not win in the playoffs with a rookie quarterback. Belichick said only that he was glad that Brady was confident. They left it at that. Then, in the AFC championship game against Pittsburgh, Brady hurt his ankle and Bledsoe came in and played well, and the Patriots won. That brought up once again the question of which player was going to start in the Super Bowl. Belichick said that he would announce his decision on the Wednesday before the game. On Tuesday he called both men in and told them that Brady would start. He told Brady, however, that he would have to be able to practice Wednesday, Thursday, and Friday, which he did.

Drew Bledsoe was not pleased. "That's what I expected you to do," he said. But among those most impressed by Belichick's decision to go with Brady was his father. Steve Belichick thought it was a very gutsy call, perhaps the most critical call his son had ever made, because the world of coaching is very conservative, and the traditional call would be the conservative one, to go with the more experienced player in so big a game. That way you were protected if it didn't work out, because you had gone with tradition and experience, and no one could criticize you. That was the call most coaches would have made, he said, under the CYA or Cover Your Ass theory of coaching. Many of his old friends disagreed with what his son was doing, he knew, but he was comfortable with it himself. When friends who were puzzled called him about it, he told them that Bill was right in what he was doing. "He's the smart one in the family, and I'm the dumb one," he would say.

Then the Patriots went out and beat the Rams in what was a singular upset, in what Belichick thought was the best coaching job of his career. Among other things, the quarterback issue was settled. The person who understood that most clearly was that same perspicacious quarterback-turned-commentator, Ron Jaworski, who a few days after the Rams game had broken down the film and understood immediately everything that Belichick had done. A great many other writers and other football people were still wondering, now that the season was over, whether Drew Bledsoe might get his job back the following year. That was not going to happen, Jaworski decided. Tom Brady knew Belichick's system too well, and Bledsoe, by contrast, was having trouble with it. Brady had stayed perfectly within the system during the Super Bowl and had never tried to do too much. He was helped by the fact that it was the only system he knew and had ever run. "He runs the play and he throws to the guy he's supposed to throw to. Coaches love that. When you look at Drew, you see a guy who's been through so many systems that it's hard to stick to the plan. He knows he's supposed to throw the square-in, but he starts thinking, 'Maybe I can hit the deep post for a touchdown.' He wants to make the spectacular play. Then when he realizes the post isn't there, it's too late for the square-in. I think that kind of doubt has crept into Drew's thinking and caused him to make some mistakes."

So they had won the first of the three Super Bowls. It was, thought their coach, something of a miracle. He had seen a lot of good football teams and coached a few of them, and this was not, in the technical sense, that good a football team. But it had played well when it mattered, and it had done the things it was supposed to do. Technically, it should have been an 8–8 or 7–9 team in the regular season, when it had a deficit in almost every statistical category. But it had scored forty-three touchdowns to only twenty-six for the opposition, and nearly one hundred more points than the other teams—a sign that when it mattered, the Patriots knew how to stop an enemy drive.

He was aware of how much luck they had enjoyed in getting to the Super Bowl, that good players had sometimes played like great players, that critical calls had gone to them (as they had not in Cleveland)—especially one against Oakland in a playoff game when a fumble on the part of Brady had been ruled an incompletion, a terrible call in the eyes of any unbiased observer. Had it gone the other way, the season would have ended then and there. He was aware that there were three or four games they had won that they could easily have lost had one critical play turned out differently. And he was aware that the one player who had made such a great difference, Tom Brady, was there mostly by luck.

◆◆◆

Belichick was also aware of how fortune had smiled at critical moments, and how thin the line in making the playoffs really was, how easy it was to fail with the exact same team. He was hardly alone in that feeling—the great Vince Lombardi, who seemed so immune to being taken down by bad bounces, had spoken in the same vein once after winning a title, remembering the bounces that had gone his way, the penalties called and not called, and the Green Bay punts that rolled out of bounds in the Coffin Corner.

CHAPTER THIRTEEN

They had won their first Super Bowl, but they were not that good yet. No one knew that better than the head coach. When it was over, he hugged his old friend Ernie Adams and asked him, "Can you believe we won the Super Bowl against the Rams with this team?" To his mind they had barely begun building the Patriots into a team with their kind of players and enough depth to withstand the usual expected injuries. In 2002, they were 9–7 and did not make the playoffs, but, ironically, Belichick thought they were a better team. They were still incomplete, but change was under way. He was steadily getting new players, ones more compatible with his system. Bledsoe was traded for a draft choice to Buffalo, a team in their own division, a decision that surprised some people but reflected Belichick's belief that Bledsoe was not a threat to him. The Patriots would have a 5–1 record against him over the next three years. Brady was coming on, getting better and better. They were picking up players that other teams did not want, but who were just right for their system. Their sense of value received for money paid out was acute.

It was increasingly obvious to people watching pro football in the middle of the 2003 season that something was coming together in New England. It was not yet a powerhouse—it did not roll over other teams—but it kept winning. The Patriots were gradually getting the right players for the system. Sal Paolantonio of ESPN, a veteran reporter who did not like the way Belichick treated the media, thought, nonetheless, that the management-coaching team being assembled in Foxboro was the most modern and sophisticated one in pro football. Robert Kraft was a shrewd owner who asked the right questions and ran a very good shop; he was a tough businessman whom people would do well not to underestimate. If there was a smarter NFL owner who understood the business side, no one was sure who he was. Belichick was the best coach of the era, and Pioli was the best player personnel man, and of course, Tom Brady was the perfect quarterback for their system. If they could keep things together, if egos or bad luck did not get in the way, and if Brady was not injured, Paolantonio thought, they had a chance of winning several additional Super Bowls before it was all over. Brady, he thought, might end up being the best ever, better even than Montana, the gold standard, in part because Montana had played in a less volatile era, with one cast of characters; Brady, because of free agency and the salary cap, was changing receivers and teammates all the time. He was, Paolantonio added, "the Eric Clapton of quarterbacks—if he works off the written music he'll never miss a note, but when you need him to improvise, he'll always amaze you."

Other observers agreed. Ron Jaworski thought that the combination of Belichick and his player personnel man, Scott Pioli, had very quickly become the best in the League, a perfect matchup of men and skills; they seemed able to finish each other's sentences. The proof of how good they were was reflected not so much in the draft choices, which were quite good, but in the way they were able to maximize free agency; how else, he asked, did you explain why so many players who had not done well elsewhere flowered in the Patriot system?

Belichick University was beginning to pay off, all those bright young men with whom he had worked, first in New York and then in Cleveland, young men who desperately wanted to be coaches and who knew about him and how good he was, were moving up in the world of football. They would work for him at cut rates—which was the only way anyone started with him. Some were working for him in New England like Pioli, or Eric Mangini, an ascending defensive coach; some had become head coaches on their own, like Kirk Ferentz at Iowa, Nick Saban at LSU, and Pat Hill at Fresno State. Most of the men Belichick had trained remained exceptionally loyal to him. If he had not paid them that much in the beginning, then he had been generous with his time, endlessly explaining to them the game as he saw it and showing them respect by listening to them. He admired Saban greatly as a defensive coach and would go down to Baton Rouge to talk to him after the season was over about changing defensive tactics and to gain more insight into potential draft picks; thus he had not only his own scouts, who were becoming more and more confident, but his own alumni association to talk with as well.

But many from Belichick University went with him to the Patriots. Eric Mangini was from Hartford and had captained the football team at Wesleyan. He had visited his brother on his junior year abroad and had ended up coaching a semipro team in Australia—the Kew Colts in Melbourne—whose players were roughly eighteen to forty-five and much given, when it was fourth and eight on their own 10, to running the ball. Mangini had not been paid, but they had asked him back when the season was over. The next year he returned and they offered to pay him $500 a game—but he couldn't take it because he would lose his college eligibility. Those were perfect credentials for Belichick University, reflecting an obvious love of the game and the willingness to take a virtual vow of poverty. He was introduced to Belichick by his college coach, Kevin Spencer, who had played lacrosse against Belichick when they were both in college, and who had stayed in touch.

Another Belichick protégé who came to the Patriots was Kirk Ferentz, who, as a bright young coach at the University of Maine, had been brought out to be interviewed for a job coaching the offensive line in Cleveland. Ferentz had somehow thought he already had the job and that the interview process would be easy, light questions about each other's children. Instead it was a grueling two-day process, and, after the end of the first day, Ferentz felt like he had been beaten up. It was like taking the oral exam for a Ph.D.; they ran film of a drill, and he had to judge how well the drill had gone; they had a clip of a potential draft choice, and he was supposed to evaluate the player, but the player was so bad that even Belichick began to laugh. Ferentz was not at all sure he had done very well, but the young man who had picked him up at the airport, another young gofer, named Pioli, took him back to his hotel that night and said, somewhat comfortingly, "Hey, don't feel too bad, you didn't do so badly." Finally they offered him the job, and Belichick lowballed him on salary—he always lowballed—but Ferentz took it. The interview process itself had proven to him how much he might be able to learn.

Ferentz was hired primarily to work with the offensive linemen, and he sensed immediately that Belichick was ahead of the curve here; he saw that Belichick had decided that of all the positions, offensive lineman was the one where you could take good, strong kids who were available in some of the lower draft rounds and, by dint of good teaching, mold them into first-rate offensive linemen. It was not technically a skilled position, and it did not demand speed; rather it demanded size, strength, football intelligence, and a willingness to learn and work very hard. The higher draft choices would go to positions that demanded greater innate athletic ability. That way you saved your higher picks. Ferentz had sensed this, and it turned out that he was absolutely right—that was how Belichick saw things, and why he had wanted him.

As Belichick brought in his own men as coaches, he started to get the players he wanted. Scott Pioli thought it started in March 2001, when they had signed Larry Izzo, a great special-teams player. Izzo was the first important free-agent signing; he had played at Rice, had not been drafted, and had ended up playing for five years on the Dolphins. He could play some linebacker, but he was a great special-teams player, a Pro Bowl–caliber one. The signing bonus, as Pioli remembered, was not especially big: $250,000. But Izzo had bought into what they were trying to do, and, if you were trying to change the culture of the team, he was an ideal player to start with. After that, a great many of the free agents, a total of twenty-three, were signed. They had tried to re-sign their own nose tackle that year, a player named Chad Eaton, but he went to Seattle, for a bonus of $3.5 million. What Pioli remembered about the signings was that they were able to sign eighteen players for less than what Eaton was paid. Some came and departed quickly and did not make a deep impression, but several turned out to be important.

There was Mike Vrabel, signed as a free agent after four years as a backup linebacker in Pittsburgh. He had come out of Ohio State, and Belichick and Pioli had been interested in him even back then, but Pittsburgh had moved more quickly. Vrabel had been what they call a tweener when he had been at Ohio State—a player caught between the physical needs of playing defensive end and linebacker; he was judged a little big for a linebacker and a little small for a defensive end in the pros. The Steelers had shrewdly moved him to linebacker, but their linebacking crew was so strong that he had played as a backup in his first four years. Belichick brought him to New England by promising that the job of outside linebacker was his to lose, though it was not necessarily his in perpetuity; but he would not begin his tour on the bench, where he had lingered for so long in Pittsburgh. That was good enough for Vrabel, and he turned out to be a perfect piece for the team—tough, smart, and versatile (eventually he would be used as a receiver in two Super Bowls); if he was not exactly a steal in player personnel terms, he was like getting a low first- or high second-round draft choice.

There were others who came aboard in similar fashion and for relatively small signing bonuses: David Patten, who had shown great speed when he had played for the Giants; and Bryan Cox, the venerable linebacker, who gave them one good year, but also brought experience and leadership to the team and tended to support the values that Belichick was trying to instill.

The other thing that was happening as they got the kind of players they wanted was that the players themselves were beginning to buy in and to enforce a winning culture. That, Belichick believed, had been the key difference between a team that had struggled like his Cleveland team and teams that succeeded like the Steelers—the best players themselves took the lead in creating a winning attitude. Now it was happening in New England. They were creating a core group of veteran players with the kind of character that he had hoped for back in Cleveland, players who were tough and serious and businesslike, men who not only pushed themselves to the limit in practice but kept on the newer players and the free agents, forcing them to become part of the culture (or get out) and staying on their case if they did not study the film, and did not know the playbook, or seemed to be coasting in practice.

There were different signs that they were pulling together and becoming more of a team each year. Before the 2003 season on one hot early preseason day, one of those awful dog days of August, Matt Light, the offensive tackle, had gone to Belichick and asked on behalf of the team for the rest of the day off for the team. "That's not the way it's done, Matt," Belichick had said, "there has to be a quid pro quo." In this case, he and Light decided, the deal would be Light's ability to catch a punt in practice—offensive tackles, of course, never fielded punts. If he caught it, the team would get the rest of the day—and the next day off. If he muffed it, they would all have to run extra sprints. The deal was accepted—by the standards of August football practice, it was a great one. The video of that day is fascinating. There is Light, surrounded by all the Patriot players who normally catch punts. The inner group of instructors includes Deion Branch, Troy Brown, and Kevin Faulk. They are showing him how to hold his hands, and how to keep them soft, and how to draw the ball in. Then they are instructing him how to look up for the ball and to move under it. Everything else on the practice field has stopped. A large area is cleared so he can maneuver easily. The tension clearly is mounting. All other drills have stopped. All eyes are on Light, at six-four and 305 not necessarily the most nimble of punt returners. Finally, a rookie punts the ball, and it floats ever so high before beginning its sudden descent. Light moves under it, not necessarily deftly, but more or less effectively, although his body seems oddly stiff. The ball seems to hang in the air for just an extra half second. On the sideline some of the players are using their own body language, trying to help bring the ball in. Light grabs it, nestles it into his body, and is suddenly surrounded by cheering teammates—only a Super Bowl victory might bring more in the way of congratulations. They seem, for a brief instant, not like a group of hardened professional football players, but like the little boys they once were. They have a day and a half off. Belichick is seen smiling. It became an annual fixture during preseason camp.

At the preseason camp in 2003, Ernie Adams felt for the first time that they were upgrading and that they had more depth, position by position. No one knew how good they might yet be, because it was always so close in the League now, the margins of victory and defeat were so thin. But Adams sensed that they were beginning to build something important at the camp, and they now had some very good football players, players who might not yet start, but who were going to play well if summoned. There had been from the start a conscious decision to build up their defensive line, because they knew they needed to control the line of scrimmage; now there was evidence this was coming together. There was, for example, a player named Jarvis Green, a defensive end who had been taken in the fourth round in the 2002 draft out of LSU; he had started seven games in 2002 for New England, and he was looking better and better. They were also building up the offensive line, and they were thrilled with the play of a young man named Dan Koppen, taken in the fifth round from Boston College; he would end up starting in the last fifteen games of the season and all three playoff games.

It was in that 2003 season that they seemed to come of age and the streak began, even though they might not yet have been the team that Belichick and the other coaches wanted—their ground game was suspect, which limited ball and clock control. They started inauspiciously, getting blown out in their season opener against Buffalo, 31–0, with their old defensive back Lawyer Milloy, a longtime Patriot favorite and a star of the first Super Bowl win, now playing for Buffalo (he had been squeezed off the roster by financial considerations). It was one of Tom Brady's worst games—he threw four interceptions—and one of Drew Bledsoe's best ones—he was by then with the Bills. They then won two games—a solid 31–10 victory in Philadelphia, against a powerful Eagles team, and then one over the Jets. Next, almost inexplicably, they lost to a troubled Washington team. At that point they were 2–2. And then they started winning. They won twelve regular season games in a row, to end up 14–2—an exemplary record, one good enough to get home-field advantage in the playoffs.

How good their defense was had showed in their regular season game against the Colts, one of their most important games. The Colts had seemed, year by year, under Peyton Manning, to be getting better and better. There was always a sense when the two teams played in the regular season that it was a tune-up for the playoffs and that it could easily determine home-field advantage. Given the different styles of the two teams, there was a huge difference between playing the Colts—a speed team with a great passer whose offense relied on timing—on their own field, a domed stadium with ear-shattering noise and artificial turf, and playing them on grass, which was so much slower, especially in the wind, cold, and possibly snow at Foxboro. What was at stake was the very tempo of the game, and a potential swing of 10 to 14 points. The regular season game was played in the dome in Indianapolis, so it tended to favor the Colts. It was Game 12 of the year and Game 11 of the streak. It had been a very good game, two very good, very different teams with very different strengths matching up. The Patriots had taken an early lead, and at one point in the third quarter they led 31–10, but the Colts, with that quick offense, had come back, and with about four minutes gone in the fourth quarter it was tied 31–31. The Patriots had scored again for a 38–31 lead, but the Colts had mounted another drive, and had come away with a field goal. The score was 38–34, when, because of a bad New England punt, the Colts got the ball on the Patriot 48 with 2:57 left to play. Manning moved the team nicely, and with forty seconds left they had a first down on the 2-yard line. Edgerrin James ran on first down and picked up a yard. Twenty-four seconds left now. On second down James tried to slip by Ted Washington, the nose guard, and failed. No gain. Eighteen seconds left now. Manning called time-out. This time they were going to pass. They threw a fade to a rookie named Aaron Moorehead, and it went over his head and out of the end zone. Fourth down now, with fourteen seconds left. They gave the ball to Edgerrin James, and Willie McGinest made a great play and stopped him cold behind the line of scrimmage. The Patriots had won, and had come of age. More important than the streak itself, they had played a very good team at home in a big game, and made the big plays when it counted.

They were still being carried by their defense, and statistically they still seemed more like an 8–8 team than a championship one; they had made one more first down than their opponents during the entire regular season, 294 to 293, and had gained fewer yards rushing, although this time they had done a little more with their passing game. But they were ready for the Colts when they came to Foxboro for the AFC championship game. Their defense was getting better, and they felt going in that they were the more physical team and could set the tone of the game. Tom Brady watched the Patriot defense against the scout team that week, and he saw the players' hunger and the variety of coverages that Belichick had in store for Manning. "I was thinking, 'Oh God, I'm glad I'm not playing quarterback [against them],'" he later said. Still the Colts seemed invincible in their own way. Coming into the game, Manning seemed to be in an almost perfect groove. In seventeen postseason possessions over two playoff games, the Colts had scored ten touchdowns; Manning himself had completed 78 percent of his passes, for eight touchdowns and no interceptions. He had been sacked only once.

On game day, the Patriots dominated the Colts offense. They hammered their receivers at the line of scrimmage, playing very physical football. "It was all about being physical, physical, physical with their receivers. We wanted to hit these guys in the mouth and let them know we are here," Rodney Harrison, the safety, said after the game. In fact, they did it with such ferocity that Bill Polian, the president of the Colts, later complained and eventually brought the issue up with the competition committee, of which he happened to be a member. (Because of the cerebral way Belichick coached, fans thought of the Patriots as a cerebral team, which they were, but they were very physical as well; they pounded other teams hard. "We know the Patriots very well here in Pittsburgh," said Kevin Spencer, one of Belichick's lacrosse opponents when they were in college and now an assistant in Pittsburgh. "We know how hard they come at you—we know they try to suffocate you. You play them as often as we play them now with as much at stake, and you realize how good they are—it's a team without an ego, all they want to do is win. In that way they're an extension of their coach.")

The Patriots disguised their coverages brilliantly and did a skillful job of disrupting the Colts' timing. There had been, in the past, quarterbacks whom Belichick wanted to keep in the pocket—Donovan McNabb and, a few years earlier, John Elway—but Manning was not one of them because he did not throw well on the move; it was the rarest of weaknesses with him. Manning was sacked four times, and threw four interceptions, three of which were caught by Ty Law. The Patriots shut the Colt offense down and led 15–0 at the half; in the second half, they were content to grind them down. They won 24–14, and the victory got them to their second Super Bowl, this time against the Carolina Panthers.

Nothing showed the volatility of the contemporary League quite so clearly as the rise of the Panthers, who were 1–15 only two years earlier. Now the Panthers were good—they had a strong defensive front four, an underrated quarterback in Jake Delhomme, and some very good receivers. They did well that season, throwing long to their top receivers, and against the Patriots in the Super Bowl they did even better: Steve Smith, Muhsin Muhammad, and Ricky Proehl caught twelve passes against them for 291 yards. Belichick spent a lot of time in practice that week before the Super Bowl working on the deep threat and the long ball. The Patriots had not given up a long ball all year, no touchdown of more than thirty yards. But in that game, they would give up three long ones, touchdown plays of thirty-nine, thirty-three, and eighty-five yards, as the Patriot secondary became a little more vulnerable than usual, after both of the starting safeties, Eugene Wilson and Rodney Harrison, went down with injuries—Wilson with a pulled groin muscle and Harrison with a broken arm—during the game.

It was a game of contradictions, starting ever so slowly, as if no one would score. The first half seemed to favor the Patriots, and the score was 14–10 at the half. Delhomme was just terrible in the beginning, completing just one of his first nine passes. Then, in the fourth quarter, the game exploded and turned into a shoot-out between Delhomme and Brady, with thirty-seven points scored in the fourth quarter alone. The Panthers scored on a thirty-three-yard run by DeShaun Foster, and it was 21–16, and then again on a stunning eighty-five-yard pass play, Delhomme to Muhammad, to take the lead 22–21. But the Patriots stayed cool, especially Brady, who went thirty-two of forty-eight that day, the thirty-two completions a Super Bowl record—for a total of 354 yards, three touchdowns, and one interception. Neither team seemed able to put the other away. Mike Vrabel, the Patriots linebacker who sometimes played tight end, caught a touchdown pass with 2:51 left, only the second touchdown catch of his career, and a successful two-point conversion put the Patriots ahead 29–22. But

Carolina came right back, and Proehl caught a twelve-yard touchdown pass to tie the game with a little more than a minute left.

Then the Patriots caught a major break, the kind they rarely handed to other teams. John Kasay, the Carolina kicker, trying a little too hard, caught the ball a little high and a little outside, and drove it out of bounds, which meant that the Patriots took it on their own 40, wonderful field position—they had the ball and could be a little looser in their choice of plays, instead of fearing what a turnover might do so near their own goal line. Brady got the ball with 1:08 on the clock, and in what seemed eerily like a repeat of the Super Bowl game two years earlier, he took his team down the field one more time, gaining thirty-seven yards in five plays. With four seconds left on the clock, and the ball on the 23, Vinatieri came in and kicked a forty-one-yard field goal for a 32–29 victory. It had been a great game, nothing like anyone had expected. "It was like Ali-Frazier out there," Vrabel said later. "That's how it felt out there. We hit them, they hit us, we hit them, they hit us."

It was the Patriots' second Super Bowl title in three years, each by three points. A six-point edge over two very good opponents after 120 minutes of football. People were beginning to use the D word again, for dynasty. The coach was wary—the D word brought more in the way of burdens than it did in assets. The X on your back got bigger. Besides, Belichick did not think he had coached that well in the second Super Bowl victory. "Truth is I thought I did a crappy job," he said afterward. "I made a really stupid mistake. I cut corners on how many defensive linemen I was going to carry, and I got caught doing it." He had carried only five. "I should have known better, because it's such a long game because of all the celebration and extravaganza. It's so draining. Your players wear down. Especially the defensive linemen, they're the first to go." He should, he said, have carried a sixth defensive lineman, Dan Klecko, a rookie they had taken out of Temple in the fourth round who had played very well all season, and who, being the son of a former professional player, Joe Klecko, did not seem to play like a rookie. Belichick still saw his own team's weaknesses—most specifically, its lack of a powerful running game, which allowed opposing defenses to concentrate too much on Brady and his receivers, and limited the capacity to run the clock when they got ahead. "Can you believe we're here," Belichick had told Ernie Adams just before that second Super Bowl started. "We can't run the ball, we can't punt the ball, and we can't snap for the field goals."

◆◆◆

After the Carolina victory, Bill Belichick went to Florida to visit with Jimmy Johnson, who he thought was the one coach out there who knew the most about what would happen once a team had shown itself able to play at so lofty a level, Johnson's Cowboys having won the Super Bowl after the 1992 and 1993 seasons. The two men were friends in the delicate sense of friendship that football coaches are allowed—in the we-may-be-on-opposite-sides-of-the-field-but-we-have-similar-problems-and-similar-enemies-and-we-may-need-each-other-yet-you-coaching-for-me-or-me-coaching-for-you kind of friendship. The friendship had started somewhat cautiously back when Johnson was the head coach at Dallas, and Belichick was at Cleveland. When Johnson was fired at Dallas (losing out in an ego contest over how much credit the coach should get compared to how much credit the owner, Jerry Jones, should get, with Jones allowed to make the final decision) and went to Miami, he had tried to hire Belichick as his defensive coordinator, though the latter had finally taken the Jets job.

But they had stayed in touch, as each morphed into a new

incarnation, Johnson as a media man and Belichick as the Patriots coach. They had talked about getting together, and after the Carolina game Belichick took Johnson up on his invitation to come down to Miami and talk, and they spent a day and a half going over the problems that accrue to the victorious. Johnson was the perfect person to visit with, Belichick thought—he was very smart, as smart as anyone in the game, and more than anyone else he had been through what Belichick was now just beginning to go through, the ordeal that came with success. Some of the issues were technical. The Patriots had a lot of draft choices in the coming draft, ten picks, and yet he already had a good team. Belichick wanted to know what to do—use them all, trade some away for futures, or what. Johnson told him to make a list of players he genuinely wanted, and draft them, but not to spend the picks just to use them, that it would be easy to trade picks now for higher picks next year. "Stay with your list," Johnson said, "and don't be tempted to pick up players outside of it, just because you can." But if there were a player that Belichick thought could help them right then, go for him. Belichick ended up using eight of the picks.

The most difficult thing, Johnson said, would be the pressure that would come with winning. When you win, everyone wants more, he said. Everything would be different. Every player and every player's agent would perceive the player as being better. The pressure to renegotiate would be immense, even for players with three years left on their contracts. Wait until the final year of the contract if at all possible, Johnson advised. It was, Belichick thought, a good philosophy, but you could not always do it, and sometimes you had to make adjustments when contracts were notoriously unfair. But a few days after their meeting, one of the players began talking publicly about his need for a bigger contract, and the fact that his contract reflected an essential disrespect for him as a player, and it brought home Johnson's lesson. The virus of higher personal expectations, Belichick called it.

The final thing Johnson mentioned was the danger of going back and trying to do the same things in the same way as before with your players. They would, Johnson warned, tune out. Football practice was built on repetition, and there was a strength and a danger in that. You've got to keep doing what you're doing, but you've got to find different ways of doing it, and you've got to find ways of making it fun. That, Belichick decided, was easier said than done, and it was hard to keep everyone focused in the preseason training camp of 2004. There was a lack of urgency to it, not quite a lethargy, but a sense that the Patriot players in some cases felt that they would be carried by their press clippings; they were champions, and they felt they should be treated as such. Thus when they played Cincinnati in their first preseason game and were beaten 31–0, Belichick was privately a bit pleased. It created a new sense of urgency.

In the off-season they made a major effort to upgrade. They had a slew of draft choices, and they traded one of them, not even a first but a second, to Cincinnati for their talented, dissident running back, Corey Dillon. To the other top teams in the NFL, those who saw themselves as potential champions and especially those in the American Conference who believed that the road to Jacksonville and the Super Bowl ran through New England, it was like a knife in the heart. The rich, it appeared, were once again getting richer. The year before, Super Bowl championship or no, the Patriots' running game had been weak, twenty-seventh in the League, and it offered a great incentive for a smart defensive coordinator to cheat against Brady, and limited Brady's own hand, and his ability to control the clock, especially against teams like the Colts, whose offenses he wanted to keep off the field. Dillon would surely change it. If the trade worked out, and there was reason to think it would work out very well, Dillon might well be the final piece for this team.

Corey Dillon was a classic power runner. He was not nifty, even though he had moves and speed, but he seemed the perfect kind of back for a team that on occasion wanted to vary its offense and needed a runner who could knock defenders down and, perhaps equally important, wear them out and use up a lot of clock in the process. Among those thrilled by the pickup were the defensive team members, who saw a chance to get a little more time on the sidelines during Patriot drives. Dillon had been in the League seven years, and he was one of only four NFL running backs who had gained over one thousand yards in each of his first six seasons. But most of those seven years had been unhappy (with good reason, thought many of his peers, since he had been forced to play for the Cincinnati Bengals) and there had always been a shadow over him. He had gotten in a good deal of trouble as a boy in Seattle. Even before he had gone to college, he was said to have an attitude problem. He had gone back and forth between junior colleges, his talent greater than his discipline, and had played for only one year at Washington before turning pro. Dillon had thought he was going to be picked in the first round by the Saints, at number ten, but they pulled back from him at the last moment because of his past problems and what they thought was a questionable attitude, so he ended up going to Cincinnati, which took him in the second round with the forty-sixth pick and which in those years was regarded as the black hole of the NFL. In sports one of the worst things that can happen to any player is to be the best player on a bad professional team, and that had been Dillon's fate. Not only do you play week after week against teams that have more weapons than your team does, but because your own team is so weak, opposing teams can concentrate all their defensive attention on you. Even worse, the hometown fans believe you are the star, and when things go badly, as they usually do on such teams, they blame you. Dillon had played hard, with marginal results, for almost all of his career, his frustration growing greater each year, and he had been heard to say on a Seattle radio show after his third season that he would rather flip burgers than play for Cincinnati any longer.

At the end of the 2003 season the Bengals were willing to let him go—the low price of a second-round pick was proof of that. The question was still his character, especially for a team like New England that prided itself now on the character of its players. He had become increasingly dissident in Cincinnati and was said to be moody and selfish. But who knew? Would Belichick or Pioli or the offensive coordinator, Charlie Weis, want to work for the Bengals as they had existed in those same years? Checking around the League, they heard quite different things, that Dillon had always played hard in what were often hopeless situations. He did not quit in games where other players might have been so inclined or in hopeless situations that seemed to occur week after week. The Patriots made their decision, in the end, based on a personal interview with Dillon. His grievances seemed legitimate for a passionate athlete who was seeking excellence but was caught in a perennial losing situation. He wanted badly to go to a winning program. He did not seem like one of those me-me-me players, but rather like someone longing to be part of a real team, where the load was shared, and where he could respect his teammates as they respected him.

The relationship worked almost from the start. The best thing about going to the Patriots, Dillon later said, was that "I knew the pressure wasn't going to be on me to strap a franchise on my back and take them to the Super Bowl. Just look at it. Without me they won two out of the last three. With me coming in, I was more relaxed in knowing we had guys who could get things done. All I had to do was focus on doing my part." He would do his part—rushing for 1635 yards in the coming season, third best in the League, and he would make Brady's job dramatically easier.

◆◆◆

So, in 2004, this time with a greatly enhanced running game, it would be time to do it again. They had ended the 2003 season winning fifteen in a row. In a League designed for parity, where it appeared the League officials liked you to lose every other week, a winning streak like that was nothing less than amazing. They picked up where they left off in the 2004 season. The opening game was with the Indianapolis Colts at home in what was now Gillette Stadium, so named when it opened in the fall of 2002. They trailed for some of the game and almost gave it away, but a blitz by Willie McGinest weakened a Colts drive at the end. The Patriots were leading, 27–24, and the Colts were moving—they had the ball just inside the Patriot 20 with 1:43 on the clock and with no Colt time-outs left. McGinest blitzed, no one picked him up, and he nailed Manning for a twelve-yard loss. With forty-two seconds left, Mike Vanderjagt came on to try the field goal; he would need a 48-yard kick, thanks to the McGinest sack. The ball went wide right, and the Patriots won. But Belichick was not entirely pleased, and he blamed himself. "We really screwed it up, or more accurately, I screwed it up—just bad coaching," he said.

He blamed himself for a flawed game plan, one that was a little old and tired—too much Cover Two, which left too much of an area open in the middle. They had gotten away with it the previous season. In the off-season he had gone down to see his pal Nick Saban, who had worked with him in Cleveland for four years, to talk about defenses and trying to stay one step ahead of opponents. Saban, then in the process of turning out some of the country's best college teams at LSU, was, Belichick thought, quite possibly the brightest young coach in the country when it came to defense, both driven and brilliant. They had talked about adding new elements of deception to the defense, showing Cover Two, but playing Cover Four. But when it came to the game itself, they had been slow in changing it, not going to Cover Four until the second half. "We knew people were going to catch on; we'd gone with it too much in the past and you can't stay static in this league. The Colts had had the entire off-season to study it, and we should have been ready for that. We went to the same well too often," Belichick said.

Still, they won, and they had won against a very good team; they had played hard, and there was no sign of complacency. It had been Corey Dillon's first game as a Patriot, and he had proven his value from the start, especially in a game where time of possession was important. He had carried fifteen times for eighty-six yards, a handsome 5.7 average per carry. There was a signature to the New England teams now. They were businesslike on the field, but they also played with genuine emotion when it was needed. One came to expect a high level of intelligence in the offensive and defensive game, and when they made a dumb play on the field, a poor call on offense, or were charged with a gratuitous penalty, or had an unnecessary turnover, one was surprised. They were much more likely to force the other team into mistakes than to make mistakes themselves. They took away from the other team—this was still the great Belichick trademark—what the other team wanted to do, and made them operate in a discomfort zone, on occasion causing the opposing quarterback to doubt what he saw and to question his own instincts. By dint of their defense and the confusion they could create even with very good teams, they tended to control the tempo of the game. The addition of Dillon made them even better at this.

Belichick thought it was easy, in fact, to underestimate how good these Patriots were becoming and how good they had become by

2004. One of the things coaches in all sports know is that when you are good in New York you are often overhyped, because it is the media center of the world, and some of the hype is virtually in the water there. Take his Patriot linebackers, he thought. They might not be as well known as the ones he had coached in New York, but they compared favorably, and he might actually have more depth with this group. Mike Vrabel had proved a very good pickup. He had come over for very little money, and he had been smart enough to know that if he got a chance to play and did well, the money would take care of itself. Belichick thought of him as being in the same class as Carl Banks, which was high praise. Tedy Bruschi was, in a way, a player outside the traditional mold, and he was not easy to categorize, but, though he was different from Pepper Johnson in physical attributes and played a different kind of game, Belichick thought him like Johnson, one of his favorite players. He was very good at pass defense, like Johnson, and could also rush the passer. Roman Phifer was exceptional at pass coverage, and Roosevelt Colvin was an uncommonly good pass rusher. Willie McGinest was a wonderful outside linebacker, a fine perimeter player, capable of making big plays precisely when they needed them. If he was not quite Lawrence Taylor, then no one else was either. If that was not enough, Belichick thought the defensive line itself was probably better than the one he had coached in New York, because of Richard Seymour, as good a front-line defensive player as he had ever coached, not to mention Ted Washington, and now Vince Wilfork, who he hoped would emerge as a dominating player.

They were not like the old New York Giants team that Belichick had coached nearly a generation earlier. Then, after a game, one tended to think more often than not of Lawrence Taylor. With the Patriots, on occasion, McGinest or Bruschi or Ty Law or some other player made a spectacular play, and a big deal was made of that immediately afterward in the locker room. But, in general, they executed as a team and won as a team, and the players seemed quite comfortable with that. They were privately quite contemptuous of other teams that squabbled over who the star was. Not many of the New England players were that well known before they came into the League; if they came from big-time programs, they usually had not been hyped by their school's publicity machinery. Once in the League, they had often bloomed slowly. Some were reclamation projects. Often, even in the middle of the Patriots' championship runs, the opposition had a goodly number of bigger names who had been higher draft choices.

But they seemed to fit well together, and the combination of so many players who knew what they were doing and who had confidence in one another was quite imposing. It made them a superior force, especially with their bench, for they were beginning to create a team with what Belichick had always wanted, replaceable parts. And when they were in a close game and it was late in the game, they had confidence in Tom Brady's ability to make good decisions (and big plays), and Adam Vinatieri's ability to kick critical field goals. Having Vinatieri on the bench late in the game was like a very good baseball team in the playoffs knowing that it had the best reliever in the game just waiting to come in.

◆◆◆

The run they had made through the regular season and especially through the playoffs in 2004 was particularly impressive. The first big playoff game for them in 2004 was once again with their old friends the Colts, one more meeting between old rivals, fortunately for the Patriots at Gillette Stadium and not the RCA Dome. The two teams now seemed destined to play against each other in big playoff games at least for as long as both Manning and Brady were the respective quarterbacks. Of Peyton Manning's brilliance, his control and command of his team, there seemed little doubt. He was a great player, playing at what seemed like an unsurpassed level. Belichick admired him greatly; he made good decisions, he had a wonderfully accurate arm, and a very quick release. Equally important, he made very few negative plays—he was rarely in the habit of beating himself. No one in the game worked harder studying film. He was a perfectionist, a man after Belichick's heart, albeit playing on the other side.

Now, for the Patriots' first game in the 2004 playoffs, once again the Colts were coming to Foxboro. Fortunately, the Patriots' record was good enough to get them a bye week at the start of the playoffs. They badly needed it. They had lost the home-field advantage for the Conference championship because of an unusually stupid series of plays in a late-season game against Miami, but they had kept the bye, and Belichick wanted it more than the home-field advantage in the Conference championship. For they were physically exhausted at the end of the season, their bodies beaten up and worn down, and they were mentally exhausted as well, and they needed an extra week to heal and to rest. They had it prior to the Colts game.

If anything, Manning seemed even better than he had been the previous year. He had broken record after record: 49 touchdown passes (a record), only 10 interceptions, 4557 regular season passing yards (an average of 284 yards a game), and a 67 percent completion average. In the 2004 season he had seemed more machine than man. The Colts were, Belichick thought, one of those golden NFL teams, not unlike the Rams when he had played against them two years earlier. The previous week, in a playoff game against Denver, Manning had completed twenty-seven of thirty-three passes, for a percentage of 81.8, 458 yards, and four touchdowns. But, once again, the Patriots dominated the Colts. Even though the referees were on red alert to watch for excessive chucking on the part of the Patriot defenders against the Colt receivers, it didn't matter. They played Cover Four, four deep men falling back, like an umbrella that was about 80 percent open, disguised as Cover Two. It looked like Cover Two, and it made it hard on any quarterback, even one as good and experienced as Manning, to determine which coverage was coming. It was a defense designed to make the quarterback doubt what he was seeing: If the quarterback thinks it's Cover Two, he'll throw the ball inside, and if he sees it's Cover Four, he can throw wide. But if it looks at first like Cover Two, and then it's Cover Four, by the time the quarterback realizes he doesn't have the inside, and gets ready to throw wide, it's too late to go to the outside receivers.

Belichick had felt they could drive the ball against the Colts defense, which was small but quick, and he had been right. Corey Dillon ran for a total of 144 yards, on twenty-three carries. In the first half they went on one long drive of sixteen plays that took 9:07 off the clock and that ended with a field goal. Then, in the second half, they went on two long touchdown drives, one of 87 yards on thirteen plays in 8:16, a lot of time off the clock, and another of 94 yards on fourteen plays in 7:24. Manning's frustration on the sidelines was palpable. They had played on a bad field, wet and in the snow, which was perfect for the Patriots, and not so perfect for the Colts. The final score was 20–3; there had been all those Colt touchdowns all season long, forty-nine of them in sixteen games, more than three a game, and then on this day when it meant so much, not one. What was even more remarkable was that the Patriots had played without two of their cornerbacks, Ty Law and Tyrone Poole, and without Richard Seymour, perhaps their premier defensive lineman.

Late in the game, Manning, the consummate professional, had started to look a little like a lost soul. It was not an upset, because everyone knew that if the Colts were good at what they did, then the Patriots were equally good at what they did, but there was something about the totality of it that was nonetheless stunning, the complete devastation by a very good defense of what seemed, at least on the morning of the game, like an equally brilliant offense. The Colts had come in looking so good, and then when it was over there had been so little left of them. Manning himself had paid the Patriots one of the highest compliments: "Most other times when you have starters down, and you are missing some Pro Bowlers, you really sort of lick your lips," he said. But with the Patriots, he said, it seems "like it doesn't really matter who is in there."

The victory over the Colts meant the Patriots would play the Conference championship against the Steelers. This was going to be a fascinating matchup: quite possibly the best team in the Conference, maybe even the best in the League, the Steelers, against the smartest team in the League, the Patriots. The Steelers had lost only one game that season, and at 15–1 they had the best record in the League. They had the home-field advantage, and they were very physical. In their regular season game, the Steelers had handled the Patriots with seeming ease, 34–20, ending New England's fabled winning streak at twenty-one and making the Patriots look ordinary. "They had," Belichick said later, "beaten the hell out of us." But New England had not been whole that day; Dillon had been out with an injury. Now, going into the championship game, Belichick thought the teams were almost equal physically, with no identifiable weaknesses on either side.

If the Patriots had an edge, it was at quarterback. The Pittsburgh quarterback was Ben Roethlisberger, a rookie who was, nevertheless, having what seemed like a career year, and was a sure rookie of the year selection. He was big and strong, and had been given fourteen starts, all of which he won. But there had been a game in the playoffs when the Jets, who had a very good defense, made him look ordinary, so Belichick thought the Patriots could confuse him. His view of the

Steelers was that they had managed over the season, because of all their strengths, to make Roethlisberger look a little better than he was. Again and again, they had placed him in situations where he was allowed to exhibit his strengths rather than reveal his weaknesses. You did not win fourteen games in a row in the NFL without having a lot of ability, but the question of what Roethlisberger would do in a supremely pressurized situation, against so strong and so varied a defense as the Patriots', was still to be answered. They were going to play at Pittsburgh, but that did not bother Belichick, because Brady was so tough-minded. He was, in his coach's phrase, "more or less road game immune—he's so mentally strong that he can shut things out. All of that comes from his inner toughness and focus."

No one was quite sure why, but before the Conference championship game against Pittsburgh, Belichick was unusually emotional in his pregame speech. Perhaps because it was the AFC championship game, perhaps because it was on the road, perhaps because Pittsburgh had the better record and so many smart football fans thought the Steelers a better team, and perhaps because the Steelers had so thoroughly defeated the Patriots during the regular season, but he was briefer and much more emotional than usual. Instead of the emphasis on more technical things they were supposed to do, the specifics of the game at hand, he spoke to them about who they were, how good he thought they were—that they were the better team, and that they had proved it by saving their best football for the end of the season against the Jets and the previous week against the Colts. All they had to do on this day was ratchet it up a notch against the Steelers. Forget the crowd, he said. Forget all those people with their yellow and black towels. "You're the better team. And the way you can prove it is by playing your best game today," he said. Then he reminded them that the only people who mattered for the next three hours, the only people who could help them, were in that room. It was a very uncharacteristic speech, but he felt it was the right moment—they needed, at that moment, not any criticism, no matter how veiled, but his belief that they were better.

Damon Hack, a writer for the *New York Times,* noted that since Belichick had come to the Patriots, there were fourteen occasions when Belichick had had a second shot in a season against a given team. His record in these second-chance encounters was a striking one: fourteen victories, no defeats. And this time Belichick had studied Roethlisberger, and he knew his weaknesses. The pressure that the New England defense applied was relentless that day. The way they went after Jerome Bettis, the feared Steeler running back, was almost savage. Roethlisberger threw two touchdowns and three interceptions, and the final score was 41–27. It was not close.

◆◆◆

Then they played the Philadelphia Eagles in the Super Bowl, and Belichick carried enough defensive linemen on the roster this time, because he knew the game would be exhausting, and he did not want what had happened in the Carolina game the year before to happen again, for it to turn into a track meet. He had become an old hand at dealing with the Super Bowl, how it exhausted everyone, four hours instead of three from start to finish, a forty-five-minute halftime instead of twelve, the primacy of entertainment instead of football, all of the things he hated and which could make things go wrong and could wear down even superbly conditioned athletes. In the locker room just before the game, he fed them a little food for energy, just so they would not wear down.

There would be two keys: containing Eagles quarterback Donovan McNabb and not letting him get outside the pocket, because he was much more dangerous outside of it when the defense began to break down than he was as a classic pocket quarterback. With Peyton Manning, a beautiful passer who did not throw well on the move, you wanted him moving outside the pocket; McNabb, a very good passer, threw well on the run, exhausting and wearing down your defense, so you wanted him inside the pocket. In addition, they did not want Brian Westbrook, the Eagles' talented running back, to get to the outside where he could do the most damage. They wanted him inside; they did not think he liked to cut back into the middle, not the way that the great Dallas Cowboys running back Emmitt Smith or some other backs did. Therefore the key for the defense was to contain the Eagles, and Belichick thought they could.

It was not one of their most artistic games. There is so much hype and fuss to the Super Bowl that it tends to work against the quality of the game, but they did what they wanted, contained both McNabb and Westbrook, controlled the tempo of the game, and were able to move the ball and score themselves. At the end, with the Eagles trailing by ten points, 24–14, they were surprised by how slowly the Eagles ran their plays. Philadelphia had gotten the ball with 5:41 left in the game, but the Eagles seemed to have no sense of urgency in their play calling or the way they came to the line of scrimmage. The Patriot strategy seemed to be working: Concede short passes, making them seem like runs, keep the Eagle receivers from getting out of bounds, and make them burn the clock. It took the Eagles eleven plays to reach the Patriot 30 with 1:48 on the clock—almost four minutes used on the drive. Belichick was more than comfortable with the pace—maybe they would get the touchdown, but they would need to grind it out if they got it, perhaps a run or two or a McNabb scramble, or two or three short passes, all the while with time coming off the clock. New England had been in this situation before, and the Patriots went to Cover Two now; they always did in situations like this—give some yards, but not too much too quickly. Belichick thought the right defensive set, Cover Two, had been called, but they did not get it set up in time, and the Eagles scored in one quick strike, making it 24–21. But that was going to be all they got. The onside kick did not work, and when the Eagles finally got one more shot at the ball, they were too deep in their territory, and it ended with a Rodney Harrison interception of a desperate McNabb pass. It was the Patriots' third Super Bowl victory in four years; they had won fifty-seven games in three seasons to get there, including the championship games themselves, thus 180 minutes of championship football, and they had won again by a field goal; three championships, nine points.

CHAPTER FOURTEEN

Bill Belichick knew all too well that with his three Super Bowl victories he was at the pinnacle, and the pinnacle was the most dangerous of places, and the reigning champion the most endangered of species. Stays at the pinnacle were traditionally brief and had, in the modern age of professional football, become even briefer. In most other professions continued success made things easier, but in coaching, it made them harder. It was very much like the NFL schedule itself: The more you won, the harder they made it. Moreover, Belichick understood that the current rules of professional football favored dislodging the champion, and that therefore residence at the top was as much a product of good fortune as it was of talent, willpower, and planning.

You got to the pinnacle because you were very good, but also because you were lucky—a ball bounced toward your player and away from another, a valuable player on your team did not get injured, or at a critical moment the referees favored you rather than your opponents with a wildly important call—as had happened against Oakland during the first Super Bowl run. They had beaten the Eagles with a badly patched defensive secondary and a wide receiver, Troy Brown, playing as a defensive back. It was bad luck that they had ended up so thin in their defensive secondary, and good luck, as well as good execution and coaching, that it had not cost them more dearly. That was, Belichick suspected, how it had always worked, a combination of good fortune blended with good players and good coaching.

As he continued to work endless hours, even in the off-season, he knew that in countless other NFL offices there were very talented men working equally long hours, studying him and his teams, looking for the tiniest of flaws. Belichick was always aware that if there was a weakness and they spotted it before he did, they would surely exploit it. The danger of being Bill Belichick was that there might be a younger Bill Belichick out there, trying to gain on him, a younger, more cold-blooded gunslinger moving in to challenge the reigning gunslinger.

Could a successful NFL coach have a life outside of football? The hours had always been killing, but now, because the rewards were even greater, they were longer than ever. Moreover, the pressures were so intense that even when you were off duty, it was hard to let go, and you were still somehow working even if you were home with your family. "Don't do it, don't go into coaching," the famed Bear Bryant had counseled young acolytes who were thinking of following him into the profession, "unless you absolutely can't live without it."

There was a constant loneliness to the job, a sense that no one else understood the pressures you faced. Each year, before the season began, Belichick would tell his team that no one else would understand the pressure on them, not even the closest members of their families.

The person in football who knew him best and longest, Ernie Adams, thought Belichick had remained remarkably true to the person he had been as a young man. Adams was a serious amateur historian, and he was not a coach who threw the word "warrior" around to describe football players, because they were football players, not warriors, and the other side did not carry Kalashnikovs. Nonetheless, he thought the intensity under which the game was now played and the degree to which that intensity separated players and coaches from everyone else, even those dear to them, was, in some way, like combat, in that you simply could not explain it to anyone who had not actually participated. It was not a profession that offered a lot in the way of tranquillity. "My wife has a question she asked me every year for ten years," Bill Parcells said back in 1993 when he was still married, "and she always worded it the same way: 'Explain to me why you must continue to do this. Because the times when you are happy are so few.' She has no concept."

There was no off-season, though there was a brief soft season, a few weeks in the spring or early summer, after the draft, when a coach might try to emulate a normal workaholic. To the degree he could, Belichick shielded his private life from the media, and he worked hard to be a family man. When George Allen, one of the most obsessive coaches of modern times, had coached at Whittier College, he once gave a birthday party for his wife, Etty, at the local country club, at which he had sat around a table with a few male friends, drawing up football plays. She was furious. "Football, football, football," she said, "even on my birthday." One of the stories that the brilliant, wonderfully obsessed Bill Walsh liked to tell was of taking his wife out to dinner on the Friday before a game, the two of them sitting at a lovely restaurant in the Bay area, and Geri Walsh had looked over at him, seeing him off in that other world, the one that was so hard to penetrate, and said, "What is it, Bill? Third and eight?" That seemed to sum up the dilemma of the football wife as much as anything: living in a world where it was always third and eight.

In 2005, Belichick and Debby, his wife of twenty-eight years, quietly and amicably separated—two nice, thoughtful people who liked each other but who had gradually gone in different directions. Belichick tried to lead a balanced life within a framework that was hopelessly imbalanced. In the summer after the third Super Bowl win, in the brief time allotted for a football coach to be a human being and have a vacation, he retreated to his home in Nantucket, where he spent as much time as he could with his kids, and with a few old friends, like Mark Fredland, who had brought him to the island in the first place. His parents were there, too; he had fixed up a house for them, and Steve Belichick got slightly irritated because, for reasons of health, he could no longer go fishing, but he was still able to putter around in his garden all day long. Bill Belichick liked more than anything else to spend his time on Nantucket with his three children: in the summer of 2005 Amanda was twenty, Stephen eighteen, and Brian thirteen. If the island in recent years had become much glitzier, he was not part of the glitz. He biked almost everywhere, dressed nattily as ever in a gray Patriots sweatshirt and, sometimes, a baseball cap. If he came into town, seven miles away, he invariably did it on his bike. A few years ago he was supposed to go fishing with Frank Gifford, the old Giant running back, and Tom Mleczko, the island's best fisherman; they were supposed to set out from Madaket, on the west end of the island, at 4:30 A.M. Belichick was not there then, and so they waited half an hour. Then, because they needed to hit the tide, Mleczko and Gifford finally left the dock, but just as they were pulling out of the harbor, Belichick showed up, and they turned back to get him. He was very apologetic; he had biked at that hour from the *east* end of the island to the other, about sixteen miles in all, setting out at 3 A.M. and had miscalculated the time. Nantucket was at its heart a small town that had been inundated in recent years by if not the rich and famous, certainly the very rich and wannabe famous. Not all of those people treated the locals with grace and courtesy, but there was a widespread admiration for Belichick for the modesty with which he behaved and the good manners he showed to everyone.

◆◆◆

Now he did much better on the public side than he had done in Cleveland. Part of the reason was that he had started to win much sooner; part of the reason was that he had learned a great deal from Cleveland about how to do the public part of the job; and part of the reason was a young man named Berj Najarian, who became his personal assistant. Najarian was a bright and winning person with an uncommonly sunny disposition. With singular grace he protected his boss from those who did not wish him well and on occasion from himself. But Super Bowl victories did not in any way bring Belichick any relief. It was not in his DNA to be complacent. He worked harder than ever, because there were more talented people out there who wanted what he had, some of them people he had helped train.

He entered the 2005 season having lost both of his senior coordinators, Romeo Crennel, the defensive coordinator, to Cleveland, where he would be head coach, and Charlie Weis, the offensive coordinator, to Notre Dame, also as head coach. In addition, one of his closest friends in the game, Nick Saban, a coach whose talents he greatly admired, especially as a defensive strategist, was now in Miami, in Belichick's own division, looking to beat him. It never got easier. Crennel had been with him in different incarnations for eighteen years, and he was a valued and admired part of a very successful team; he was also a man caught in the difficult position of being the defensive coordinator on a team where everyone believed the great defensive mind was that of the head coach and therefore no one was sure how much was his work and how much was Belichick's. Weis was in a more enviable position, because the offense was generally judged to be less Belichick's handiwork, and because Weis was credited with helping shape Brady into the formidable quarterback he so quickly became. But their departure did not seem to shake Belichick that much—he knew it was going to happen sooner or later, and because he did not like surprises, he had been preparing for more than two years, moving other good people into the slots right beneath them.

In the end the reward for what he and the staff and the players had done was the right to try and do it again under even more pressure. They had to be ready for the 2005 season, trying to win again while escaping the shadow and the burdens of the D word. When the Eagles game was over, the coaching staff had started immediately shaping the roster for the coming season. The draft and the free agent struggles were coming upon them soon, and they were trying as best they could to protect their own roster. Everyone now wanted a Patriot type of player—tough, intelligent, a man who controlled his ego—and the most likely place to find one was on the Patriot roster. Belichick knew they had to rotate a few new players in each year, and a few older ones out, and sometimes he had to do it before the older players actually needed to be let go, in order to fight off the tendency of successful teams to grow old overnight. He liked the players he took in the 2005 draft. Though he did not normally draft offensive linemen that high, the Patriots took Logan Mankins from Fresno State in the first round, because, of the available players, he best met their needs, and because of the recommendation of his coach, Pat Hill, who was, of course, a graduate of Belichick University. He was a guard, but Belichick loved versatility in his players, and if Mankins could play tackle as well, that would be a major plus.

He was the best in the contemporary game. No one, it was acknowledged, did his job better. Because of the salary cap, because of the League-driven equity, thought Sal Paolantonio, he had had a great advantage, because so many games were going to be so close, and it would come down in so many games—not unlike the AFC Championship games against the Steelers—to a question of which team's quarterback played better. No one, believed Paolantonio, did a better job of attacking the other team's quarterback than Belichick. If anything, he had given the football world a new definition of what a coach should be, and now everyone wanted The Next Belichick. Professionally, he could be cold and unsentimental, which was, in effect, what the League mandated, in an age of the salary cap. Besides, Cleveland had given him, as his friend Ernie Adams said, the hide of a rhino. If he had become, professionally, a hard man, then much of that hardness was built into the job description.

What a curious, complicated, contradictory man, a hard man to reach and to understand completely. He was completely dedicated to fighting off the virus caused by too much ego, all too aware of what it could do to his dominating purpose—playing championship-level team football. But a man like that, who was so driven to win, and who excelled again and again at such a high level, was hardly without ego. Instead, he had learned how to make his ego work for him, and to keep it from being a negative force. What he had excelled at was taking his ambition and talent and fusing it into something larger than himself. He gloried in the purpose of a successful season, not as so many others did in modern American sports, with so many cameras running live all the time, in personal celebration. Most of the fruits of victory—the ever larger salary, around $4 million a year, the handsomely paid lectures before assembled CEOs who wanted to know his secret of leadership—moved him not at all. He might accept those rewards, as part of his due, but they were not what he sought, or needed. He took the money, but he also seemed curiously immune to it.

Would you like him as a friend? someone asked the writer. Quite possibly you would like him more as a friend if you never knew what he did for a living, knew him away from football, and had just stumbled into the friendship, through being a neighbor. But you would need to earn both his trust and his respect, and that was a complicated matter, especially as he became more successful, and thus in some ways warier and more self-protective. Oddly enough, the best case for his value as a coach and a man was eventually made in Boston not by one of the city's sportswriters but by a political columnist named Joan Vennochi, who rarely wrote about sports. Belichick, she noted, wasn't "glib or glitzy. At press conferences he sometimes seems a little goofy and is often way too grim. But he is a leader without the swagger, selfishness, and pomposity that so many men in business, politics, and sports embrace as an entitlement of their gender and position."

He was still often found lacking as a public figure by the media. The charisma gap still existed, and if he had his way, it would probably be larger every year. Part of the problem was his failure to become someone different from himself, the kind of person who fulfills the larger role the public expected of a coach, someone with a certain amount of avuncular charm, mixed in with a certain obvious toughness of spirit, able to employ a few catchphrases that showed that he had the team ready for the big one. It would help if he had a better jawline, a chin that jutted out a bit more. "Most owners in this league don't really care what their coaches do as long as they look like the Marlboro man out there on the sidelines," George Young had once told Ernie Adams. In that case, thought Adams, it might have been better for Belichick to hire an actor, someone like, say, George C. Scott, if he were still alive, who had played George Patton so well, to play the public role of the coach for him. If that had happened, it might all have worked better for him along the way in his coaching odyssey. But all they got in Cleveland was him and all they were going to get in New England was him, and that would have to be enough.

In his professional role—it was particularly true of him when he was at Cleveland—he thought he had to win football games, not hearts and minds. Because of that he had slipped at a critical moment in his career. That which made him most human and revealed his personality, he shielded from the public. In a way, thought a talented writer named Peter Richmond, who watched him closely and later wrote about him, what sometimes bothered the media was that he was too straight, that he had so little in the way of artifice. "What's interesting about him, and was judged a weakness in Cleveland," Richmond said, "was that he did not play any games. There's nothing fake, and there never was. He is what he is. There is no pretense, and he is utterly authentic in a world where because of television there is more and more which is inauthentic. What is troubling about all this is that a lot of people are more comfortable with the inauthentic, if it is reassuring, than they are with the truth, if it is not reassuring. He doesn't play the role of the coach. Instead he is the coach."

Belichick once told a reporter that what he had always sought, from players, peers, and the general public, was respect. Well, he had that now. It was easy to oversimplify him, to think of him as the smart grind, who was better at his homework than many of the other kids in the class. Certainly, it was possible that he was the kid who loved doing homework. But the world of professional football had rarely been a hospitable place for someone who was merely a smart grind; it demanded, in the end, a totality of knowledge and experience, and the ability to assess human behavior, including your own. It also demanded a staggering amount of discipline.

As a coach the most critical thing in his relationship with players was that in the end they believed in the mantra: Stay with him, even if he seems a little different from what you expected in a coach;

believe in what he says, even if it's different from what you expected to hear; sustain your belief for an acceptable period of time, and surely good things will happen, not perhaps in the first year or even the second, but sooner than anyone expected. It was as if he were a man of a certain kind of secular faith: faith in a certain kind of football coached in a certain kind of way, and in his ability in an age of so many football infidels to assemble a group of players who would willingly honor one another and play that type of football. It was, of course, a fragile kind of faith, not easy to sustain in an age with so many potential corruptions, and Belichick was all too aware that it could be shattered at any moment. But finally, and it had taken a long time, for it was the sum of his career, everything had come together and his players had shared the faith.

ACKNOWLEDGMENTS

Bill Belichick and I more or less stumbled into the doing of this book. By chance we both have houses on Nantucket, a small island off Cape Cod, I for thirty-six years, he for twenty-five. We had never met, but I had admired him at a distance from the time he had been a young defensive coach with the New York Giants, the team I had watched and rooted for faithfully since my boyhood. More, I had always been intrigued by him, and by the fact that he was so innovative, his game plans so original. I was intrigued as well by how uncoachlike he was, or at least different from the stereotype of what a coach was supposed to look and sound like.

We finally met in the summer of 2004. He, it turned out, was a serious reader of nonfiction and had several of my books in his voluminous collection of sports books. Ironically, the first book of mine he had read was not a sports book, but *The Best and the Brightest*, to which he had been introduced by our mutual friend Bobby Knight. When we finally met, I suggested that there might be a book in the education of a coach, especially since the most important teacher in his life was his father, Steve—a coach's coach. It was an idea that interested him, and eventually he agreed to cooperate—most of my reporting to be done in the rare slack time in a coach's life, in late May and June of 2005. There would be no financial participation on his part, although I suggested that we might take a share of the royalties and commit them to a charity of his choice, and we have agreed to do that, to AccesSportAmerica, an extraordinary group to which the Belichick family is committed, which brings formidable athletic challenges—windsurfing, outrigger canoeing, and water-skiing—to children and adults with serious physical or developmental disabilities.

At the time he agreed to cooperate on the book, Bill Belichick was already at the pinnacle of his profession, two Super Bowls won in three years. In the season that followed, a third championship was added. So the given of the book was: How did he get to where he was from where he started, and what did the world of football and coaching football look like to someone who had excelled in it for three decades (and lived within it for his entire life)? Of America's three main sports, football was the one I had never written a book about and whose inner workings seemed most mysterious to me. The given was also that the book would be mine, but that the football insights would be largely his. It was also agreed upon that he would not review the book when it was finished. In a way it is a book about two journeys: his family's journey into the center of American life after his paternal grandparents arrived here from Croatia, and his own journey to the top in the world of professional football. He kept his word about cooperating with me and was remarkably available for a long series of marathon interviews we had in May and June. I am grateful for that cooperation, and the fact that—as a great many people, primarily his players, have found out before me—he is an uncommonly good teacher.

The interviewing process for any book is almost always the most fun, the best part of what has been for me over a fifty-year period a continuing learning process, and the interviews for this book were unusually pleasant. A number of people, most notably Ernie Adams and Scott Pioli, were good enough to hold what became informal seminars, as they explained to an outsider the changing nature of the professional game and the brutal pressures on elite coaches.

There are two other people to whom I am especially indebted: Berj Najarian is Belichick's personal assistant, in effect an ambassador from the rest of the world to Belichick and from Belichick to the rest of the world. He is bright, enthusiastic, as disciplined as his boss, and very good at knowing when the windows of opportunity will appear so a writer can plan his schedule dealing with Belichick. Neil Cornrich, Belichick's attorney as well as his friend, was equally helpful, and from the start he saw his job as making sure that the book happened, and for that I am extremely grateful.

Among those I interviewed were Ernie Adams, Marvin Bass, Maxie Baughan, Bill Belichick, Jeannette Belichick, Steve Belichick, Buzz Bissinger, Evan Bonds, Bruce Bruckmann, Kevin Byrne, Mary Kay Cabot, Tim Callard, Dave Campbell, Michael Carlisle, Barry Carter, Johnny Clark, Vinnie Colelli, Casey Coleman, Joe Collier, Dorothy (Laramore) Coyle, Pete Dawkins, Dick Duden, Kirk Ferentz, Rick Forzano, Mark Fredland, Don Gleisner, Al Groh, Tony Grossi, Wayne Hardin, Louis Hoitsma, Terry Jackson, Gene Janecko, Ron Jaworski, Dave Jennings, Pepper Johnson, Ken Keuffel, Bob Kraft, Bruce Laird, Eric Mangini, Ted Marchibroda, Judy (Mrs. Rich) McCabe, Berj Najarian, Judge John T. Nixon, Sal Paolantonio, Dean Pees, Ray Perkins, Scott Pioli, Bruce Poliquin, Floyd Reese, Peter Richmond, Jay Robertson, Mac Robinson, George Seifert, Ken

Shipp, Peter Sorota, Philip Sorota, Stephanie Sorota, Kevin Spencer, Bill Walsh, Joe Wennik, and Stan White.

I am indebted to a large number of people who helped me, including Casey O'Connell and Stacey James of the Patriots media staff, and Nancy Meier from Scott Pioli's office, and to Laura London of www.allthingsbillbelichick.com. From Andover, Theresa Pease and Linda Capodilupo were invaluable in checking out information. Charles Roos was the Mariano Rivera of computer counselors, registering save after save when the text of the book seemed so magically—and effortlessly—to disappear from this technophobe's screen. My friend Sam Roberts was very helpful in backstopping me on several parts of the book. Alex Stern, the resident football expert of the Elias Sports Bureau, walks around knowing every single thing that happened in the world of the New York Giants over the last twenty-five years. Rod Williamson of Vanderbilt's Athletic Media Relations Staff was very helpful under deadline pressures.

Among those who helped in different ways were my own support team, Bob Solomon and Marty Garbus, Doug Stumpf and Fred Turner, and Justin Bishop as a checker; from my publishers, Hyperion, Will Schwalbe, Emily Gould, Bob Miller, Ellen Archer, Jane Comins, Katie Wainwright, Beth Dickey, Charlie Davidson, Phil Rose, and Caroline Riordan; Bob Plapinger found out-of-print books for me; and among others who helped in different stages were Linda Torraco and Chris Holden; and our friends Ken Starr and John Phelan.

I am indebted to all the beat reporters from the *Boston Globe,* the *Boston Herald* (an interview Gerry Callahan of the *Herald* did with Ron Jaworski after the first Super Bowl win was unusually valuable and helped connect me to Jaworski's exceptional insights into some key games), the *New York Times,* and *Sports Illustrated,* whose work made my job so much easier. In addition, a number of books on professional football were very helpful, including *Football Scouting Methods,* by Steve Belichick (actually written by Jeannette Belichick, the book that originally connected Ernie Adams to Bill Belichick); *PB: The Paul Brown Story,* Paul Brown's autobiography with Jack Clary, a story weakened by the fact that the principal never seems to feel he has been wrong about anything; *The Future Is Now,* by William Gildea and Kenneth Turan, about George Allen in his Redskins incarnation, charmingly and informatively written; *Parcells,* a biography by Bill Gutman; *Parcells,* an autobiography with Mike Lupica, a book that quite skillfully captures Parcells's own voice; *Patriot Reign*, by Michael Holley, a well-done, quite shrewd account of the Patriots' first championship season; *Where Else Would You Rather Be?* by Marv Levy; *America's Game*, by Michael McCambridge, an extremely valuable, almost encyclopedic history of the League, required reading for any other football writer; *Tales from the New York Giants Sideline*, by Paul Schwartz; *LT: Over the Edge,* a very graphic account of the underside of his own football life by Lawrence Taylor, with Steve Serby; *Roger Staubach, Captain America,* by Mike Towle; and *All Things Possible,* by Kurt Warner (with Michael Silver—whose writing for *Sports Illustrated* was also very helpful).